Western Welfare in Decline

Western Welfare in Decline

Globalization and Women's Poverty

Edited by
Catherine Kingfisher

PENN

University of Pennsylvania Press

Philadelphia

10 9 8 7 6 5 4 3 2 1

Published by
University of Pennsylvania Press
Philadelphia, Pennsylvania 19104-4011

Library of Congress Cataloging-in-Publication Data
Western welfare in decline : globalization and women's poverty /
edited by Catherine Kingfisher.
    p. cm.
  Includes bibliographical references and index.
  ISBN 0-8122-3668-8 (cloth : alk. paper) —
  ISBN 0-8122-1812-4 (pbk. : alk. paper)
  1. Public welfare.   2. Social policy.   3. Poor women—
Government policy.   4. Welfare recipients—Government
policy.   I. Kingfisher, Catherine Pélissier.
HV51 .W47   2002
361.6′5—dc21   2002020309

For
John Pélissier
and
R. L. B. (1957–1991)

Contents

Part I
The Big Picture
GLOBALIZATION, NEOLIBERALISM, AND THE FEMINIZATION OF POVERTY

Chapter 1
Introduction

The Global Feminization of Poverty

Catherine Kingfisher

The 1992 World Bank Report argued that "Women must not be regarded as mere recipients of public support. They are, first and foremost,
economic agents" (IBRD 1992:60). This claim captures a key discursive
shift in the currently unfolding transformation from Keynesian and de-
velopmental to neoliberal forms of governance. In this transformation,
which is witnessing exponential growth in the feminization of poverty,[1]
low-income and poor women in both developed and developing countries are being reconstituted in new political discourses and practices
as already or potentially able-bodied workers and entrepreneurs, while
other identities, in particular, those of mother and dependent housewife, take on increasingly negative salience.[2] While skyrocketing poverty
rates among women in the South can be said to result from structural adjustment programs initiated by external agents such as the World Bank
and the International Monetary Fund,[3] similar increases in poverty rates
among women in advanced welfare state societies may be interpreted in
relation to an analogous, internally initiated restructuring, usually entailing cuts in social provisioning. In both cases, public services are put
under threat, and in both cases it is poor women who disproportionately
shoulder the burden of service reductions while they struggle to fill in
the gaps left by a retreating state. These parallels may in turn be situated in the larger context of the global spread of neoliberal approaches
to economic, social, and state organization.

Although situated in the context of a global feminization of poverty,
the focus of this book is on restructuring and women's poverty in western
welfare states, with particular emphasis on the situation of poor single
mothers.[4] While there is a significant literature on poverty, gender, and
structural adjustment in the Third World (e.g., Afshar and Dennis 1992;
Beneria and Feldman 1992; Elson 1995; Thomas-Emeagwali 1995), only

recently has a literature begun to develop on the comparative analysis of gender and the western welfare state (see especially Orloff 1993; Casper, McLanahan, and Garfinkel 1994); and, more importantly for the purposes of this collection, on the comparative analysis of gender and welfare state restructuring (see especially Bakker 1994b, 1996; O'Connor, Orloff, and Shaver 1999; Sainsbury 1996).

This collection contributes to this groundbreaking and now burgeoning literature on women's well being in restructuring welfare states in two ways. First, it takes what I refer to as the *culture of neoliberalism* as a particular focus of investigation, both theoretically and practically: theoretically, by exploring the gendered nature of the basic tenets of neoliberalism, and practically, by documenting how neoliberalism articulates with local/national cultures in specific relation to poverty policy. Secondly, the book works to situate the analysis of neoliberal culture in the context of economic and cultural *globalization*; in other words, globalization, frequently mentioned in passing in the literature on welfare reform, becomes, like neoliberalism, a focus of investigation in itself. The general argument that neoliberalism and globalization are inextricably tied is maintained throughout the book. Briefly, the argument claims that a key feature of economic and cultural globalization is the spread of specifically neoliberal forms of governance (Gill 1995; Mishra 1999; Teeple 1995), characterized by an international shift in the direction of increasing marketization, a redrawing of the public/private distinction, valorization of possessive individualism, and shifts in state expenditure (often accompanied by increasing state interference) in social arenas. An understanding of the global feminization of poverty thus requires an analysis of neoliberalism: analysis of neoliberalism as a cultural system, analyses both of neoliberalism as a movement and of the movement of neoliberalism across cultural space (globalization), and an analysis of its contradictions and disjunctures that provide entry points for intervention and resistance.

With reference to their situatedness in a specifically global terrain, then, this book explores the discourses and practices of welfare state restructuring in relation to poor single mothers in the United States, Canada, Britain, Australia and Aotearoa/New Zealand.[5] The goal is to provide a comparative analysis of welfare reform programs currently being instituted in these countries, with particular emphasis on their economic and social goals, and on the discourses of labor, gendered subjectivity, and public versus private which inform them and which they attempt to deploy. Such a comparative focus serves to generate insight into the convergences and divergences among and between welfare state reforms of provisioning for single mothers in light of the globalization of neoliberalism across historically and culturally unique national settings. Again, it is important to underscore that the analysis here is situated in terms not just of comparison, but also specifically of *globalization.* While comparative frameworks endeavor to uncover similarities and differences, they do not tend, in general, to situate these relationships in terms of transnational patterns (although see Esping-Andersen 1996; Mishra 1999). Theories of globalization—of increasing and accelerated transnational interdependencies and cross-fertilizations of politics, culture, and economics—provide this situatedness and also create a space for theorizing the underpinnings of the similarities and differences that comprise the focus of the comparative project.

It is also crucial to point out that policy, as analyzed here, is theorized as inherently *cultural,* insofar as it is based on culturally and historically specific discourses of gender, the division of labor, public and private, and whatever other phenomena happen to be locally relevant. Identities, roles, needs, and dependencies—and the various approaches taken to encourage, support, or ameliorate them—must be recognized as cultural constructions, reflecting and instantiating locally received and contested views that are always already reflective of and in conversation with other (perhaps globalizing) constructions. This collection is thus one response to the call for an anthropology of welfare (Russell and Edgar 1998); that is, for an approach that emphasizes the construction, negotiation, and contestation of meanings that underlie, inform, and reflect the material realities of welfare systems—which are, after all, "a product of, and . . . response to, power relationships in society" (Russell and Edgar 1998:2).

Restructuring Is to the "West" What Structural Adjustment Is to the "Rest"

Marshall Sahlins (1972) uses a "west/rest" binary to distinguish between the role of money in the west and kinship in "the rest." This formulation may be used here to refer to gross parallels in processes of structural adjustment (the rest) and welfare state restructuring (the west). This is not to claim that either the west or the rest is homogeneous. Indeed, there is enough heterogeneity within each category to render the categories themselves useless except as limited heuristic devices; and a key goal of this collection is, in fact, to explore precisely the heterogeneity within and among western welfare states. However, just as a west/rest binary is of limited value, so a homogeneity/heterogeneity opposition can lead to an unfortunate partiality that fails to capture complexity and nuance. On the other hand, it remains the case that west/rest and homogeneity/heterogeneity binaries can serve as useful points of entry or departure. My intent here is to do both: to capture both similarities and differences, to explore both generalities and specificities, rather than only one or the other. This requires a willingness to live with a fundamentally unresolvable but hopefully illuminating tension.

I begin with the overall patterns of similarity that have allowed analysts to make the general claim that it is women, specifically, who "have borne the brunt of restructuring—economically, socially, physically" (Sparr 1995:18). First, feminists early recognized that women were suffering in the development process in the Third World to the extent that they were being excluded from development programs that constructed men as heads of households and thus as the main contributors to economic development, particularly in rural areas (e.g., Boserup 1970; Rogers 1980; Tinker 1976, 1982; see Kabeer 1994 for a comprehensive review). Women's contributions to economic activity were construed as secondary to those of (often absent or nonexistent) male heads of household; and their roles as "housewives" (Mies 1986) were accentuated while their reproductive work paradoxically remained hidden. A specifically middle-class, western, and idealized view of the gender division of labor (male breadwinner, dependent wife) permeated the development theory that was exported to the Third World, materially manifesting itself in the differential targeting of development aid among women and men.

More recently, scholars and commentators have noted the gendered nature of structural adjustment programs (e.g., Afshar and Dennis 1992; Beneria and Feldman 1992; Elson 1992; Thomas-Emeagwali 1995). In her discussion of women and poverty in Africa, for instance, Daphne Topouzis (1990) argues that austerity measures increase poor women's work and caring burdens by decreasing their access to health, education, and employment services and opportunities. In reducing or eliminating public services, structural adjustment programs work to "privatize" or "rationalize" responsibility for protection and care by devolving it to the level of the community, household, or individual. This devolution presumes and valorizes women's "efficiency," "entrepreneurship," and "infinite elasticity" (Elson 1995).

The situation in western welfare states is characterized by similar valorizations and elisions. Economic globalization, such as that represented by the World Trade Organization (WTO) has been coupled in the west with shifts to a market-oriented neoliberalism at the domestic level, characterized by, among other things, attacks on the welfare state. These assaults are justified on two grounds. First is the claim that public relief is too expensive along a number of dimensions, including national debt and "the extra costs of reducing inequality," such as the higher tax rates needed to finance redistribution (Hum 1993:107). Coupled with this economic justification is a moral argument which claims that the receipt of welfare disempowers the poor, sapping their motivation to achieve self-reliance and undermining their self-respect (e.g., Green 1996; Mead 1986; Murray 1984; Plant 1993; see also Kingfisher 1999). The argument of this book is that such attacks, though seemingly gender neutral, are in fact gendered in nature and have particularly negative consequences for the well being of poor single mothers and their children.

The parallels in reforms being proposed and instituted in western welfare states regarding policy provisions for poor single mothers are remarkable. In 1996, for example, the United States instituted the Personal Responsibility and Work Opportunity Reconciliation Act (PRWORA), which places lifetime limits on the receipt of assistance and makes rigid stipulations regarding recipients' participation in work-related activities. Significantly, the act eliminates the federal program Aid to Families with Dependent Children (AFDC), implemented with the passage of the 1935 Social Security Act. AFDC has been replaced with Temporary Assistance for Needy Families (TANF), and assistance has been devolved to individual states (Ozawa and Kirk 1997). The Canadian government made similar changes when it replaced the 1966 Canada Assistance Plan Act (CAP), which provided federal dollars to the provinces and set national standards for social programs, with Canada Health and Social Transfer (CHST), introduced in 1995 and effective in 1996. CHST eliminates all but the vaguest national standards, reduces the amount of federal dollars available to the provinces for social programs, and provides whatever funding is available in the form of block grants, which are intended to provide coverage for health and education as well as for poverty related assistance. Provinces may now also institute their own workfare programs (Muscovitch 1996). As a final example, in 1997, as a result of the 1996 Tax Reduction and Social Policy Bill, Aotearoa/New Zealand instituted a series of workfare related reforms, including worktests for recipients of the Domestic Purposes Benefit (DPB) with children over the age of fourteen (Stephens 1999; Higgins 1999). These Canadian, New Zealand, and U.S. reforms, while varying in terms of specific provisions, all entail reductions in state provisioning for the poor. As such, they are one manifestation of a privatization of the public realm.

However, while welfare state restructuring is often described in terms of a "shrinking" or "rolling back" of the state, shifts in levels of state funding and interference are, in fact, selective, and certain sectors, such as the police or the military—or particular arms of the welfare bureaucracy—may, in fact, expand. Restructuring must therefore be conceptualized as a realignment of the public and the private (Brodie 1994), or as a shift in relative focus, rather than as a generalized and evenhanded reduction in the orbit of the state. Even the shrinking of those arms of the state concerned with social welfare may perhaps be best conceived of in terms of transformation, insofar as the "shrinking"—the cutbacks in benefits—may entail a simultaneous increase in bureaucratization and surveillance, with all the expenditures that these require. The concern here is thus with nation-states' *reconceptualizations* of the role of the state in the provision of social services in general, and in the provision of financial assistance for single mothers in particular, the latter of whom are increasingly predominant among the ranks of the poor.

This emphasis on nation-states' reconceptualizations of their roles in relation to those of the market and the individual or family provides the general framework within which the heterogeneity mentioned at the beginning of this section may be situated and explored. Such an emphasis also underscores the need to keep *the state* clearly in view. The role of the state is often diminished in discussions of globalization that tend to emphasize its demise and/or focus on global/local relations that seem to bypass the national level. The state, however, plays a pivotal role, both in the orchestration of "globalization," and in the everyday lives of the poor (Maskovsky and Kingfisher 2001; see Chapters 3 and 4, this volume, for further discussion). This is one reason why the case study chapters in Part II are organized by nation-state rather than thematically.

The Feminization of Poverty

In a now classic article published in 1978, Diane Pearce coined the phrase "the feminization of poverty" to refer to the fact that "it is women who account for an increasingly large proportion of the economically disadvantaged" (Pearce 1978:28). Discussion since has continued to focus on occupational segregation and women's responsibilities for childcare as key contributors to this phenomenon (Casper, McLanahan, and Garfinkel 1994; England et al. 1998). Specifically, it is the combination of various forms of discrimination in the workplace with the fact that women are more likely to have sole custody of dependent children that engenders their greater vulnerability to poverty (England et al. 1998; Starrels, Bould, and Nicholas 1994).[6]

Two claims with regard to the gender division of labor are particularly noteworthy in the context of current welfare state restructuring and women's poverty. The first is the assertion that the public realm of paid work depends on women's unpaid work in the private sphere, a claim long made by Marxist feminists (Jaggar 1983; Sargent 1981). The second is that it is women, in particular, who must negotiate the gap between the public and the private; women embody (physiologically and socially) and negotiate the contradictions between market and nonmarket structures by engaging in part-time work, home work, and casualized or illegal labor and by stretching to meet more needs with fewer resources. This provides evidence, perhaps, of Jenny Shaw's (1995) assertion, based on Claude Lévi-Strauss's (1969) analysis of the exchange of women and Gregory Bateson's (1972) discussion of the doublebind, that women seem to be the universal mediators of contradiction.

Restructuring clearly works to heighten the contradictions and tensions between market and nonmarket discourses and domains. Entailing ostensibly neutral macroeconomic changes, restructuring in fact depends on unpaid domestic labor (usually done by women), on the invisibility of this labor, and on women's ability and willingness to take on more and more work, whether it consists of paid labor or the labor involved in producing more with less. Restructuring in western welfare states, like austerity measures in developing countries, is thus a gendered phenomenon, with specifically gendered impacts on poverty rates. What connects these two seemingly disparate phenomena is their roots in economic and philosophic neoliberalism, the theoretical and situated analyses of which provide the focus of this book.

Gendering the Welfare State

Ann Orloff defines the welfare state most generally as consisting of "interventions by the state in civil society to alter social forces" (Orloff 1996:52), including market forces (Orloff 1993:304). Specifically, the welfare state may be characterized by institutionalized interventions in such areas as labor, health, and economic inequality (Bryson 1992; see also Esping-Andersen 1990 and Mishra 1984). As a phenomenon inextricably tied to capitalism, moreover, the welfare state is

a capitalist *society* in which the state has intervened in the form of social policies, programs, standards, and regulations in order to mitigate class conflict *and* to provide for, answer, or accommodate certain social needs for which the capitalist mode of production in itself has no solution or makes no provision. (Teeple 1995:15, emphasis in original)

Welfare state interventions are not, however, uniform, but diverge along the lines of class, ethnicity, age, and most important for the analysis here, gender. The welfare state constitutes women and men as different kinds of persons and has different expectations of how they are to live their lives, as reflected in its provision of gendered incentives and services.[7] Traditionally, men have been constructed as workers while women have been constructed as mothers, and these constructions have been enacted and reinforced in the services and programs each has had access to, for example, "workmen's compensation" versus "mothers' allowances." Thus current welfare state restructuring may be read to a large degree as "a restructuring around gender" (O'Connor 1996:8). Insofar as the welfare state has always been in the business of constructing gendered identities and needs, along with appropriate responses to them (Fraser 1989), restructuring accordingly reflects an ongoing (re)construction of genders and needs.

There is, of course, no paradigmatic welfare state, and early feminist work on the welfare state has been criticized for generalizing from one welfare state to all welfare states (Orloff 1996; Sainsbury 1996). This tendency to universalization has been usurped in recent years by an increasing emphasis on comparative analyses that highlight difference and variation. The focus is no longer on how women as a unified category fare in the welfare state in general, but on the differences that welfare state variations make for different groups of women, as well as for women and men (Sainsbury 1996:9).

Despite this emphasis on difference and variation—a highly productive emphasis in which this collection participates—there are nevertheless some patterns that seem to cut across a number of welfare states and that are therefore worth keeping in mind. Most notable for the purposes of this collection is the fact that "Nowhere in the industrialized West can . . . mothers choose *not* to engage in caring and domestic labor (unless they are wealthy enough to purchase the services of others)" (Orloff 1993:313, emphasis in original). Welfare states may have subsidized this caring work for some women on some occasions, but such subsidization has always been partial and has always reflected the state's constitution of women as dependent housewives—a constitution, as already noted, that has served to buttress the public sphere.

This pattern is continuing in the current phase of restructuring, with added stress generated by an increasing disengagement of the state from responsibility for welfare and the greater burden on women for remunerated and unpaid domestic work that this retreat engenders. In this context, commodification (access to paid work) becomes a problem for poor women not only in light of the kinds of employment they have access to—which is often marginal in terms of pay, security, benefits, and status—but also in relation to the additional pressures placed on them domestically. There is a certain poignancy, then, to Julia O'Connor's plea for state acknowledgment

that independence is the key to full citizenship, that employment is the key to independence in contemporary welfare states, and that *equal access to, and participation in, employment is dependent on social policy strategies that recognize that individuals have care-giving responsibilities or may be care-dependent, or both.* Without this recognition the emphasis on employment excludes a major part of the work on which the functioning of society depends, that is, unpaid care-giving work and service. (O'Connor 1996:102, emphasis added)

In addition, while feminists have often decried the fact that women in welfare states have been defined as dependents, and have accordingly pushed for increasing individualization, individualization, like commodification, may be problematic for some women. The question here, according to Diane Sainsbury, is "whether individualization results in an equalization of social rights [between women and men] or their elimination" (1996:174). In analyzing particular cases of restructuring, then, the extent to which the reforms entailed either enhance or undermine women's capacities to demand social rights must be interrogated.[8] Current welfare state restructuring, which places increased burdens on women to be both breadwinners and primary caretakers, may in fact serve to undermine women's capacities to "demand and utilize social rights" (Orloff 1993:309)—despite the fact that many reforms are ostensibly designed to buttress women's capacities as "individuals."

Outline of the Book

A great deal of the literature on welfare state restructuring emphasizes either theory or empirical case study, or at least weighs one more heavily than the other. This collection represents an attempt to intervene in this somewhat unfortunate, albeit traditional and conventional, binary by giving equal weight to both theoretical and empirical analyses.

Part I, which provides theoretical framing, outlines a preliminary grammar of neoliberalism in specific relation to restructuring and single mothers' poverty, and, by implication, that of their children.[9] Chapter 2 explores neoliberalism as a cultural (symbolic meaning) system that serves to organize society in highly gendered ways, with particular emphasis on the neoliberal conceptualization of personhood and its articulation with welfare reform agendas. I explore the neoliberal "individual" as a cultural and historical construction based on idealizations of the experiences of an elite group of white European males, and argue that as long as reform measures are based on such a construction of the person, they will undermine efforts to reduce the incidence of poverty rather than the number of people on the welfare rolls, and will serve to hinder, rather than enhance, single mother's "independence."

Chapter 3 focuses on a second and closely related key concept of neoliberal culture, the free market. Following the approach taken in Chapter 2, I analyze the free market and its globalizing tendencies as historical and cultural phenomena with highly gendered implications in the context of welfare state restructuring. Together, Chapters 2 and 3 argue that neoliberalism provides the basis for discourses and practices of restructuring. In giving equal weight to the person and the market, moreover, I am attempting to bypass foundationalism in favor of a focus on key linkages. The issue is not one of cause and effect, but of interrelation, of mutual implication and constitution. This applies not only to "economics" versus "philosophy" (materialism versus mentalism), but also to other categories of analysis, for example, gender and race.

Chapter 4, which serves as a bridge between Parts I and II, explores the conceptualization of globalization as hybridity, as cross-fertilization or mélange. This conceptualization, which creates space not only for the analysis of mixture per se, but specifically for that of power-laden processes of mélange, creates a framework for the specificities analyzed in the case study chapters which follow.

The idea of hybridity underscores the crucial point that the preliminary grammar of neoliberalism presented in Chapters 2 and 3 is just that—preliminary, a launching pad, provisional in the loosest sense. It is, in fact, only in the circulation of neoliberal related meanings and their articulation with other meaning systems that neoliberalism takes on its multiple and contradictory lives. These particular and unique instantiations are accordingly taken up in Part II, which is devoted to analyses of welfare state restructuring in five historically linked, English-speaking countries that have been engaged, to one degree or another, in reforms that participate in the neoliberal project: the United States, Canada, Britain, Australia, and Aotearoa/New Zealand. Each country has had a different relationship to the global economy, followed its own trajectory of welfare state development (although with different levels of independence vis-à-vis other nation-states), and exhibited unique gender and racial/ethic regimes—all of which have served to comprise their particular "national cultures," themselves characterized by various lines of both fracture and unity. The country chapters thus provide examples of "glocalization," or the articulation of what we refer to as local and the global.[10]

Exploration of how the neoliberal project articulates with various forms of national culture and specific programs of restructuring is strategically as well as theoretically relevant. In a situation in which many women seem to be the losers, the search for both particularities and similarities must be grafted onto a political agenda, namely, a search for points of intervention. Disjunctures and contradictions, revealed by means of the comparative project, provide potential sites of such intervention. Accordingly, and following the lead provided by such openings, Chapter 10 explores possible avenues for asserting the social rights of poor single mothers currently being denied at the level of the nation-state.

Chapter 2
Neoliberalism I

Discourses of Personhood and Welfare Reform

Catherine Kingfisher

The goal of this chapter is to outline features of the cultural context within which the developments outlined in Chapter 1 must be situated. As I argued in that chapter, welfare state restructuring must be understood in relation to the globalization of neoliberal approaches to economic, social, and state organization. Accordingly, in this chapter I describe what I mean when I refer to neoliberalism as a cultural system, outline a preliminary grammar of neoliberalism with particular reference to the neoliberal constitution of subjectivity, and discuss some features of welfare reform in neoliberal culture. Although the relationship between a specific geographic territory and culture is becoming increasingly problematic (Appadurai 1996b; Hannerz 1996; Kearney 1995; Tomlinson 1999), in referring to neoliberalism as a cultural system I am attempting to locate it, to contextualize its genesis in a western philosophical tradition, with particular reference in this context to that of the English-speaking west. Locating neoliberalism in this way opens up possibilities for analyses of its ethnocentric and racist characteristics. In addition, I want to explore the ways in which neoliberalism is not only specifically western, but also specifically gendered. Ostensibly neutral, neoliberal understandings and prescriptions regarding the market, the proper role of the state, and the nature of personhood are not only ethnocentric, but also androcentric.

By cultural system, I mean a framework, or paradigm, for understanding and organizing the world and for informing our practice in it. Neoliberalism is not, then, simply an *idea*, or a way of thinking about economics, but an approach to the world, which includes in its purview not only economics, but also politics; not only the public, but also the private; not only what kinds of institutions we should have, but also what kinds of subjects we should be.

John and Jean Comaroff define culture as

the semantic space, the field of signs and practices, in which human beings construct and represent themselves and others, and hence their societies and histories. It is not merely an abstract order of signs, or relations among signs. Nor is it just the sum of habitual practices. Neither pure langue nor pure parole, it never constitutes a closed, entirely coherent system. Quite the contrary: Culture always contains within it polyvalent, potentially contestable messages, images, and actions. It is, in short, a historically situated, historically unfolding ensemble of signifiers-in-action, signifiers at once material and symbolic, social and aesthetic. (Comaroff and Comaroff 1992:27)

In conceptualizing neoliberalism as a cultural system, I wish to highlight the constructed, contingent, and contradictory nature of culture to which the Comaroffs refer.[1] First, neoliberalism is a social construction, insofar as we understand all cultural systems to be constructions or fabrications, elements of which have been naturalized. This is not to claim that it is easily deconstructed, but rather to point out that it is a human invention, the artifact of particular historical and material practices and struggles. This view of a historically situated and unfolding phenomenon leads to the second point, namely, that neoliberalism is contingent. Like any culture, it is never a fait accompli, but is always in need of accomplishment. Finally, neoliberalism is not a "monolithic apparatus that is completely knowable and in full control of the 'New Right'" (Larner 1993:13); it is not coherent, but contradictory. Thus the Comaroffs' point that "Culture always contains within it polyvalent, potentially contestable messages, images, and actions" (1992:27). This potential contestability points, in turn, to the power relationships inherent in culture, power here relating to both "the force of meaning and the meaning of force" (ibid.).

A brief sketch of the parameters of neoliberalism in relation to gender and poverty will set the stage for a more detailed elucidation of some of its features. I do not, however, intend to simply replace a monolith we refer to as the "world capitalist system" with a monolith called "neoliberalism" and argue for an analysis of its relative penetration. What I want to sketch and interrogate is not a unitary system or essence moving across the globe like a cancer (or savior, depending on one's perspective), but one among numerous philosophies and worldviews in circulation, which has, itself, various permutations. I have to begin somewhere, however, so I begin with the general and the abstract. The following outline of a grammar that does not exist in any pure form, but only in its numerous very particular forms, is thus intended as a launching point only, the end goal of which is to track the circulation of neoliberal-related meanings across cultural space. A similar point may be made about gender as a category of analysis. Thinking at the level of grammar moves the discussion from one focused specifically on poor single mothers to one focused on gender in its most general and abstract senses; but again, as with neoliberalism, the end goal is to track the movement and instantiations of gendered meanings "on the ground," which is the task of Part II of this collection.

Neoliberal conceptualizations of personhood, market, and state lead to particular sets of economic and social prescriptions, the most notable in this context being the establishment of a minimalist state. Ruth Smith's (1990) discussion of the naturalization of poverty provides a useful analysis of the relationship of this project to gender and poverty. In short, Smith claims that the existence of poverty challenges the basic assumptions of liberal society, among which are included individual autonomy and self-sufficiency (1990:212). Her exploration of the liberal bourgeois symbolizations of poverty and society highlights a nonpoor/poor binary in which the nonpoor represent society and civilization, "good" (that is, controllable) nature, order, autonomy and freedom, intentionality, independence, universality, morality, and rationality; and the poor represent nature and savagery,[2] "bad" (uncontrollable) nature, disorder, need and necessity, want, desire, particularity, dependence, immorality, and irrationality. As the following list indicates, gender is a key axis of this set of binaries, with the various attributes on the masculine side having a positive valence in relation to those on the feminine side, which are hierarchically and definitionally secondary.

Nonpoor (masculine)	*Poor* (feminine)
society	nature
"good" nature (controllable)	"bad" nature (uncontrollable)
order	disorder
autonomy/freedom	need/necessity
interests	wants (absences)
intent	desire
universal	particular
independence	dependence
moral	immoral
rational	irrational

Women are thus representative of irrationality, dependence, desire, and so on. The intent/desire split is particularly important in this context in that it points to sexuality, and, in particular, to issues of (un)controllability and reproduction.

In their attack on the assumptions and organization of liberal bourgeois society, the feminized poor, by their very existence, serve to define the boundaries of ordered society, becoming in the process a pedagogical instrument in our own identity and social formation. They are not benign teachers, however, but rather represent the abject, threatening the boundary (Sibley 1995:14; Kristeva 1984; see also Kingfisher 1999). This boundary, moreover, is fluid and permeable. The divide between the nonpoor and the poor shifts with economic change, and while certain groups are clearly more "at risk"—for example, women, people of color, immigrants, the elderly, and the disabled—the risks of poverty, and, in particular, of various forms of dependency, are within each of us. The risk, in other words, "traverse[s] each and every member of the population. . . . It does not divide populations by a single division (the dangerous classes versus the labouring classes) so much as follow the warp and weft of risk within a population. . . . the entire population remains the primary locus of risk" (Dean 1997:219).

Personhood and Culture

The gendered and somewhat fluid set of binaries outlined above provides one basis for arguments in favor of a minimalist state, that is, a state whose role is confined to enabling the free exchange of goods and services between rational, independent individuals. The "rational, independent individual"—neoliberalism's quintessential human being—is key to this endeavor. Thus the shift away from the interventionist state and toward a free market social structure has entailed attacks on the welfare state that are based, at least in part, on the claims regarding "proper"(masculine) personhood alluded to above. Just as poverty policy is devolved from central government to the state, provincial, or municipal level, so responsibility for poverty is increasingly devolved to the level of the individual. A more detailed analysis of the neoliberal construction of personhood is thus in order.

I begin with two qualifications. First, when I refer to the neoliberal construction of the person as a specifically western construction, I am not intending to claim that this construction is the only western construction of personhood. The west, as a historical and ideological construct in opposition to "the rest" (Sahlins 1972), is, as pointed out in Chapter 1, neither temporally, geographically, nor culturally homogeneous: "the Western intellectual tradition" is, as Brian Morris (1991:1) points out, expressive of numerous conceptualizations of personhood (see also Lukes 1973); poststructuralist views challenging the idea of unified subjectivity are also gaining currency (see, e.g., B. Davies 1991; Lannaman 1991). The individualism at issue here thus represents only one strand of thought, and a highly contested one, not the least by feminists, a point to which I will return. It is thus most useful to conceptualize the neoliberal construction of the individual as a particular variant of western individualism,[3] specifically, the variant that has been inscribed in poverty-related policies.

It is also important to qualify in what sense I am referring to personhood or to the individual. There is a large literature in anthropology concerning the analytic concepts and uses of "individual," "person," and "self." Grace Gredys Harris (1989), in particular, argues that we need to distinguish between (culturally based) biologistic, psychologistic, and sociologistic concepts; distinctions must also be made between representations of the person/individual, on the one hand, and individuals' self-representations on the other (see also Fogelson 1982; Spiro 1993). In this context, I restrict my focus to what Melford Spiro (1993:114) refers to as the "cultural conception of the person or individual." Mechanisms for the constitution of these conceptions are here taken to include historical and economic forces, the state, various media, and welfare institutions. In keeping with the Comaroffs' (1992) emphasis on the power relations inherent in culture, these cultural models of the person/individual must be viewed in political terms: they are, particularly in the context of welfare reform, politically motivated and deployed. As Michel Foucault states:

I don't think we should consider the "modern state" as an entity which was developed above individuals, ignoring what they are and even their very existence, but on the contrary as a very sophisticated structure, in which individuals can be integrated, under one condition: that this individuality would be shaped in a new form, and submitted to a set of very specific patterns. (1982:214)

In other words, there is no such thing as an enduring, presocial, preconstituted individual or person that is then acted upon by external sources of power. Particular forms of governmentality—the conduct of conduct (Foucault 1979)—entail particular constructions of subjectivity, which are specifically historical and cultural in nature. In this sense, Foucault's analysis of power emphasizes not the "negation of the vitality and capacities of individuals," but "the creation, shaping and utilization of human beings *as* subjects. Power, that is to say, works through, and not against subjectivity" (Rose 1989:142). And in the case of neoliberalism, "this respecification of the ethics of personhood, is perhaps the most fundamental, and most generalizable, characteristic of these new rationalities of government" (Rose 1996a:60). The (re)constitution of (gendered) subjectivity is thus particularly germane to the neoliberal project of welfare reform (Kingfisher and Goldsmith 2001; see also Larner 1997).

With these qualifications in mind, it can be argued that the neoliberal discourse of individualism, while not the only discourse of personhood in circulation, is highly salient, if not hegemonic, in contemporary

neoliberal culture. With roots in Enlightenment philosophers' efforts
to challenge the hegemony of traditional church and aristocratic state
authority, contemporary neoliberal individuals are viewed as the center of morality, agency, and intentionality (Cushman 1995). Alan Mac-
Farlane describes this (particularly English) individualism as characterized by "the view that society is constituted of autonomous, equal units,
namely separate individuals and that such individuals are more important, ultimately, than any larger constituent group. It is reflected in the
concept of individual private property, in the political and legal liberty
of the individual, in the idea of the individual's direct communication
with God" (1978:5, cited in La Fontaine 1985:124). There is a correla-
tion between this broader definition of individualism and economic individualism, which asserts that "a spontaneous economic system, based on
private property, the market, and freedom of production, contract and
exchange, and on the unfettered self-interest of individuals, tends to be
more or less self-adjusting; and that it conduces to the maximum satisfaction of individuals and to (individual and social) progress (Lukes
1973:89). Autonomy, the pursuit of rational self-interest, and the market
are mutually constitutive in this formulation. In one of its more popular
current neoliberal manifestations, there is an equivalence between individualism and self sufficiency, an equivalence that translates into having
a "well paid secure good job" (Young 1997:126), and thereby being able
to take care of oneself (Polanyi 1989:153). The result is a detached—that
is, self-sufficient—independence.

Many anthropologists have argued that this philosophy of individualism is a particularly western phenomenon. In his seminal essay, "A Category of the Human Mind: The Notion of Person; the Notion of Self,"
Marcel Mauss ([1938] 1985) argued that the theory of individualism was
both culturally specific, that is, western, and of relatively recent historical origin (see also Weber [1930] 1958).[4] Nations, he argued, "who have
made of the human person a complete entity, independent of all others
save God, are rare" (Mauss [1938] 1985:14). It is in this regard that J. S.
La Fontaine makes a case for "recognition that concepts of the person
are embedded in a social context," and are related to "a particular concept of society as a whole" (1985:137–38)—a point that serves to clarify
the connection between the individual and the market alluded to above.
Specifically, La Fontaine claims that the western concept of society draws
on the idea of the nation-state, in relationship to which conceptualizations of persons as autonomous entities and of the individual as "a constituent unit of society" must be situated.[5]

The general distinction anthropologists tend to make between the
west and "the rest" with regard to ideas of personhood is one between
individualist conceptions, on the one hand, and sociocentric or "holis-

tic" conceptions on the other (Carrithers, Collins, and Lukes 1985; Dumont 1980; Morris 1994).[6] This is somewhat simplistic. It is not that individualism does not exist outside the west or that sociocentrism is completely absent in the west (Morris 1994; see especially Hollan 1992 and Spiro 1993 for discussions of cross-cultural similarities and intracultural variation). But as a gross distinction, and in the context of welfare state restructuring, it may have heuristic value. Clifford Geertz provides a useful starting point. He writes that

The Western conception of the person as a bounded, unique, more or less integrated motivational and cognitive universe, a dynamic center of awareness, emotion, judgment, and action organized into a distinctive whole and set contrastively against other such wholes and against other social and natural background is, however incorrigible it might seem to us, a rather peculiar idea within the context of the world's cultures. (1975:48)

Two examples from the vast literature on cross-cultural conceptualizations of personhood will serve to illustrate Geertz's point. The first is from Bradd Shore's comparison of Samoan and western constructs of the person. He states:

While the European concept of the integrated, coherent, and "rounded" personality suggests the metaphor of a sphere, that most perfectly "integrated" of objects, the contrasting Samoan metaphor implicit in the Samoan conception of the person is a many-faceted gem. A sphere maintains its shape, its integrity, by a denial of sides, or what is called in contemporary American slang by "getting it all together" [or, more currently, "centering"]. By contrast, a faceted gem maintains its own form through differentiation, a maintenance of distinct sides, as a denial of that integration which would render it without sides. (1982:141)

The European idea(l) of the personality as an integrated whole underscores the individualist attributes of separateness and autonomy. These attributes, however, are problematic in Samoan culture, within which they give rise to either loneliness or antisociality.

Catherine Lutz provides a second example. In her analysis of the cultural construction of emotion in Euramerican culture, on the one hand, and among the Ifaluk in the Caroline Islands, on the other, she claims that westerners

work initially from our own sense of the person as divided into a thinking part and a feeling part, which is private and set off distinctively from a social world of others, from whom we are ideally markedly independent. The emphasis on the distinction between mind and body and the view of the person as above all a sovereign individual help structure the concept of emotion as commonly used by Americans and help organize experience itself. In contrast, the ethnopsychological beliefs that surround and structure Ifaluk emotional life include the notion that the person is first and foremost a social creature and only secondarily, and in a limited way, an autonomous individual. Daily conversations of Ifaluk are pervaded by the assumption that people are oriented primarily toward each other rather than toward an inner world of individually constituted goals and thoughts. (1988:81)

It is not my intention here to explore the strengths and weaknesses of the culture and personality school of anthropology, which makes its own claims about the nature of the person as more or less essentially "plastic" and thus molded by (albeit in the process also molding) the culture in which she or he is placed. Nor am I concerned with the reality of any particular cultural claim about the nature of the person. Rather, I refer to this literature in order to make two points. The first is simply that conceptualizations of personhood are culturally and historically variable. This is, in some ways, and in some circles, unremarkable. But this does not mean that it is not worthy of explicit recognition and, in the current climate of reform, frequent repetition.

The ostensibly unremarkable point that western neoliberal conceptualizations of the person are historical and cultural constructions raises the question of naturalization. In an attempt to avoid ethnocentric interpretations that served to naturalize particular cultural constructs, Louis Dumont (1980) argued against the imposition of western ideas of individualism on interpretations of nonindividualistic oriented cultures. Bronislaw Malinowski ([1922] 1961) made the same point in reference to western readings of the "primitive" Trobriand culture. Dumont's and Malinowski's insight was that ethnocentric projections onto "primitive" cultures lay the groundwork for readings which naturalized indigenous western concepts, in this case, those to do with individualism and "economic man." Friedrich von Hayek (1948:134) did just this when he claimed that, "Even though in the pre-industrial society the great majority also spent most of their lives within the familial organization which was the unit of all economic activity, the heads of the households saw society as a network of family units connected by the markets"—as if (cultural constructions of) *family* and *market* are pancultural, ahistorical facts. The point here is that neoliberalism implicitly challenges the view that personhood is socially and culturally constructed by asserting that the autonomous and rational monad of western thought is "natural" and that any other versions of personhood are more ideological than cultural (Fairclough 1991; Rose 1989).

Cultural conceptions are also naturalized by removing from the social order, or othering, those who do not fulfill its prescriptions. This points to the second issue I want to raise in reference to the cross-cultural literature on personhood; namely, that conceptions of personhood entail conceptions of nonpersonhood, a point crucial to the understanding of contemporary constructions of poor single mothers. Returning again to the anthropological literature, Mauss ([1938] 1985:17; see also Pateman 1988) points out that, among the Romans, slaves were not constituted as persons; and Meyer Fortes states that, among the Tallensi (Ghana), women "can never attain the complete personhood that a male can attain, especially if he reaches elderhood or becomes the holder of a ritual or political office. Certainly for the Tallensi the ideal of the complete person is an adult male who has reached old age and lineage eldership [and] who has male descendants in the patrilineal line" (1987:264, cited in Morris 1994:128).

In contemporary western culture, distinctions are often made between the complete personhood of adults and the partial personhood of children, the elderly, and servants—distinctions that are linguistically marked by the relative appropriateness of referring to members of the latter groups in the third person in their presence. The existence of such distinctions indicates a fluidity by means of which individuals may move in and out of relative positions of personhood[7] This fluidity with regard to poor single mothers is discussed in more detail below. For now it is important to note that binaries of personhood/nonpersonhood, or complete personhood/incomplete personhood, clearly describe "systems of domination" within which "one term has a positive status and an existence independent of the other; the other term is purely negatively defined, and has no contours of its own; its limiting boundaries are those which define the positive term" (Grosz 1989:xvi). Thus the culturally disvalued dimensions of personhood must be examined alongside its valorized dimensions, particularly with regard to their mutual constitution and articulation (Hollan 1992:294).

In the U.S. context, Lawrence Mead (1992:136), a prominent conservative analyst, argues that the "nonworking poor" lack rationality "in the usual sense," insofar as they do not work even though there are opportunities to do so, and are therefore "less responsive to economic incentives than the better-off." He relates this lack of "usual rationality" to inadequate parenting, itself the result of particular historical experiences, most notably those of slavery for African Americans, and of "Third World" origins for immigrants. Of the latter he states:

One of the basic distinctions between the West and non-West is that, in modern times, only the former has consistently taken an activist attitude toward economic activity. Industrialism developed first in the West. People in the West commonly seek to justify themselves through material achievement, and Western societies have a dynamic, ever-changing character. The non-West has typically been less interested in economic progress, suspicious of individual striving, and slower to change. Except for Japan and a few other Asian countries, these societies are still "premodern" or "developing" in Western terms. (Mead 1992:136)

In Mead's view, the "nonworking poor" suffer from attitudes of defeat-ism and helplessness, refusing "to believe that opportunity exists, even when it does." He refers to this defeatism as having "little inner sense of freedom" (1992:145). What such people need—indeed, want—is exter-nal control: "they want norms enforced exactly *because* of their tendency to deviate. . . . They actually desire control, which they typically have not had enough of" (156; emphasis in original).

The construction of poor single mothers is even more telling. In both policy discussion and mass media, poor single mothers are constructed as "strangers in our midst" (Katz 1989:7; cited in de Goede 1996:331), as deviant with regard to mainstream norms of work, childbearing, and self-sufficiency. In their "chosen" dependency on the state, poor women are reconstituted as normative strangers, as not fully adult, even not fully human. (As one U.S. representative claimed, welfare programs "have made generations of Americans nothing more than animals in the Gov-ernment barn"; U.S. Congress 1995.) Poor single mothers, then, consti-tute a population whose subjectivity needs to be reformed (or "disci-plined," in the Foucaultian sense).

Smith's analysis of the naturalization of poverty, mentioned earlier, is worth returning to at this point. As she puts it,

The liberal belief in the freedom of all individuals to participate in citizenship and the marketplace makes it necessary for liberal theories to account for those who do not easily participate in these institutions. At the same time, this liberal belief makes attempts at such explanations difficult because the possibility that citizenship and the market are restrictive defies the terms of freedom and uni-versality that constitute liberal explanation itself. Nowhere is this conflict more evident than in the liberal discussion of poverty. (Smith 1990:209)

As already noted, Smith argues that this conflict is addressed by means of constructions of the poor that situate them outside the realm of ordered liberal society. Welfare and its various bureaucratic forms accordingly function to "surround the poor, to symbolize their outsiderness, to sug-gest that, since this group lacks the ability to get their private property from the market, we will create a structure that distributes commodities 'unnaturally'" (Smith 1990:227). The welfare system thus provides "an ordered way for society to think about the poor" (212). The poor hover on the outskirts of society, and welfare institutions police the boundary. Workfare, in this formulation, like the workhouses of the seventeenth and eighteenth centuries, represents yet another attempt to transform the poor, to "realign . . . them with freedom" (210).

This connection between individualism and freedom is worth pursu-ing, insofar as individual freedom constitutes "liberalism's fundamental moral and political value," leading to an emphasis on "the value of individual autonomy, respect for individual judgement and the importance of individuals pursuing their own self-interested desires as they define them" (Ramsay 1997:38). The unfreedom of the poor, however, is of a particular nature. In recent welfare reform debates in the U.S. Congress, for instance, welfare recipients were described as "enslaved," and welfare reform was touted as the road to "individual liberty" (U.S. Congress 1995). In this formulation, it is not poverty as such but the receipt of relief that renders the poor unfree (see Rose 1996a). As Hayek put it, "There is all the difference in the world between treating people equally and attempting to make them equal. While the first is the condition of a free society, the second means, as De Tocqueville described it, 'a new form of servitude'" (1948:16). Relief, in other words, serves to undermine "some essential human characteristics, in particular self-respect and independence as well as motivation to achieve these things" (Plant 1993:33). It creates unfreedom.

Personhood, Gender, and Race

C. B. Macpherson's (1962) analysis of possessive individualism indicates that freedom, self-possession, market society, and a minimalist state are inextricably tied in the seventeenth century political philosophy which provides one basis of current neoliberal culture. This constellation of philosophies and prescriptions underscores the extent to which neoliberalism is gendered as well as culturally specific. According to Macpherson, possessive individualism is characterized by

a conception of the individual as essentially the proprietor of his [*sic*][8] own person or capacities, owing nothing to society for them. The individual was seen neither as a moral whole, nor as part of a larger social whole, but as an owner of himself. The relationship of ownership, having become for more and more men the critically important relation determining their actual freedom and actual prospect of realizing their full potentialities, was read back into the nature of the individual. The individual, it was thought, is free inasmuch as he is proprietor of his person and capacities. The human essence is freedom from dependence on the wills of others, and freedom is a function of possession. Society becomes a lot of free equal individuals related to each other as proprietors of their own capacities and of what they have acquired by their exercise. Society consists of relations of exchange between proprietors. Political society becomes a calculated device for the protection of this property and for the maintenance of an orderly relation of exchange. (1962:3)

As the history of women's battles to protect their bodily integrity indicates, this notion of the possession of one's own person is clearly gendered, as is the related organization of society and exchange. First, the biological nature of the human species entails a fundamental sociality which problematizes views of the individual as separate, autonomous, and self-sufficient. Both pregnancy, characterized by fuzzy boundaries between the pregnant woman and her fetus (Young 1990a), and lactation, during which the boundaries shift but nevertheless remain fuzzy, belie the myth of separateness and independence (Jaggar 1983). Second, and as feminists have well rehearsed, the "individual" of liberal theory is not a generic individual, but a specifically male individual, whose independent individuality is predicated on women's dependence and subservience. As Nancy Fraser and Linda Gordon (1994) point out in their genealogy of dependency, dependence has both gender and race subtexts. The feminization of the concept is related to the historical development of the "housewife" and the hegemony of the "family wage," both rooted in the period of industrialization; while the racialization of the concept has its roots in industrial justifications of colonization and slavery. "Independence" is thus representative of the free Anglo male earning a family wage, and takes its specific meaning in relation to its opposite, "dependence," represented by the wife, the enslaved, and the colonized. The dependence of free Anglo wage-earning men is thereby erased.

In this construction, "independence" is displayed in the public realm, while "dependence" is sequestered to the private sphere. The public/private divide is thus strongly implicated in the constitution of masculinist individualism (Pateman 1988, 1989): the public, civil society generated by means of the social contract is predicated on the simultaneous generation of a private sphere, into which is jettisoned all that which is not amenable to contract—most notably women, who are not "endowed with the attributes and capacities necessary to enter into contracts" (Pateman 1988:5). Full personhood is thus achieved in civil society, with a marked "liberal resistance to recognizing personhood inside the household" (Brown 1995:181).[9]

In their association with the private sphere, and in their corresponding responsibility for (but not authority over) what goes on there—in particular, childbearing and rearing, and meeting the various messy and embodied needs of male heads of households—women underwrite male development of the capacities requisite to their constitution as "individuals." In so doing, however, they forfeit their own possibilities of achieving this status. This is clearly exemplified by women's relationship to the public realm of paid work, which is constrained by their "private" duties and constituted as secondary in importance to both these responsibilities and their men's public functioning (as constituted by means of the family wage, for instance). Women's contribution in the patriarchal welfare state thus becomes the provision of private (unpaid) welfare—a contribution simultaneously upheld and obscured (Pateman 1989).

The implications of this public/private, independent/dependent binary are twofold. First is the impact on women's citizenship status. The
public sphere is the realm in which full personhood is achieved and prac-
ticed, and, in being the domain of politics, it is thus the realm of citizenship, which is as exclusive as it is inclusive (Lister 1997a). In the context
of the divisions I have just outlined, citizenship is accorded to those who
achieve full personhood by means of their participation in the public
realm: the citizen is specifically the citizen-worker. Given their circumscribed access to the public realm of work, then, women are, as Ruth
Lister (1997a:68) puts it, placed in "exile."

Women's circumscribed relationship to paid labor, and their resulting
status as secondary citizens, has had implications, in turn, for their relationship to the welfare state. Whereas men have made claims against
the state on the basis of their identities as public, rights bearing citizens,
women's claims against the state have usually been made on the basis of
their identities as private persons, as dependent "clients" (Fraser 1989;
Pateman 1989). In some cases (most notably in the United States, but
also in Europe; see Cannan 1995), this distinction has been materially
manifested in a two-channel welfare state characterized by contributory
social insurance programs, on the one hand, and noncontributory welfare programs, on the other. This divide is based on the so-called "contributions" recipients have or have not made by means of participation
in paid labor. Hayek's point about utility and remuneration is instructive here. He states that "any workable individualist order must be so
framed not only that the relative remunerations the individual can expect from the different uses of his [*sic*] abilities and resources correspond
to the relative utility of the result of his efforts to others but also that
these remunerations correspond to the objective results of his efforts
rather than to their subjective merits" (1948:21). The concepts of utility
and merit in this formulation are restricted to the market, clearly illus-
trating Marilyn Waring's (1989, 1990) point that neoclassical economics
fails to account for, and thus place value on, unpaid work in the private
sphere—work done primarily by women (see also England 1993). Such
distinctions and restrictions have served to reinscribe women's status as
second-order individuals. Returning again to Smith's (1990) discussion
of the symbolic alignment of the poor and women, the feminization of
poverty thus refers not only to an exponential rise in the numbers of
poor women, but also to a characterization of the poor, as a category, as
feminine, as suffering from the feminine attributes of disorder, emotion,
irrationality, need, lack, desire, and passion.

These negative attributes of the poor are raced as well as gendered. In
tracing the construction of African-American women over time, for instance, Evelyn Brooks Higginbotham (1996:193) points out that, histori-

cally, "black women's bodies epitomized centuries-long European perceptions of Africans as primitive, animal-like, and savage." She refers in
various contexts to the "pervasive belief in black female promiscuity"
(194), and to an emphasis on "black immorality" (195). Somewhat parallel points have been made about Eurocentric constructions of, among
others, Native Americans in North America (Lomawaima 1993) and
Maori in Aotearoa/New Zealand (McArdell 1992).

The construction of racialized others as "savages" is particularly telling, underscoring a Eurocentric distinction between its civilized self and
the various uncivilized "primitives" inhabiting the non-European world
(or non-European enclaves within the European world, e.g., in the North
American colonies). While the meaning of the term *savage*, like that
of any concept, is subject to historical and cultural variation, several
general features of western constructs of "savages" are discernible, including references to pagan immorality, irrationality, inability to defer
gratification, and a particular relationship with "nature," as opposed to
"culture" (Berkhoffer 1978; Pandian 1985; Sibley 1995; Todorov 1984;
see Kingfisher 1999 for further discussion). While western constructions
of "savages" have included positive elements—thus the concept of the
"noble savage"—it is the negative constructions of "savages" that I wish
to underscore here, insofar as they are predominant in racialized/racist
constructions of welfare recipients.

Stereotypes of the poor and of welfare recipients, then, are thus often
both gendered and raced, and the "dependent" nonperson on welfare is
often a specifically nonwhite woman. As Higginbotham explains, again
in the U.S. context,

the metaphoric and metonymic identification of welfare with the black population by the American public has resulted in tremendous generalization about the
supposed unwillingness of many blacks to work. Welfare immediately conjures
up images of black female-headed families, despite the fact that the aggregate
number of poor persons who receive benefits in the form of aid to dependent
children or medicare is predominantly white. (1996:185)

Thus, in the United States "the black solo mother [has] come to epito-
mize welfare dependency. As a result, the new discourse about welfare
draws on older symbolic currents that linked dependency with racist
ideologies," for example, colonization and slavery (Fraser and Gordon
1994:17). This stereotype of the single black (teenage) welfare mother
"partakes of virtually every quality that has been coded historically as
antithetical to independence" (Fraser and Gordon 1994:18). As Ruth
Lister indicates in Chapter 7 of this volume, the situation in Britain is
somewhat similar, although it is worth pointing out that the racialized

components of stereotypes of welfare dependents are variable across contexts and must be investigated in terms of their unique instantiations.

Women and Welfare Reform in Neoliberal Culture

The ascendancy of neoliberalism's "new regime of the self" (Rose 1996: 60a), as characterized by responsibility, autonomy, self-sufficiency, and independence, signals a shift in the relationship between poor women and state provision. If feminism has struggled with the contradictions between the welfare state's construction of women as mothers and dependents, and thus as secondary citizens, on the one hand, and its contribution to women's independence from abusive relationships with men, on the other, neoliberalism has responded to these struggles and critiques by "degendering" individuals' relationships to state provisioning. In its hypervalorization of the "individual," neoliberalism works to erase all negative and "undeserving" forms of dependency and invites women as well as men to participate in this erasure. Now women, too, can be counted as separate, autonomous individuals whose very individuality provides them with the means to achieve self-sufficiency.

Insofar as the neoliberal erasure of private sphere dependency is nominal, however, women in general, and poor women in particular, cannot function as separate, autonomous "individuals." Neoliberal reform thus works to "degender women and obscure the gendered division of labour by defining them as employable individuals instead of as mothers, and then regenders them as welfare 'dependents' in need of therapeutic intervention" (Brodie 1996b:133). Poor women, in other words, fail to fulfill the requirements of full individuality and autonomy; indeed of citizenship. This "failure," however, is not constituted as one of a particular political or economic system; nor is it seen to be a feature of a gender regime that works to produce male citizens and incomplete dependent women. Rather, the failure is attributed to individuals (women), who are always already incomplete and dependent, with the result that poverty policy is directed at the reformation of individuals rather than structures. The problem, in other words, is not "capitalism, racism and inequality," but "the order of the self and the way we govern ourselves" (Cruikshank 1996:231). The result is that poverty policy is directed at the reformation of individuals rather than structures. Current discourses of empowerment, self-esteem, and self-help accordingly reflect a form of governance in which "the question of governance becomes a question of self-governance" (Cruikshank 1996:232; see also Rose 1996b). As central government programs are devolved to smaller bodies, "welfare dependency" is devolved to individuals who are now constructed as pathological and deficient (Cruikshank 1996; Fraser and Gordon 1994). The ideal neoliberal individual, then, is not just the individual of early liberal philosophy, but a specifically post-Keynesian (neo)liberal individual—one who can transcend the "dependency" engendered by a Keynesian welfare state that was designed to cushion individuals from the vagaries of the market.

This shift from Keynesian to post-Keynesian personhood is marked not only by the pathologizing of "welfare dependence," but also by changes in the various labels attached to those who receive welfare payments—recipients, beneficiaries, clients—each of which marks a particular status. Most notable in this regard is the recent shift from beneficiary or recipient to *customer*. As James Carrier (1997:18) puts it, in the current climate, "Treating citizens as customers of government services is good." This new label gives the impression of *choice*, a keyword of consumer culture, indicating a discursive shift in which recipients of financial support are no longer the beneficiaries of charity, but parties to a contract—a shift, in other words, that serves to obfuscate the inequality between welfare recipients and the welfare bureaucracy (see below for further discussion of contract).

Insofar as poverty is constituted as a reflection of an individual, feminized and/or racialized incapacity, the responses of the neoliberal state are channeled in two specific directions. One is the route of outright cuts, including benefit reductions and limitations, restrictions on eligibility, and increased targeting and means-testing. This route is particularly attractive if the existence of the poor is constituted as reflective of an individualized incapacity that is perhaps not only inherent, but specifically enhanced by welfare programs that have encouraged dependency. In other words, if freedom requires the absence (or at least the minimization) of interference—what is known in liberal theory as negative liberty (Ramsay 1997)—then welfare provisions undermine recipients' liberty, as well as that of taxpayers who are forced to contribute to welfare programs. What Sainsbury (1996:198) refers to as "residualization" thus becomes a key strategy of reform.

A second route to reform draws on a more positive version of freedom in recognizing that freedom requires the resources necessary to pursue one's own individual ends (Ramsay 1997). In this case, the state is seen as responsible for providing some of these resources. The resources it provides must be of a very particular nature, however, if the result is not to be a disabling, disempowering interference. Specifically, the resources provided must be designed so as to enhance individuals' abilities to exercise autonomy, self-sufficiency, and independence. So-called "incentive" programs, which are highly interventionist (certainly with respect to surveillance), punitive, and in many respects illiberal, result from this position. Sanctions for children's nonattendance at school and for out-of-wedlock births, and lifetime limits on the receipt of benefits (in the U.S. case) are constituted as appropriate "incentives" in this framework. Most notable, however, is workfare.[10] "Work," as Foucault (1977:242) quotes Léon Faucher (1838), is "the providence of the modern peoples; it replaces morality, fills the gaps left by beliefs and is regarded as the principle of all good." Workfare, in this regard, functions "as a means of promoting the personal capacities required for the exercise of autonomy" (Hindess 1997:25), positively contributing to poor people's "ethical reconstruction as active citizens" (Rose 1996b:60).

This second option draws heavily on the idea of contract. The kind of contract to which welfare recipients have access, however, is not characterized by exchange among equals, but, rather, by "the exchange of obedience for protection" (Pateman 1988:58; see also Yeatman 2000). The parties to this kind of "contract" are thus specifically unequal, and the "less equal" party must acquiesce to the terms put forward by the "more equal" party (Pateman 1988:58–59; see also Fraser and Gordon 1992). The relevance of this insight for women's relationship to state provisioning is obvious: perversely, women must depend for protection on that from which they must most fear violation (see Brown 1995).

The veneer of equality, however, remains central to the model of contract deployed in welfare reform measures, and this supposed equality is often set in opposition to charity—a curious modern day take-off on what Henry S. Maine ([1861] 1998) described in terms of the oppressions of status. In the contract model of exchange—the paradigmatic example of which is the exchange of labor for wages—equal parties exchange equivalents. Charity, on the other hand, is not about exchange, but about gifts given without return. Historically, according to Fraser and Gordon (1992), noncontractual exchange and obligation have gradually been restricted to the domestic or private sphere, becoming defined as "female" and as "charity." Contractual exchange, on the other hand, occurring in the public, male sphere, has become the more prevalent, and accepted, mode of interaction between individuals and parties. Again, however, as Carol Pateman (1988) has demonstrated, the assumption that parties to a contract are full contractual persons (Yeatman 1997) is erroneous. And whereas liberal theory previously awarded "protection" and charity to those deemed to be less than full contractual persons, such protection is no longer acceptable under neoliberal regimes. Indeed, it is deemed to be patronizing and disempowering, contributing to the creation of a particularly insidious form of unfreedom.

Instead, with the help of the disciplinary measures of cuts and so-called incentives, poor single mothers on welfare are being reconstituted as potential able-bodied workers—as potentially empowerable and equal individuals. The move is one from dependence to enterprise, the latter characterized by a valorization of "autonomy, responsibility, initiative, self-reliance, independence, a willingness to take risks, see opportunities, and take responsibility for one's own actions" (Cannan 1995:162). With their reconstitution as enterprising subjects, poor women are being compelled to enter the public realm to an even greater extent than previously (since many already combine welfare with low wage labor). Despite the increasing material and discursive movement of women into the public sphere, however, women do not enter as equal citizens, as the dearth of effective equality legislation indicates (Sainsbury 1996). Simultaneously, moreover, privatization is contributing to an expansion of the realm of private welfare, for which women continue to be held responsible.

Conclusions

I have focused in this chapter on a conception of personhood that is at the center of neoliberal theorizing. It is on the basis of this neoliberal "individual" that a particular portrait of society is drawn—a portrait, as Pateman so eloquently points out, that depends on, but does not include within its purview, the private sphere. The neoliberal "individual" is also at the center of contract theory, on which current ideas of "contracts" between welfare institutions and recipients are drawn.

My goal in this chapter has been to argue that this particular view of personhood, and of the societal relationships developed on its basis —particularly those related to welfare reform—are ethnocentric, masculinist, and racist; and that its current deployments reflect a particular form of governance that relies on self surveillance and self-governance (Barry, Osborne, and Rose 1996). Insofar as women are less able to conform to its prescriptions, this neoliberal discourse of individualism is inimical to their interests, particularly when they have sole responsibility for the care of dependent children. The potency of this discourse, and its refusal to recognize various forms and levels of "dependence" and "independence" (Fraser and Gordon 1994), is such that single mothers in western neoliberal states often find themselves the targets of new welfare programs focused on reforming the "undeserving" poor by bringing them more in line with the tenets of neoliberal individualism. This targeting of single mothers clearly points to the gendered subtext of social citizenship (Brodie 1996b), which requires attachment to the labor market for recognition. In this formulation, childrearing is neither recognized as "work," nor counted as contributory to society (Fraser and Gordon 1992). Moreover, in the context of economic globalization (see Chapter 3), economic citizenship, as a social right to economic well-being and survival, is no longer the property of individuals, but one of firms and markets—of what Saskia Sassen (1996a:38) refers to as "global economic actors."

How this grammar of neoliberal individualism articulates with various forms of national welfare culture and specific programs of reform is the project of Part II of this collection. First, however, I turn to a second key theme in the neoliberal project of welfare reform; namely, the proliferation of ideas and practices related to market society. If neoliberal conceptualizations of personhood are fundamental to the discourse of welfare reform, conceptualizations of the market are equally relevant; indeed, the two are inextricably tied. The market, and the globalizing implications of the "free" market (which, not coincidentally, has close ties to ideas of "free" individuals), are, accordingly, the focus of the following chapter.

Chapter 3
Neoliberalism II

The Global Free Market

Catherine Kingfisher

> [A] growing body of evidence signals that economic globalization has hit at some of the major conditions that have hitherto supported the evolution of citizenship and particularly the formation of social rights.
>
> —Saskia Sassen, *Losing Control?*

Through the processes of globalization, the one-time mutual dependence of the wealthy and poor (or, most importantly, the dependence of the wealthy on the poor)[1] has been disestablished: "Creation of wealth is on the way to finally emancipating itself from the old, constraining and vexing connections with making things, processing materials, creating jobs and managing people" (Bauman 1998:44). The welfare state, as an artifact of this mutual dependence, is thus no longer necessary, and its obsolescence is proclaimed in calls for simultaneous cuts in welfare benefits for the poor and in taxes for the rich. Theorists of an informational society similarly note the increasing surperfluousness of the poor (e.g., Castells 1996, 1997; see Susser 1997 for summary).

The argument has also been made that the welfare state was an artifact of the Cold War, a strategy for dampening the allure of socialism (Seabrook 1997). Now that the Cold War is over, so the reasoning goes, the raison d'être for the welfare state has been eliminated. From this perspective, the welfare state has not been a simple matter of generosity and caring, of concern with the well-being of the population; rather, it has reflected a form of governance interested in, as Foucault (1979:10) cites Guillaume de La Perrière, "the right disposition of things, arranged so as to lead to a convenient end," namely, the constitution of particular subjectivities and social systems in a bipolar world.[2]

Regardless of their respective merits, both arguments serve to situate welfare state processes in a global milieu. As I argued in Chapter 1, and as will be demonstrated in the case study chapters in Part II, there are cross-national patterns in the restructuring of welfare states. The obvious point is that welfare reform does not just take place in nation-states in isolation, but in the larger context of nation-states' relationships with each other, and with other transnational nonstate actors or forces (e.g., multinationals, transnationals, international organizations such as the World Bank, the International Monetary Fund [IMF], the International Labor Organization [ILO], and the World Trade Organization [WTO]; and trade agreements such as the North American Free Trade Agreement [NAFTA] and the Australian—New Zealand Closer Economic Relationship [CER]). Welfare reform measures undertaken in particular nation-states must therefore be situated in the context of a global political and cultural economy. This global political and cultural economy is typically referred to by the term *globalization*, which indexes two inextricably tied processes: on the one hand, economic globalization, or the "rapid growth of transactions and institutions that are outside the framework of interstate relations" (Sassen 1998:100); and, on the other hand, the globalization of culture, which refers to the increasing mobility of people, ideas, and practices.

In this chapter, I continue to outline a preliminary grammar of neoliberalism by working to situate our understanding of welfare state restructuring in relation to "globalization," with specific emphasis on a neoliberal culture of economics. The argument I make is that global trends in welfare state restructuring are dependent not only on the spread of specifically gendered notions of personhood, but also, to a large degree, on the mobilization of gendered sources of cheap labor and of unpaid domestic and volunteer work; in other words, on one gender's—women's—"infinite elasticity" (Elson 1995). All of these trends, or emphases, are inextricably tied to ideas and practices of a free market that is inherently global in orientation. Globalization and the restructurings that accompany it are thus underwritten, at least in part, by women. My goal in this chapter is therefore to *gender* the globalization of neoliberal economics and to *gender* the related restructuring of the welfare state. Those who suffer the greatest negative impacts of these processes, I will argue, are low-income and poor women—either literally, or as persons who have otherwise been "feminized."[3]

Globalization and the Market

In his now famous "Disjuncture and Difference in the Global Cultural Economy," Appadurai (1996a) outlines five *scapes* whose "fluid, irregular shapes" characterize the disjunctive nature of what he refers to as the current "global cultural economy" (1996a:32–33).[4] I begin my discussion with reference to two of these *scapes*, technoscapes and financescapes, which Appadurai defines as follows:

> By *technoscape*, I mean the global configuration . . . ever fluid, of technology and the fact that technology, both high and low, both mechanical and informational, now moves at high speeds across various kinds of previously impervious boundaries. . . .
>
> . . . *financescapes* [refer to] the disposition of global capital . . . [to the fact that] currency markets, national stock exchanges, and commodity speculations move megamonies through national turnstiles at blinding speed, with vast, absolute implications for small differences in percentage points and time units. (1996a: 34–35)

Together, technoscapes and financescapes, related as they are to both production and trade/exchange, encompass key features of economic globalization. As Sassen (1998) points out, however, economic globalization is neither theoretically nor operationally neutral. Yet, many models portray globalization as a purely impartial economic phenomenon. How is this culture-free dispassionate economic enterprise envisioned and constructed?

Definitions of economic globalization, drawing on neoclassical economics, most often refer to the increasing intensification of global economic interdependencies. Richard Higgott, for example, defines globalization simply as "greater international economic integration" (1999:25). Hans-Peter Martin and Harold Schuman refer similarly to a single world market, which they critically characterize as "turbo-capitalism" (1996:9). Perhaps most comprehensively, Dean Baker, Gene Epstein and Robert Pollin view economic globalization as "an accelerating rate and/or a higher level of economic interaction between people of different countries, leading to a qualitative shift in the relationship between nation-states and national economies" (1998:5). This "greater international economic integration" means that technology, production, finance, and trade are ever less oriented or accountable to national borders and are increasingly able to move at the behest of nonstate forces or actors. It means that the unit of analysis for economic decisions is no longer the nation-state (Hart and Prakash 1997), but the transnational—that which cuts across, supersedes, or subsumes national borders. It is in this light that Masao Miyoshi (1993) refers to transnational corporations as the new (neo)colonials, answerable only to themselves. Discourses and practices of economic globalization thus endeavor to enhance the supremacy of the market vis-à-vis the state.[5] A laissez faire model—Adam Smith's "invisible hand"—is valorized over state interference (Keynesianism). This idealized market is a sphere of activity characterized by exchange relations between equal individuals, based on the forces of supply and demand.

In the neoclassical model, Michele Pujol points out, "the market provides the central mechanism for resource allocation, production decisions and income distribution. By assuming perfectly competitive conditions, utility maximization (for individuals) and profit maximization (for firms), the market mechanism is shown to provide the most economically efficient, maximizing outcome" (1992:6). The free market, then, produces a self-regulating economy, the potential benefits of which—for all citizens—are susceptible to being undermined by state interference, whether that interference takes the form of social programs or trade barriers:

The state regulation of industry and collective welfare provisions are to be minimized as they are seen as impediments to liberty and the freedom of the individual to define, pursue and satisfy their own wants and preferences. Public power is to be restricted to maintaining or expanding the framework of private property, competition and trade which guarantee free scope for private enterprise. The implicit normative claims are that in an unfettered market these institutions are self-adjusting leading to an equilibrium of supply and demand, and that they are conducive to maximizing satisfaction. Economists claim that, on the basis of a given distribution of income and resources, the perfect market economy would represent the realization of individual choice for goods and services, and would maximize this choice equitably and efficiently. (Ramsay 1997:238; see also Elson 1994)

In other words, threaded through this construction of the "free market" is "a claim and belief that a certain sort of buying and selling benefits all those involved economically, politically, socially and even morally" (Carrier 1997:vii). This reasoning provides justification for restructuring. Indeed, it was precisely such thinking that underwrote Reaganomics in the United States, Thatcherism in the United Kingdom and Rogernomics in New Zealand, all of which were based on the promulgation of what Macpherson referred to as "possessive market society," the postulates of which are as follows:

1. There is no authoritative allocation of work.
2. There is no authoritative provision of rewards for work.

3. There is authoritative definition and enforcement of contracts.
4. All individuals seek rationally to maximize their utilities.
5. Each individual's capacity to labour is his [*sic*] own property and is alienable.
6. Land and resources are owned by individuals and are alienable.
7. Some individuals want a higher level of utilities or power than they have.
8. Some individuals have more energy, skill, or possessions, than others (Macpherson 1962:53–54).

Insofar as economic globalization entails the spread of this model of competitive market society across national boundaries, it requires the removal of barriers to its reach—in this case, public goods and social support systems. Only then can the market function in a free and unfettered fashion. Indeed, according to many proponents of welfare reform, the lack of an empirical free market is precisely the problem. As Fredric Jameson states more generally, "In the view of many neoliberals, not only do we not yet have a free market, but what we have in its place . . .— namely, a mutual compromise and buying off of pressure groups, special interests, and the like—is in itself . . . a structure absolutely inimical to the real free market and its establishment" (1991:266).

The Free Market as Cultural Construction

It is arguable that this model of the market has become the lingua franca of globalization (Carrier 1997). As Jameson points out, however, the market is "at one and the same time an ideology and a set of practical institutional problems" (1991:260). The market, he claims, "turns out finally to be as Utopian as socialism has recently been held to be" (278). There is no such thing—in an empirical as opposed to an ideological sense—as a free market, the market is "'a superstition,' a 'self-validating essay in logic'" (E. P. Thompson 1971:91; cited in Carrier 1997:8).

Given its status as an ideological construct, then, and like the construction of personhood outlined in Chapter 2, the free market is not "natural"; it is not "a reflection or expression of some pan-human propensity to truck, barter and exchange" (Carrier 1997:26). As anthropologists from Malinowski ([1922] 1961) to Sahlins (1972, 1976) have noted, "rational" economic behavior, like "rationality" itself, is not a cultural universal, but a cultural and historical construction. In a western context, the relationship between the idea of the market outlined above and the construction of personhood explored in Chapter 2 is succinctly summarized by Joel Kahn:

As a discourse, the "Market model" represents not just a defence of "markets," but an elaborated "theory" about human nature and the best means of promoting human emancipation. Within that model, those who populate this cultural world of the Market are taken as free individuals with their eyes securely on material reward. Whatever sorts of people they may be in their private lives, once they enter the economic realm their manner is one of self-regard and material calculation. In the Smithian version, public life is—or, perhaps better, should be—characterised by impersonal interactions: neither who one is or considerations of morality should be allowed to influence public behaviour. Indeed, precisely this liberation from social and ethical norms is what constitutes human emancipation in the discourse of the Market. (Kahn 1997:75; see also Carrier 1997:8–9, 20–21)

The mutual dependence of possessive individualism and competitive market society thus reveals the gendered nature of both. Insofar as the globalization of neoliberalism and neoliberalism as a globalizing force are dependent on the spread of these highly gendered discourses, it is arguable, as I claimed at the beginning of this chapter, that globalization, as discourse and practice, is itself highly gendered—that economic and cultural globalization carry gender subtexts (some of which are not so sub).

Consideration of the specifically gendered nature of both possessive individualism and the free market serves to highlight the selective nature of arguments for reduced state funding and interference. In "reinvigorat[ing] the market sector" (Bryson 1992:179), rationalist economic policies work to the advantage of particular groups and to the disadvantage of others (e.g., women, the poor, people of color). Recall from Chapter 2, for instance, Hayek's (1948) argument that remuneration be based on the "objective" value of what individuals produce. On the contrary, Maureen Ramsay notes that

Demand is a poor guide to the contributions people value, because some of the things people value do not register as demands on the market, because the market does not supply them (they are not marketable); and because people can be manipulated into demanding things which bring them little benefit. *The market does not measure a person's contribution. It merely reflects how much that contribution can be sold for.* (1997:77, emphasis added)

In other words, the invisible hand of the market, based on the forces of supply and demand which will supposedly lead to a natural equilibrium, actually works to render some phenomena visible and others invisible—some things count while others do not. For a phenomenon to be included in the market, it must be traded in the marketplace, it must have monetary value. Otherwise, it does not figure as part of the market, which has come to stand in for the economy. The result is that what constitutes work, trade, production, and so on becomes very narrowly defined (Waring 1989, 1990; Strassman 1993). "Macro-economics," Elson (1994:42) argues, "has a one-sided view of the macro-economy: it considers only the monetary aggregates of the 'productive economy.' It ignores the human resource aggregates of the 'reproductive economy.'" What is jettisoned in the process of articulating this model of the market with the neoliberal project of welfare reform is not only particular kinds or spheres of activity, however, but also the particular subjectivities of those who engage in these activities and live in these spheres. The individuals carrying these subjectivities are erased not as persons per se, but as particular kinds of persons—(poor) mothers—with particular kinds of attributes. Their subjectivities are then reconstituted, such that they can be seen—and treated as—possessive individuals who can/must now freely enter the marketplace.

Cultural Constructions and Policy

. . . the Market model provides the vocabulary and conceptual equipment that make it relatively easy to define certain sorts of things as problems and relatively hard to define other sorts of things that way. Just as it influences the sort of problems that can be addressed, so it influences what is likely to appear as an acceptable, plausible solution. (Carrier 1997:51)

People do not produce meanings within some entirely separate interpretative channel which, as it were, runs parallel with other social practices but leaves them untouched. Cultural signification and interpretation constantly orientates people, individually and collectively, towards particular actions. (Tomlinson 1999:24)

In adopting particular discourses, we construct specific orientations to the world, with direct implications for how we operate in the world. Discourse, in other words, sets the parameters of what is statable, of what is visible, and therefore, of what, in fact, "exists"—or should exist (Foucault 1972, 1978). Thinking about the market in particular ways, then, has real material consequences. The impact of free market discourse on public policy accordingly warrants interrogation.

Nancy Fraser (1989) discusses the connection between discourse (or interpretation) and practice in direct relationship to policy formation, arguing that the latter is not simply a response to already constituted needs, but rather entails the constitution (interpretation) of needs, and the construction of appropriate ways of addressing these newly defined needs. The process is permeated, through and through, with discursive struggle. In this sense it is difficult to "distinguish clearly between economics and culture, economic analysis and policy prescription" (Carrier 1997:15).

The global spread of neoclassical economic models valorizing the free market may be referred to as "global neoliberalism" (DeMartino 1999: 343), "neoliberal globalization" (Gill 1995:400), or, perhaps most insightfully, "neoliberal market civilisation" (Gill 1995:399). What shape, however, does this phenomenon take at the level of the nation-state? Although claiming the reality of economic regionalism over that of globalization (see especially Hirst and Thompson 1996), Vicente Navarro outlines four key features of the neoliberal "orthodoxy" that characterize the current thinking of many neoliberal regimes:

1. Public deficits are intrinsically negative.
2. State regulation of the labor market is also intrinsically negative.
3. Social protection guaranteed by the welfare state and its redistributive policies hinders economic growth.
4. The state should not intervene in regulating foreign trade or international financial markets. (1998:608–9)

As adopted differently by various nation-states, the outcomes of these orthodoxies may be said to characterize economic globalization. Together, they comprise the orientation that provides economic justification for the reform of welfare provisioning. The first point to be made here, then, is that the nation-state is pivotal to the removal of the barriers considered inimical to economic globalization. Indeed, Roland Robertson (1992) argues that the processes of globalization had their genesis in the emergence and consolidation of the nation-state. Accordingly, the nation-state is constitutive of the global.[6] Moreover, as Sassen (1996a, 1998) elucidates, globalization *requires* the nation-state. Globalization is always, she claims, territorially situated, and that situatedness has as much to do with the state as it does with the transnational, insofar as multi- and transnationals depend for their functioning on the legal instruments of the state.

Returning to Navarro's orthodoxy, welfare state restructuring, construed by the state as a way of addressing budget deficits and increasing international economic competitiveness, has tended to focus on cutting costs, rather than raising revenues (Bakker 1994a:7). The rhetoric of many states resembles the following: "In order to compete, national economies must become efficient, which means reducing fiscal and regulatory burdens on industry and lowering expectations about the role of the state both in terms of protecting national economies from global pressures and providing social welfare" (Brodie 1994:48; see also Cerny 1994).[7]

Examples from Aotearoa/New Zealand and the United States will serve to illustrate how this argument works.[8] Both countries have experienced changes in recent decades reflective of their changing sovereignty in a global political-cultural economy. Ida Susser (1997:396) accordingly situates the 1996 U.S. Personal Responsibility and Work Opportunity Reconciliation Act (PRWORA) in the context of a worldwide "expansion of the industrial labor force." What we now find in the United States, she claims, is "an informational economy, accompanied by enfeebled unions, less security for most workers, a growing informal labor force, the shrinking of the welfare state and increasing inequality."

Several factors have also altered Aotearoa/New Zealand's political and economic relations with the "outside world" and made it more open to external influences of the sort that globalization theory highlights. First, with Britain's entry into and growing commitment to the European Community, access to the major market for the sorts of commodities that New Zealand traditionally produced (meat, wool, and dairy products) could no longer be taken for granted. Second, the Australian and New Zealand labor and commodity markets became much more integrated through the creation of an instrument known as the Closer Economic Relationship (CER), thus exposing New Zealand to its much larger neighbor. Third, the rise of the East Asian "tiger'" economies opened up new markets for new and traditional export products. Finally, and partly as a response to these developments, New Zealand's own trade barriers have been progressively dismantled, its economic and financial sectors have been deregulated, and many state assets have been sold to local and (especially) international interests (Jesson 1987; Kelsey 1993, 1995, 1999; Easton 1997, 1999).

In response to these changes, proponents of the economic argument against welfare in both countries claim that public relief has become too expensive and that it has failed to relieve poverty. In a July 1996 speech, for instance, then New Zealand Minister of Social Welfare Peter Gresham provided background and justification for the 1991 benefit cuts, which reduced the benefit for a single adult with one child by $25 per week and also transformed a system of more or less universal benefits into one of increasingly targeted benefits. One rationale for the cuts was that New Zealanders could simply "no longer sustain the cost of their comprehensive social security scheme"; that in the face of a depressed economy, the government had to reduce expenditure (New Zealand Executive Government Speech Archive, July 30, 1996). Calls for cutting welfare spending in Aotearoa/New Zealand have also been made in the name of "inter-generational equity" (Kelsey 1995: 281).

Similar sentiments regarding runaway costs of welfare programs have been expressed in debates on welfare reform in the United States Congress. In support of the 1996 PRWORA, for instance, Senator John Ashcroft stated that, "In spite of the good intentions of the welfare program, which we have poured billions of dollars into, hundreds of billions of dollars, we have ended up trapping people at their lowest and least rather than calling people or prompting people to their highest and best" (U.S. Congress 1996). In an earlier debate, Representative David Funderburk also pointed to the financial incentives for welfare reform: "Let me tell you where we will be if we do not put a brake on the runaway welfare train. Today Federal welfare spending stands at $387 billion, by 2000 we will spend $537 billion on welfare entitlements. This madness has to stop" (U.S. Congress 1995). Finally, as vice chairman of the 1996 welfare reconciliation conference, Senator Pete Domenici echoed Funderburk's fiscal incentive, stating that the bill would save the American taxpayers $55 billion dollars in its first six years (U.S. Congress 1996).

This approach represents a form of economic rationalism, in which claims that "social problems can progressively be solved by the application of rationally devised state-implemented social policies" are seen as both unaffordable and inefficacious (Bryson 1992:178; see also Macdonald 1995). In economic arguments, the suffering body is the economy, not the individual poor body;[9] accordingly, resources must be diverted to, or reclaimed by, the larger body, and in so doing the longer-term interests of the individual poor will be better served. It is an argument, in other words, for "trickle-down" welfare. This trickle-down approach is exemplified by Winton Bates (1996; cited in Boston, St. John, and Stephens 1996:3), who claimed that in New Zealand, "Continuation down the free-market track will strengthen the basis for widespread opportunity and a high degree of personal security through growth of the economy." Similar arguments have been made in other nation-states.

In a cautionary remark, Gøsta Esping-Andersen argues that, while we "should not exaggerate the degree to which global forces overdetermine the fate of national welfare states" (1996:5), it is clear that "global competition does narrow the field of domestic policy choice" (1996:2; see also Cerny 1994). Most notable in the case of welfare state restructuring in countries like the United States and Aotearoa/New Zealand, for instance, is "a strategy of deregulating wages and the labour market, combined with a certain degree of welfare state erosion" (Esping-Andersen 1996:10). The processes of economic globalization thus indicate that the sovereignty of the nation-state, in terms of its ability to control what goes on materially and ideologically within its territory, is not what it used to be and is in the process of transformation—although no one is quite clear as to the results of this transformation. In addition, the challenges to the welfare state identified by Esping-Andersen—changing economic conditions and demographic trends, and a disjuncture between the current social order and that for which the welfare state was designed (1996:6–9)—must themselves be situated in a global context. The changing economic conditions to which Esping-Andersen refers clearly occur in reference to the changes in the international division of labor noted by Susser (1997). In addition, shifts away from an ideal homogeneous population composed of homogeneous nuclear-family units reflect, at least in part, the movement across cultural space of ideas of heterogeneity and difference.[10]

In his comparison of the United States and various European Union countries, however, Navarro (1998) argues that economically determinist or reductionist arguments are problematic insofar as the tenets of neoliberalism have not proven to be beneficial. Specifically, neoliberal programs have failed to stimulate economic growth, and in fact have engendered increased social inequality and polarization (see also Gill 1995). In this context, the economic justification for welfare reform is simply that—a justification. As the case study chapters in Part II indicate, nation-states *do* have some element of choice in relation to how they deal with the pressures of economic globalization, with which, as I have already indicated, they are often complicit.

The Cultural Politics of Globalization

Globalization is clearly not just about the economic, but also about the political and the cultural. It entails not only a transformation of "territorial organization and economic activity," but also a transformation "in the organization of political power" (Sassen 1998:92).[11] Accordingly, analysts are increasingly noting the relationship between economics and other aspects of social organization. Higgott (1999:23), for example, refers to the need to put the political back into political economy, Navarro (1998), as already pointed out, claims that economically based arguments for the retrenchment of the welfare state are in fact more political than economic, Roger Tooze and Craig Murphy (1996:689) refer to the invisibility of populations whose activities fall outside of the realm of the "rationality of the neoliberal market," and so forth. There is recognition, in other words, that economic phenomena are not "outside" of culture and society, and of power relations in particular.

This recognition is particularly evident in the more encompassing theories of globalization that have been generated by anthropologists, sociologists, and cultural studies scholars. These theorizations point to the contexts within which neoliberal ideas travel, and perhaps can best be summarized by Eric Hobsbawm's (1994; cited in Gill 1995: 404–5) definition of globalization as "a single, increasingly integrated and universal world economy largely operating across state frontiers ('transnationally') and therefore increasingly across the frontiers of state ideology." Thus Robertson (1992) emphasizes not only global "compression" (material interdependence) but also reflexivity (a global self-consciousness), both of which draw the world closer to some kind of "unicity" (Tomlinson 1999). Particularly relevant in this context is Robertson's specification of the increasingly global definition of persons as autonomous entities.[12]

Like Robertson, Anthony Giddens (1990) underscores the reflexive features of globalization. He points additionally to "time-space distanciation," the differentiation of time from space that allows for the stretching of social relationships across great distances and the "disembedding" of social relations from local contexts. In a somewhat different reading, David Harvey (1989) stresses time-space compression, rather than distanciation, in which space is removed rather than stretched, and in which time is shortened.

These theorists all emphasize the relationship between the social, cultural, and political aspects of globalization, on the one hand, and economic systems, on the other: Giddens, for instance, argues that through the processes of globalization the world economy becomes a capitalist world economy; while Harvey relates postmodernity and time-space compression to the move from Fordist to post-Fordist regimes of accumulation. Stuart Hall (1997) also combines economic analysis, for instance of flexible specialization, with analyses of a shift in global cultural centers from England to the United States. Many of these theorists draw on Scott Lash and John Urry's (1987) work on disorganized capitalism, which, in contrast to an organized capitalism in which the flows of finance and commodities are tightly organized by corporations and states, is characterized by an increasing international expansion and velocity in which commodities are more mobile and finance becomes dematerialized (Waters 1995:52–53). The political, social, and cultural concomitants of disorganized capitalism then become the subject of analysis, especially insofar as what are now produced, as much as or more than material objects, are systems of meaning, or signs (Lash and Urry 1987).

Appadurai's (1996a) *mediascapes, ideoscapes,* and *ethnoscapes* become particularly relevant here. *Mediascapes* refers "both to the distribution of the electronic capabilities to produce and disseminate information . . . and to the images of the world created by these media" (1996:35)—that is, to the images carried by television, newspapers, and so on. More narrowly, *ideoscapes* refers to particular sets of traveling images that are

often directly political and frequently have to do with the ideologies of states and the counterideologies of movements explicitly oriented to capturing state power or a piece of it. These ideoscapes are composed of elements of the Enlightenment worldview, which consists of a chain of ideas, terms, and images, including *freedom, welfare, rights, sovereignty, representation, and the master term democracy.* (Appadurai 1996a:36, emphasis in original)

Finally, by *ethnoscape*, Appadurai (1996a:33) means "the landscape of persons who constitute the shifting world in which we live: tourists, immigrants, refugees, exiles, guest workers, and other moving groups and individuals."

These three *scapes* frame the movement and (re)conceptualizations of discourses across cultural space. One example from the United States and Aotearoa/New Zealand,[13] also discussed by Wendy Larner (this volume), will serve to illustrate the heuristic power of these *scapes* for investigating how ideas of the free market and possessive individualism travel—in other words, how neoliberal globalization is produced. In early 1997, the New Zealand Social Welfare Department sponsored a "Beyond Dependency" conference, in which high-ranking proponents of welfare reform in the United States were featured as key speakers. Particular emphasis was placed on WisconsinWorks, a program widely known for its stringent emphasis on "personal responsibility," "independence," and workfare. This conference laid the groundwork for the New Zealand government's production, in 1998, of a proposed "Code of Social and Family Responsibility," which outlined a code of individual and family—that is, private—responsibility for economic, social, and physical well-being. The code mirrored in many ways the discourse of welfare reform in the United States, from which it got its inspiration. In Chapter 7 of this volume, Ruth Lister also tracks the travel of the discourses of dependency and the underclass from the United States to Britain, via local sponsorship of Charles Murray's analyses.

Although Appadurai has been criticized for what is considered to be an overly humanistic orientation that neglects political economy, his *scapes* in fact encompass both political *and* cultural economy, insofar as they recognize that "political economy [is] inseparable from a range of cultural processes" (Ong 1999:16).[14] Thus globalization is perhaps best viewed as an intensification and transformation of international interdependencies and worldwide relations in the broadest possible sense (Hall 1997; Nederveen Pieterse 1995; Sassen 1998).

Globalization, Gender, and Welfare State Restructuring

A feminist critique of economic policy reform at the macro-level can be developed in terms of an analysis of how economic policy reform treats the interdependence between the "productive economy" and the "reproductive economy," between making a profit and meeting needs, between covering costs and sustaining human beings. (Elson 1994:41)

One thread that runs through the current phase of globalization is the role of gender in underwriting the twinned processes of marketization and privatization.[15] As Aihwa Ong (1999:11) notes, however, "Besides the poor, women, who are half of humanity, are frequently absent in studies of transnationalism." As yet another intervention in this problematic "conceptual silence" (Bakker 1994a:1), in the remainder of this chapter I provide a brief framework for conceptualizing the relationship between globalization and gender, and between welfare state restructuring and gender, with emphasis on both women in general, and single mothers in particular. It is noteworthy in this regard that the poor and the women to whom Ong (1999) refers are often one and the same.

As I noted in Chapter 1, analysts of gender and labor in the so-called "First" and "Third" worlds have noted that women in both contexts tend to occupy the least secure, lowest paying, and often most dangerous positions in the labor force (Enloe 1989; Mies 1986; Mies, Bennholdt-Thomsen, and von Werlhof 1988). This phenomenon seems to have been intensified in the current phase of economic globalization; indeed, it is arguably the case that the First/Third World distinction is becoming increasingly artificial—that the Third World, or South, is increasingly present in the First World, or North (Sparr 1995; Stavrianos 1981).

In her discussion of the intertwined processes of the overvalorization and devalorization of particular forms of production, outputs, and workers in global cities,[16] Sassen (1988) points out that women and "female-typed" jobs tend to predominate in devalued sectors. What mainstream analyses of economic globalization glorify—in particular, "the new finance and services-led economy," characterized by "extremely high profit-making capabilities"—is dependent on and serves to devalorize the "[l]ow-value-added services and urban-based manufacturing . . . where [poor] women and immigrants predominate" (Sassen 1998:88–89). In this regard, Claire Turenne Sjolander indicates that the internationalization of production, a key marker of contemporary globalization, has brought with it an internationalization of service industries,[17] which comprise 90 to 95 percent of new jobs created in the industrialized countries (1996:607). The problematics of women's predominance in the low-value-added service sector, known for its insecurity, low rates of remuneration, and often difficult to manage schedules in relation to childcare needs, are well known (Sjolander 1996.:612). The result is that globalization produces an "increased polarization of society" (609), which entails a particular process of othering—of constructing and consolidating differences that matter. This, in turn, generates the view that the immiseration of certain segments of the population "is justifiable to support the economic restructuring 'demanded' by globalization" (614). Sjolander states further that

The construction of "others" who can be compromised by the exigencies of globalization is not restricted to the other-national worker [Third World workers].

The national "welfare cheats" are equally to be decried because they do not share our value for hard work and manicured lawns. . . . While the poor have to some extent always been constructed as "other," the homogenizing processes of globalization reveal their "difference" all the more starkly. (1996:615)

In a related analysis of the production of devalorization—indeed, erasure—of the gendered foundations of globalization, Linda McDowell (1991) claims that major theorists of globalization have neglected to explicitly include gender in their analyses while simultaneously making particular assumptions about gender relations. Focusing on the transition from Fordist to post-Fordist regimes of accumulation, McDowell analyzes the work of the French Regulation School[18] and analysts of flexible specialization. Both, she finds, ignore the essential role of gender in restructuring, in terms not only of women's role in reproduction (which is often taken for granted), but also of women's increasing significance to paid labor. For instance, despite the connections that regulation theorists make between the spheres of production and reproduction and between the labor market and family form, the school fails to adequately analyze the change in gender regimes marked by the move from Fordism to post-Fordism; namely, from a male breadwinner/unpaid female domestic worker nuclear family model, to one characterized by "the withdrawal of the state from the collective provision of goods and services," and in which "State concern with social reproduction of labour power is reduced as the core workers increasingly rely on specialist and privatised forms of provision in the market" (McDowell 1991:403). Sassen (1998:90) rightly asks in this regard whether "the 'systematic abandonment,' that is, radical economic marginalization, of a growing segment of households—specifically, low-income female-headed households—[is] completely unconnected to this reorganization of consumption and social reproduction?"

Welfare state restructuring is thus clearly part and parcel of neoliberal globalization. The rhetoric of international competitiveness and of the benefits of a free market society in which the state is reduced to a "night watchman" role, and the resulting tenets of neoliberalism articulated at the state level (as outlined by Navarro 1998; see above), place poor single mothers in a situation in which they must increasingly compete for the devalorized jobs Sassen mentions while their responsibility for an ever-widening and deepening domestic/private sphere increases. What is visible to the state in relation to reproduction and to its own responsibilities is increasingly narrowed: not only is the role of low-income and poor women in underwriting the vaunted aspects of globalization erased (as we glorify high finance and other super profit making sectors), but the role of women in reproduction is simultaneously blocked from view (see Gallin 1998). In the new economic order, according to McDowell (1991:408), "neither the father nor the sons appear to need domestic labour . . . or perhaps more accurately they are not prepared to pay the cost of its provision."[19]

Despite the emphasis in welfare reform on workfare—on the reconstitution of women as potential able-bodied workers, as the new unemployed—"women continue to be constructed as marginal labour with particular characteristics that mean that their attachment to the labour market is temporary or flexible" (McDowell 1991:410).[20] The basic contradiction is that globalization and restructuring entail a simultaneous increase in, dependence on, and yet devalorization of female-typed labor *and* a twined decrease in state support and therefore increase of pressure on women's reproductive labor. This, according to McDowell (1991:412), makes the system "inherently less stable." By placing women "simultaneously in the workforce and in the home," in other words, restructuring "provides a formula for a crisis in social reproduction" (Brodie 1994:58).

It is crucial to note that the erasure of the building demands on women's domestic labor that accompany the restructuring of the welfare state places particular burdens not only on women, but also on children. As poor mothers lose access to resources, so their children will suffer greater misery (Susser 1997; see also Elson 1994:41–42).[21] In the United States, for instance, more than 40 percent of the poor are children (Sparr 1995).

In a particularly insightful analysis, however, Rita Gallin argues that this situation does not necessarily reflect disinterest in the domestic sphere on the part of state actors, but rather their attempt to influence the domestic sphere and its reproductive functions in particular ways:

The fact that the state in countries of both the core and periphery are increasingly retreating from responsibility for the well-being of their citizens does not mean that it is disinterested in the household and women's position in it. . . . [T]he state has systematically intervened in the domestic sphere, controlling women's bodies, appropriating their presumed "underused" and "unused" labor, and repatriating to the household the responsibility for sustaining itself. Moreover, the state has provided strong ideological support for "self-help." (1998: 15–16)

Here Gallin indicates that women have not simply been omitted from economic analysis or policymaking, or that any such omission is purely accidental. Again, women's roles are *assumed*, yet unacknowledged (McDowell 1991). What has *not* changed during the current transition is women's responsibilities for reproduction. What *has* changed is both the state's willingness to support (poor) women in this role and its acknowledgment of this role—of the role of (poor) women as *mothers*. Rather, as indicated in Chapter 2, states are working to reconstitute poor women's subjectivity such that they become ungendered—that is, male—persons, or individuals.

Summary: Back to Market

In reconstituting poor women as (male) able-bodied workers and stripping them—discursively, but not practically—of their roles in reproduction, proponents of market-oriented restructuring fail to acknowledge that the market is not purely economic, but fundamentally embedded in cultural, and therefore power, relations. They fail to realize that "the unpaid work of reproduction and maintenance of human resources contributes to the realization of formal market relations," that nonmarket relations provide the grounds on which people engage with the market, that there is a "dialectical relationship between market and non-market activity" (Bakker 1994a:5).

In so valorizing the market, the costs of reproduction are shifted from the public to the private realm. Thus "neoliberal market civilization" (Gill 1995:399) entails redrawing the line between the public and the private such that much of what the state supported in terms of reproduction (including not only direct welfare benefits, but also housing subsidies and educational and health-care programs) is jettisoned, or "reprivatized" (Fraser 1989:172).[22] Reprivatization serves to cover, or erase, that which has been reprivatized from public (that is, state, or policymaking) view. In their reconstitution as gender-neutral workers, poor single mothers become increasingly exposed to exploitative working conditions and are increasingly forced to purchase, as consumers, goods and services that were formerly *public* goods and services—or else provide them on their own. Welfare state restructuring, then, and the reprivatization that it entails, assumes women's "infinite elasticity" (Elson 1994, 1995). While feminists have decried this assumption, the assumption is nevertheless correct (Gallin 1998): women *will* stretch to meet the needs left by a retreating state. And this stretching will hamper their abilities to enter the market as rational, utility-maximizing individuals.[23] At this level, "the very ability of a person to function as an economic individual—that is, an individual able to enter into voluntary contracts to exchange goods and services—is constituted by the state" (Elson 1994:35). Specific state strategies in this regard are the focus of the country study chapters in Part II.

Chapter 4
Globalization as Hybridity

Catherine Kingfisher

> Much of the time, cultural process will be shaped . . . by the way that
> fairly different habitats of meaning are made to intersect.
> —Ulf Hannerz, *Transnational Connections*

> [Globalization] symbolizes the blurring of traditional territorial and
> social boundaries through the interpenetration of local and distant
> influences, therefore requiring hybrid and multi-polar solutions.
> —Ash Amin, "Placing Globalization"

In the previous two chapters, I outlined a preliminary grammar of neoliberal culture, with particular reference to two keywords, or concepts,
of neoliberalism: the person and the free market. Underlying both concepts is what is perhaps neoliberalism's inherent globality, its tendency
to totalize and universalize. Possessive individualism is viewed, within
the context of neoliberal culture, as descriptive of human nature per se,
rather than as representative of a historical and cultural construction;
it is, that is to say, naturalized. Similarly, the free market, if one were
to believe Hayek, for instance, is also a natural phenomenon, which, if
left to its own devices, offers the best possible mechanism for the (self-)
management of social interaction. In both cases, the normalized and the
normative are conflated.

It is these two concepts—person and market—that underpin the cross-
national patterns currently at work in welfare state restructuring. As Appadurai (1996a:17) states, however, "if the genealogy of cultural forms
is about their circulation across regions, the history of these forms is
about their ongoing domestication into local practice." Relatedly, Sassen
(1996, 1998, 2000) highlights the problems of a global—local/national
dualism which assumes that one ends where the other begins. Instead,

she asserts, we need to recognize that all so-called global processes are territorially situated, that the global is always, and only, manifested in local specificities. The global, in other words, is always already local and the local is, perhaps, always already global: each is implicated in, and constitutive of, the other.

These insights generate a number of questions with regard to gender, poverty, and welfare reform that require an analytic movement from the general to the specific. For instance, what shape does neoliberal restructuring take in nation-states with a collectivist or communitarian history—say, Aotearoa/New Zealand or, to a lesser degree, Canada—versus nation-states with a more individualist ethos, such as the United States? Put another way, how does welfare reform manifest itself in states with a history of universal provisioning versus those characterized as minimalist or residualist? Do the discursive similarities among sites—the ubiquity of the rhetoric of independence, responsibility, motivation, self-discipline, and, of course, "tough love"—signal precise similarities in welfare reform practices? Or are "independence" and "tough love" refracted through different local lenses, resulting in a proliferation of family resemblances rather than exact replicas—or possibly in radically divergent practices? We need to be careful, in other words, "not to confuse similarity with convergence" (Cox 1998:13). And, finally, we must recognize that variations and differences are not only international, but also intranational. We thus need to inquire as to how the culture of neoliberalism and neoliberal reform articulate with various minority cultures in western welfare states, for example, Aboriginal or African-American cultures.

The story of neoliberalism's globalization is, therefore, not "the story of cultural homogenization" (Appadurai 1996a:11). Rather, it is a series of stories characterized by disjointed, disjunctured articulations. In this sense, neoliberalism as a mode of thought or culture is best "collapsed into and made an integral part of parallel, related local situations rather than something monolithic or external to them" (Marcus 1995:102). It is in this regard that an understanding of welfare state restructuring and women's poverty requires a comparative, globally situated, analysis. Given the general similarities in the structure and outcome of restructuring across nation-states, it becomes strategically crucial to avoid isolated, single-site interpretations. At another level, and as discussed in Chapter 3, we need to keep in mind that global economic and cultural flows (Appadurai 1996a) have altered (rather than dismantled) the economic, political, and cultural sovereignty of the nation-state. This signals that it is not only strategically, but also theoretically, crucial to move beyond single-site analyses. The imagery of flows indicates movement and shift, admonishing against approaches that posit a fixed, stable, monolithic, and unitary global economic/cultural system, in favor of an emphasis on the "circulation of cultural meanings, objects, and identities in diffuse time-space" (Marcus 1995:96). What is needed, then, is an analytic framework that begins simultaneously with both the global and the national/local, that traces connections, articulations, and manifestations of the phenomenon of welfare reform and various women's poverty across national and cultural boundaries.

Another way to think of this project is in terms of "eventalization," which Mitchell Dean (1992:217), following Foucault, describes as a process involving "the definition and attempted understanding of an event or episode in its singularity." While both Foucault and Dean employ this method specifically in relation to particular historical events, such as, in Dean's case, the emergence of pauperism, the method might be used contemporarily to begin to analyze the currently unfolding global and patterned shift in the discourse and organization of relief away from Keynesianism and toward neoliberalism.

Dean's (1992:217) methodological emphasis is on the "identification of singular assemblages of social and institutional practices and forms of knowledge and discourse . . . the [analysis of] these into the elements from which they are composed, and . . . [the construction of] the specific processes of formation of those elements." Applied comparatively, this resonates with George Marcus's (1995) proposal that multi-sited analysis (in his case, ethnography) begin with an object, idea, person, story, conflict—in other words, that the analysis begin with some phenomenon of interest—and proceed to follow it across sites (recognizing, of course that the "it" doesn't exist externally to those sites). The goal is to explore what it is that is traveling in terms of the specific shapes that it takes, and the hows of its travels, more so than the whys (Dean 1992:228), although the whys are by no means irrelevant.

This is the project of Part II of this collection. The preliminary grammar of neoliberalism outlined in Chapters 2 and 3 thus provides a framework, or launching point, for the following analyses of restructuring in the United States, Canada, Britain, Australia, and Aotearoa/New Zealand. Each case study chapter is an example of "eventalization" and presents a diachronic analysis of the formation of current neoliberal regimes that emphasizes both their constituent elements and their articulation. Before presenting the country study chapters, however, I briefly discuss what Appadurai might mean by indigenization, with particular reference to two key terms in the literature on globalization; namely, glocalization and hybridity. Together, these terms provide framing for the specificities of the case study chapters.

In discussions of globalization, the global is often taken to be "out there," as opposed to the "in here" of the local. The concept of *glocal-*

ization attempts to move beyond this binary by recognizing the dialectical nature of the so-called global and local, in order to make visible what Amin (1997) conceives of as "out there—in here connectivity" (see also Hall 1997; Sjolander 1996; Tomlinson 1999). Appropriated from Japanese business discourse by Robertson (1995), the term *glocalization* challenges the idea that the global, that which is "out there," overrides the local—that globalization is a process entailing an externally imposed homogenization, to which the local is always in a position of reaction. In arguing against the equation of globalization with homogenization, Robertson refers to: (1) the flow of ideas from periphery to center; (2) the fact that so-called national symbolic resources, such as the concept of democracy, are available internationally; (3) niche marketing; and (4) the reality that cultural messages are differentially received and interpreted—all of which points are also made by Appadurai (1996b). "The local," according to Ulf Hannerz (1996:28), "is an arena where various people's habitats of meaning intersect, and where the global, or what has been local somewhere else, also has some chance of making itself at home. At this intersection, things are forever working themselves out, so that this year's change is next year's continuity." Such a notion of intersection (or dialectic; see Tomlinson 1999:26) brings to mind the idea of an ongoing "conversation," to which each interlocutor—the "global" and the "local"—makes some contribution.

The point is to collapse the global/local binary, and glocalization provides a useful heuristic in this regard. Perhaps even more useful, however, is Jan Nederveen Pieterse's (1995) theorization of globalization as hybridity—as mélange, or crossover. In this framework, there is no "global" or "local," but only phenomena which are always already mixed. Globalization becomes a process of accelerated mixture, with a concomitant production of new forms. Returning to the metaphor of conversation, each interlocutor is in itself complex and becomes increasingly so through time and interaction. In other words, not only is globalization not a process of homogenization, but what we take to be the "global" and the "local" are themselves not homogeneous, but heterogeneous (in which heterogeneity is taken as an ongoing process, rather than a state). Thus the western cultural, economic, and political forms that are said to be homogenizing the world—here, the neoliberal conceptualizations of person and market—are themselves hybrids, which then interact with "local" national cultures, also hybrid in form.

Processes of hybridity, however, are not free of power relations, and the parties to the conversation of hybridity are not necessarily (or even often) equal. We are not dealing with an ideal communicative situation à la Habermas, and it would be a mistake to conceive of border crossings as neutral and symmetrical. In this regard Nederveen Pieterse (1995:56–

57) points to "a continuum of hybridities: on the one end, an assimilationist hybridity that leans over towards the center, adopts the canon and mimics the hegemony, and, at the other end, a destabilizing hybridity that blurs the canon, reverses the current, subverts the center." Power is never absent.

A key problem with the idea of hybridity, of course—as Nederveen Pieterse himself points out—is that it assumes an initial purity, which brings us back to the binary.[1] However, it is not my goal here to overcome the problem of binaries, which continually haunts even the most sophisticated social theory.[2] The relevant point in this context is that in exploring neoliberal welfare reform, we must not mis-take neoliberalism as a fait accompli, a point to which I return in Chapter 10. The concepts of glocalization and hybridity provide the tools to avoid this error and to recognize the unique features of each case while simultaneously holding on to what might be similar across sites. This both/and approach provides for a more sophisticated and nuanced analysis of neoliberalism, that, as I pointed out in Chapter 1, is not only theoretically, but also potentially politically, beneficial.

Overview of Country Chapters

The discourses and practices of welfare reform in the United States, Canada, Britain, Australia, and Aotearoa/New Zealand share a number of key features. Although historically situated at different points along a residualist, institutional welfare regime continuum, they have all shared, at the most general level, a male breadwinner/dependent wife model of social and state organization. In addition, with the ascendancy of neoliberal reform in each country, there has been a move from the construction of poor single mothers as *mothers*, to their construction as potential able-bodied *workers*, where the category *worker* is constituted to exclude those who engage in unpaid childcare or domestic labor. This has entailed a process of degendering (evident in the Australian case, for example, by a shift in referents to welfare beneficiaries from "mother" to "parent") and an increasing emphasis on paid labor as the foundational requirement of social citizenship. In many cases, the latter has been reflected in a transformation in discussions of welfare provisioning from "entitlement" to "obligation," where, following the discourse of contract, recipients are now required to provide something in return for their benefit, where "return," like "work," does not include the business of raising children. Degendering, the ascendancy of worker-citizenship, and the discourse of contract and obligation in relation to welfare provisioning have occurred, in all cases, in the context of a valorization of the market and of supposed reductions in the orbit of the state—both ostensibly working to increase competitiveness and therefore, supposedly, well-being in a globalized economy. These valorizations and devalorizations have been accompanied by a marked favoring of individualized as opposed to social-structural explanations of poverty.

The chapters in Part II work to historically contextualize and situate these transitions to neoliberal governance in each country. In so doing, they allow for the emergence of two general points: first, and most obviously, all of these countries are indeed undergoing this transition (homogenization, in a globalization framework); and second, equally obvious from a juxtaposition of the case studies, the historical and cultural specificities of the transition are unique in each instance (heterogeneity).

In addition to the historical context, all of the case study chapters emphasize the *discursive* nature of the shift to neoliberal governance; that is, they all emphasize the importance of particular constructions of poverty, gender, race, work, and so on, to the emergence and implementation of neoliberal policies. This serves to underscore the relationship between material and ideological forces and formations.

A final theme that emerges in all of the chapters is that of race. Judith Goode and Wendy Larner in particular focus on this issue, outlining the ways in which discourses of race are imbricated with/in discourses of poverty and welfare reform in the United States (Goode); and how discourses of indigeneity were complicit in the dismantling of the welfare state in Aotearoa/New Zealand, while, at the same time, the negative material impacts of welfare state restructuring in that country have fallen disproportionately on the shoulders of Maori and Pacific Island women (Larner). Although also clearly relevant in Canada, Britain, and Australia, race does not seem to be quite as salient in discourses of change in these countries. Thus the different emphases on race in the case study chapters reflect, perhaps, variations in the discourses associated with the ongoing transition to neoliberal governance in each context. Given the different historical contexts, in other words, different features of the terrain become more salient while others wane in importance. Thus, in the United States, specifically racialized (or, more to the point, African-Americanized) discourses of poverty, behavior, morals, and so on dominate the terrain; while in Canada, for instance, and in this context, discourses of race, while certainly not unimportant, trail behind debates about gender and equity.

What the issue of race points out very clearly, however, despite its relative salience in different contexts, is that our analyses of the transition to neoliberal governance must foreground both intra- and international similarities and differences. Just as the differing experiences of the case study countries reflect, in part, the hierarchical relationships among them (with the United States generally at the top); so the impact of restructuring within any particular nation-state will be differentiated according to (and sometimes serve to accentuate) already existing hierarchies of race and gender. Larner's chapter is particularly clear in this regard.

Various themes, then, play out differently in different national contexts. Thus each of the following five chapters explores an instance of hybridity. I therefore conclude this chapter with a brief overview of some of the hybrid characteristics of each case.

I begin with a note on the national as opposed to thematic organization of Part II. It is hoped that this organization will accomplish two things. First, a privileging of the nation-state over individual themes can serve as a reminder that, as I pointed out in Chapter 1, the state continues to play a central role in the lives of those living within its boundaries, especially in the lives of the poor. We must not mistake transformations in state sovereignty for a loss of power in all areas; nor should we fall prey to reading the "local" as somehow bypassing (or undermining) the state. The state can be the "local," just as it can be the "global," depending on the level and orientation of analysis. Second, a state by state analysis serves to maintain the integrity of the national cultures being explored—which is not to construct them as tightly bounded entities, but to recognize that there is, at a most general and abstract level, something that we can still refer to as national culture, here reflected in particular policy prescriptions. The differences accentuated by each case study thus reflect not only the particular interests of the authors (whose disciplinary affiliations range from anthropology to sociology to political science to education), but also the specific cultural geographies of those countries. Rather than ask each author to address particular issues, which presupposes (and imposes) an understanding of what the key issues are in all contexts, or organize the case studies according to theme, exploring how one theme at a time plays out in each context, I asked contributors to focus on what they felt to be most salient in their particular country. My concern, again, has been to avoid abstracting issues from their contexts of occurrence. The point is not simply one of what, for instance, occupational segregation or childcare looks like in different national contexts, but, rather, what the *constellation* of contextually salient issues looks like, and how the issues interact with each other to constitute that specific constellation. This orientation and the ensuing organization may decrease the ability to make straightforward comparisons among the countries, but what is lost in terms of a clear-cut comparison is more than made up for in the rich nuances of each unique case.

A note on the sequence of the chapters is also in order. Judith Goode's chapter on the United States leads the case study chapters for several reasons. First, the U.S. reforms are the most draconian among those covered in this collection; they express the most extreme institutionalization of the neoliberal tenets of personhood and market. Second, the discourses of welfare reform in the other countries included in this collection have often taken their inspiration from (or, by some accounts, been imposed by) the United States (or U.S.-dominated interests), as Ruth Lister and Wendy Larner explicitly point to in reference to Britain and Aotearoa/New Zealand, for instance. Finally, following a sequence that begins with North America and ends with Aotearoa/New Zealand allows for a tracing of neoliberal reform from the historically most residualist of the welfare regimes (the United States), to the historically most institutionalized (Aotearoa/New Zealand). It is worth noting in this regard that while the 1996 reforms in the United States are the most severe of the reforms analyzed in this collection, the country which has experienced perhaps the greatest ideological shift has been Aotearoa/New Zealand.

Goode's chapter interrogates the role of neoliberal discourses of personhood, state and market in recent welfare reforms in the United States, all of which have had a negative impact on the well-being of poor single mothers and their children insofar as they have endeavored to erase poor mother's childcare responsibilities in favor of their roles as members of the paid workforce. Goode situates the stipulations of the 1996 Personal Responsibility and Work Opportunity Reconciliation Act (PRWORA) within their historical contexts, arguing that PRWORA represents a continuation of trends already set in motion through prior legislation (especially the Family Support Act of 1988), and builds on discourses of race, morality, and the individual that have deep roots in mainstream U.S. culture.

Goode's particular emphasis is on the racialized aspects of welfare-related discourses, in which constructions of poor single motherhood are built on stereotypes of indigent, inner-city, young (teenage) African-American mothers. These stereotypes not only fail to consider both structural factors generating poverty and the creativity of poor women's survival strategies, but are also extended to cover all poor mothers, the general category of which is constructed as immoral, lazy, and so on. The othering of this category of (non)person has been accomplished by, among other means, attempts to measure poor people's supposed inability to defer gratification, clearly marking them as "different" from "normal" adults whose future orientation provides the willpower to temporarily suspend desire.

The discursive constitution of the racialized poor as "other" in the U.S. context closely articulates with a particularly American discourse of morality. In the context of PRWORA, this discourse is evident in arguments claiming that welfare reform is not just about economics (i.e., saving government and taxpayer monies), but also about individual empowerment, or "liberation," from the shackles of dependency. Thus Goode describes popular representations of welfare-to-work "success stories" that draw on ideologies of personal uplift and an almost religious conversion.

A final theme running through U.S. discourses and practices of welfare reform is that of "dependency"—a key concept that flows through all the discourses of welfare reform examined in this collection. Here is where neoliberal emphases on the market and a minimalist state articulate with neoconservative discourses of "family values," where the goal becomes to reprivatize dependency, through encouraging, by means of a variety of positive and negative sanctions, nuclear family formation. This goal is clearly different from that of enhancing individual (women's) empowerment.

Janine Brodie's chapter on Canada broadly surveys changes in governance over the past twenty years that have served to simultaneously erase issues of gender equality from public and policy discourses at the same time as poverty has become increasingly gendered. She explores four tenets of neoliberal governance as it has taken shape in Canada: performativity, which engenders increasing displacement of the public onto the market or the individual/community; privatization; decentralization; and individualization. The valorization of possessive individualism and of the market discussed in Chapters 2 and 3 are manifested in the Canadian context in Canada Health and Social Transfer (CHST), the outcomes of which have included the development of workfare in a country in which social assistance was formerly provided solely on the basis of need, and a marked rise in poverty, particularly among single mothers, elderly women, and members of visible minority groups.

Brodie contextualizes the current form of neoliberal governance in Canada in reference to various strands of the liberal progressive discourse characteristic of the Canadian welfare state from the 1930s/40s until the current ascendancy of neoliberalism, and which also informed the Canadian women's movement. The hegemony of neoliberal governance has engendered an eclipsing of liberal progressive feminist concerns, which, as Brodie discusses, enjoyed considerable political influence in the 1970s and early to mid-1980s. In the current gender order, in contrast, poor single mothers are vilified and accordingly jettisoned from the category of the "deserving" poor into that of the "undeserving" poor, while poor children, abstracted from the familial and social structural contexts in which they experience poverty, are constituted as the last remaining "deserving" poor. According to Brodie, the contradictions and paradoxes thrown up as a result of this and other processes entailed in the establishment of neoliberal governance will be the challenge of "all equality seeking groups in the new millennium."

In her chapter, Ruth Lister tracks the movement of welfare discourse —most notably, that of "welfare dependency"—from the United States to the United Kingdom. The adoption of U.S. discourse was facilitated by the British press and by the Institute of Economic Affairs' Health and Welfare Unit, a neoliberal think tank that has locally sponsored the writings and speeches of Charles Murray, a prominent U.S. proponent of welfare reform. Interestingly, one of the British commentators to whom Lister refers, David Green, has had work published in Aotearoa/New Zealand under the auspices of the right-wing Business Roundtable. Appadurai's (1996a) *ethnoscapes* and *ideoscapes* provide useful heuristics here. And, again following Appadurai, we can also note the indigenization of these discourses. In its travel from the United States to Britain, for instance, the concept of the "underclass" lost its more rigid U.S. racialization (although, as Lister points out, welfare discourse in Britain is nevertheless raced).

Lister tracks not only the movement of ideas across space, but also their movement across time, with particular regard to the social construction of single motherhood. Under the Thatcher regime, poor single mothers were maligned in precisely the way in which Ruth Smith (1990) claims liberal bourgeois society deals with the poor in general: they were constructed as a threat to the social order. If not subnormal as a category of person, they certainly failed to fulfill "normal" expectations of motherhood. As Lister points out, conservative views of single mothers as a social threat took on moral overtones: the good mother versus the "not good enough" mother who was guilty of "spawning juvenile criminals." Interestingly, this demonization was also directed, although perhaps not as virulently, at absent fathers.

The construction of poor single mothers as a threat to the social order has, however, been softened under the Blair regime, although poor single mothers continue to constitute a "problem." Thus in the British case there is an articulation of neoliberal discourses of personhood with a more "modern" discourse that eschews "Victorian hypocrisy about sex, women's employment or sexuality" (Blair 1997b; cited in Lister, this volume). As Lister points out, however, a subtextual privileging of the "normal" nuclear family nevertheless dominates Blair's "third way."

In contrast to the situation in the United States and in some Canadian provinces, and thus closely resembling the material realities of Aotearoa/New Zealand, welfare-to-work schemes in Britain remain voluntary; the only requirement currently being discussed consists of work-focused interviews with welfare bureaucrats. It is here where the distinction between discourse and practice takes on meaning. While the language of responsibility and citizenship obligation may be similar in the United States and Britain (the emphasis in Britain, Lister points out, is on a tripartite responsibility, inclusion, opportunity), the practices of workfare arising from this discourse vary. The erasure of women's roles in reproduction discussed in Chapters 2 and 3 is thus clearly relative in practice, highlighting the different ways in which the tensions between different constructions of women—as mothers *or* workers, or as both mothers *and* workers—are played out.

Like Brodie in the Canadian context, Susan Robertson's analysis of the Australian welfare state focuses on the dual process of "occlusion and intensification" of the gendered nature of reform and restructuring. In detailing this process, Robertson tracks a situation that is becoming increasingly dismal for poor single mothers. The trajectory of the Australian welfare state, Robertson argues, must be analyzed in relation to the articulation of the discourses of globalization and neoliberalism with Australia's unique history as a "workingman's welfare state" premised on full employment among male heads of households comprised of dependent wives and children—a history that has had particular implications for both women's participation in paid labor and for the (in)visibility in policymaking of their unpaid labor. In keeping with the discussion of personhood in Chapter 2, Robertson argues that Australian masculine "independence" and citizenship have been historically predicated and dependent on women's "dependence."

Robertson outlines two phases of welfare reform in Australia: a pre-1996 phase consisting of a relatively gentle restructuring represented by the Accord between organized labor and the Australian Labour Party; and a post-1996 phase characterized by more rigorous privatization and marketization, with a marked promulgation of the discourses of employability, responsibility, flexibility, and choice—and a marked vilification of families headed by a single parent as "decayed," or "nonintact." In keeping with neoliberal discourses of personhood that function to erase gender, the discourses and practices of privatization and marketization have increasingly worked over these two phases to shift responsibility for childcare from the government (which under the Jobs, Education and Training program is limited to twelve weeks) to the market, that is, to enterprise and individual bargaining. Given their labor market situation, however, low-income and poor mothers are not in strong bargaining positions. As Robertson puts it, "within this new more individualized and contractualized discursive and practical frame . . . sole mothers find themselves multiply jeopardized. In the labor market they have been further peripheralized and marginalized, while in the household their labor is neither compensated for nor augmented by the state." Simultaneously, however, individuals are increasingly expected to engage in paid labor in order to gain full social citizenship. Thus the Australian response to globalization includes a "clever country" strategy that requires social welfare recipients to be available for training and work. Without concerted government effort to increase the availability of both well-paying jobs and affordable and adequate childcare, the situation of poor single mothers and their children will only worsen.

Finally, Larner's chapter illustrates both hybridity and neoliberal hegemony in Aotearoa/New Zealand, where neoliberal discourses of personhood and market have articulated with local, indigenous Maori discourses of *tino rangatiratanga* (self-determination) to produce both salutary and negative effects: salutary insofar as Maori have won at least nominal self-determination in particular arenas, and negative insofar as the discourse of *tino rangatiratanga* has been appropriated to justify neoliberal style government retreat, with concomitant marketization and privatization—a set of phenomena from which Maori and Pacific Island single mothers seem to be suffering the greatest repercussions. On the other hand, Maori have also appropriated neo-liberal discourses for their own purposes, indicating a level of dialogue that precludes complete neoliberal hegemony. And finally, there is a third discourse at work, that of neoconservativism, contributing to an emphasis on traditional family forms. Ultimately, Larner admits, neoliberal discourses have predominated since the election of a National government in 1990. The result is a greater racialization of the feminization of poverty and increasing class differences both among and between Maori, Pacific Island, Pakeha (European), and other women.

While emphasizing the particularities of the discourses of neoliberalism and *tino rangatiratanga* in Aotearoa/New Zealand, Larner also situates them, and their shifts over time, in a global context in which the emphasis on economic discourse has been influenced by moral discourses, having their genesis in the United States; and in which the discourse of *tino rangatiratanga* has been influenced by the transnational circulation of various discourses of indigeneity. Thus the specificities of restructuring in Aotearoa/New Zealand reflect a hybrid of the articulation of local discourses with each other and with their nonlocal variants.

Finally, Larner's discussion of the articulation of the discourses of neoliberalism and *tino rangatiratanga* not only makes the point that neoliberalism—as a process, and as *contingent* process—is always in conversation with other discourses; it also makes the point that the discourse of welfare state restructuring is not always "simply a top-down discourse driven by neoliberal ideologues." This insight is crucial to our understanding of how neoliberal discourses gain currency: what about neoliberalism do people find appealing? Choice and individual empowerment are not unattractive ideas.

Despite parallels in discourse and legislation, each country, the United States, Canada, Britain, Australia, and Aotearoa/New Zealand, is following its own trajectory of welfare state restructuring. It is worth noting, however, that each case represents a more assimilationist than destabilizing instance of hybridity (Nederveen Pieterse 1995), at least at this current historical juncture, a point to which I return in Chapter 10.

Part II
On The Ground
CASE STUDIES IN THE ARTICULATION OF (GENDERED) NEOLIBERALISM WITH (GENDERED) LOCAL CULTURE

Chapter 5
From New Deal to Bad Deal

Racial and Political Implications of U.S. Welfare Reform

Judith Goode

In 1996, the United States legislature passed the Personal Responsibility and Work Opportunity Reconciliation Act (PRWORA), which abrogated the sixty-one year social contract between the state and poor women that had been put in place as part of the Keynesian New Deal. Placing a finite time limit on the receipt of federally supported cash assistance as well as imposing other limits in eligibility,[1] this law virtually eliminated previous state obligations to maintain poor women as mothers responsible for social reproduction.

While these changes are in line with a general neoliberal shift from supporting mothers to making workers, they are more severe than similar changes in other nation-states. What made this possible was a long history of suppressing discussions of the role of the political economy in producing poverty in favor of emphasizing behavioral causes which racialized and "othered" the poor. In this chapter I address two issues. First, I argue that the political will for such a drastic elimination of the social safety net was made possible by increasingly racialized constructions of poor women which became scientifically and institutionally legitimized during the War on Poverty in the 1960s. When postwar racial dynamics led to the conflation of race and poverty, the particular U.S. racial hierarchy was mapped onto a preexisting emphasis on invidious moral/behavioral distinctions between the deserving and undeserving poor. The conflation of race and class worked against any notion of social citizenship or legitimate entitlement as a racially marked poor population came to be seen as increasingly different from the rest of us, not quite *of* the nation.

My second point is that discourses of welfare reform have a major depoliticizing effect on poor women's collective activism which is part of a larger political demobilization (Goode and Maskovsky 2001). In the interests of regulating poor women, moral discourses about them will-fully ignored their actual family and community lives and thus their social competence and political agency. While policymakers and practi-tioners construct poor women as passive and socially incompetent, this is strongly challenged by the political agency they have developed by extending their family roles to those of politicized community activists. I will demonstrate how the privatization of welfare-to-work programs, an aspect of neoliberal practice in the new policy, is working to dis-able women's political consciousness and practice. The very way in which social provisioning has been privatized through the implementation of new legislation further empowers male dominated structures and dis-ables women's political ability to make claims on the state.

The discursive underpinnings of this shift away from social provision-ing are produced by the contingent playing out of several historically pervasive U.S. discourses whose contradictions have come to a head under the current material conditions of economic globalization. Social provisioning in the United States has always disfavored reliance on the state in favor of voluntary charity (Katz 1986) or privatized insurance benefits through the workplace. Moreover, the private market has domi-nated the distribution of social goods such as housing and health care to a greater extent than in most industrialized countries.[2] Furthermore, the heavy emphasis on individual morality and behavior as the cause of poverty and the avoidance of political economic analysis has promoted moral judgments about poor people's work ethics and sexuality. These judgments have historically created invidious moral distinctions between the deserving and undeserving poor (ibid.).

For a brief historic moment, New Deal discourses and programs contradicted these major discursive formulations and practices. As a response to the magnitude of an international depression which had widespread impact on the U.S. population, structural explanations of the economic crisis dominated over individually based behavioral/moral ex-planations. During this first state recognition of responsibility for safe-guarding people against the volatile market forces of capitalism, the nation came closest to a shared notion of social citizenship (Fraser and Gordon 1992), or the human right to be free from need without stigma. Yet, racial minorities were largely excluded from these programs since the agriculture and domestic work sectors of the economy were not covered by New Deal programs. Black workers were consequently also left out of the dominant imagery of the deserving victims of the De-pression, such as that represented in *The Grapes of Wrath* and the famous Dorothea Lange photos.

Gendering the Social Contract

It was policies of the New Deal that inscribed preexisting gender assumptions into the social contract. Nancy Fraser and Linda Gordon (1994) and Gwendolyn Mink (1995) have pointed out that social policy in the United States has been strongly gendered and premised until now on the ideal of men as breadwinners and women as family caretakers dependent on men for livelihood. Work is clearly privileged as redemptive and inextricably validates morality and inclusion in the nation. Men's benefits (Social Security, Workers' Compensation, Unemployment Insurance) are based on the idea of contract through reciprocal exchange. One makes contributions through the workplace and receives benefits in return. Moreover, many social benefits, such as health care, are tied to employment, thereby further stigmatizing recipients of public aid as nonworkers.

In contrast, women's programs, since the Mothers' Pensions of 1911, are based on women's roles as mothers and their corollary dependence on men. Their citizenship is linked to their maternalist role in producing citizens of the nation. This was institutionalized in the automatic subsidies that "deserving" widows received through Social Security survivor's benefits, in contrast to the stigmatized charity of the New Deal program of Aid to Dependent Children (ADC) received by divorced and never married women.[3]

While the charity on which most social provisioning had been based prior to the New Deal had been private and voluntary, ADC implicitly recognized the state's obligation to women as unpaid caretakers of children in the service of the state. Yet as in cases of charity as opposed to contract, there was no reciprocal exchange. Instead, women recipients had to submit to means tests, intrusive surveillance, and moral judgments, in other words, to a loss of liberty and full citizenship.[4]

The War on Poverty

Unlike the New Deal, the War on Poverty in the 1960s took place during a period of economic expansion and technocratic optimism before major shifts in the international economy created uncertainty about the economic future. Poverty was seen as a limited, residual, but serious problem which could easily be eliminated in an affluent society. The assumption was that by using the scientific knowledge of emerging "policy science," the "leftover poor" could be put on the path to upward mobility, thereby bolstering the consumer demand necessary for capital expansion.

Michael Harrington (1962), who "rediscovered" American poverty amid postwar affluence in his book *The Other America*, emphasized the limited, uneven occurrence of poverty among certain regions and industries in the nation, but argued that such inequities in opportunity should be easy to fix. He also used examples from the white poor of Appalachia, thus avoiding a racialization of the poor.

The Political Economy of Race and Racialized Images of the Poor

Race has always been a major factor in U.S. discourses of morality and belonging to the nation. Recent analyses have demonstrated a process through which, during the formation of the industrial working class in the nineteenth century, white workers identified with white privilege as they were placed in increasingly race segregated labor markets, foreclosing labor solidarity (Roediger 1990; Ignatiev 1996).

The New Deal created the first legal protections for collective bargaining for industrial workers. In the postwar era, unions helped move white male skilled workers solidly into the ranks of middle-class consumers and depoliticized labor-based social movements for structural change. In the 1950s, the American Dream of easy upward mobility for the hardworking individual was bolstered by the GI Bill which is now recognized as the largest state affirmative action program in U.S. history. This legislation, produced in a context of concern about unrest among returning veterans, subsidized university educations and mortgages for the children of the "not quite white" turn of the century labor immigrants from eastern and southern Europe. While this population was "whitened" and brought solidly into the middle class, people of color were informally excluded from the benefits (Brodkin 1998).

Poverty talk related to War on Poverty programs in the 1960s was heavily raced in contrast to what had seemed to be an inclusive, universalistic New Deal discourse that had silently excluded minorities in practice. The War on Poverty itself developed under Lyndon Johnson partially in response to the social unrest of the civil rights and National Welfare Rights movements. During the simultaneous campaigns for the Civil Rights Act of 1964 and for antipoverty programs, race and poverty were conflated as people of color, especially blacks, were visible participants arguing for inclusion and social citizenship.

In many ways, nonblack racial minorities who also faced high rates of immiseration were largely invisible on the national scene although their civil rights movements had regional impacts. Latinos, Asian-Americans, and Native Americans had long been subjected to differential labor market treatment and state policies of control (Takaki 1979). Yet the issue of slavery had haunted the nation since its formation, leading to civil war and a contested aftermath. Most discussions of "civil rights" were associated with a series of critical events led by blacks throughout the nation which were publicly visible through significant media coverage. In the public sphere, blacks represented racial minorities.

In addition, postwar policies had created new patterns of racial segregation and spatial exclusion which made the black poor and the black "slum" or ghetto increasingly visible images for suburban whites, especially under conditions of urban unrest in the 1960s. State-sponsored investment patterns produced both mortgage redlining in older city centers and suburbanization and white flight, which were coupled with increasing migration of blacks from the rural south to urban industrial cities. This produced the racially segregated older inner cities. The state-sponsored suburbanization and upward mobility of working-class whites also created demand for blacks in the declining unionized urban labor force, but such work was precarious. Blacks were seriously disadvantaged as the last hired and first fired when production moved to the suburbs, Sunbelt, and other nations. Under these conditions of retrenchment, poor blacks became an increasing proportion of welfare recipients (DeParle 1998).

Putting a Scientific Gloss on Behavioral Explanations of the "Leftover" Poor

The Cold War context contributed to the avoidance of political economic explanations of poverty during the 1960s. In a situation where labor had pragmatically been incorporated into the political structure and where the heightened anti-Communism of the Cold War further silenced any discussions about the nature of class inequalities, this was not surprising.

With the increasingly intense focus on individual behavior, racialized views of poverty were bolstered by several scholarly narratives which were widely disseminated to the expanded, suburbanized professional and managerial classes. Like much of the new policy science, these relied on individual psychologistic explanations which scientifically legitimized the already strong relationship between individual moral behavior and the persistence of poverty. For example, social psychological experimental studies attempted to measure "mental traits" linked to explanations of the persistence of poverty. One such effort attempted to measure a so-called Non-Deferred Gratification Pattern (NDGP) in low-income people. Here, artificially constructed exercises using offers of money with subjects of different income levels were performed in an effort to demonstrate that poor people could not defer their desires to the future. Ignoring the situational contingencies of the real contexts in which people actually make such calculations, results were taken to be "scientific proof" of NDGP as a part of low-income mentality (Miller, Reissman, and Seagull 1968).

Oscar Lewis's "culture of poverty" formulation was highly influential in "othering" the American poor. While he saw poverty as a consequence of the political and economic processes associated with capitalist development, his widely disseminated concept of the "culture of poverty" saw *some* of the poor as enmeshed in an intergenerationally reproduced quagmire of dysfunctional values and behaviors which kept them poor. His article "The Culture of Poverty" (Lewis 1996) appeared in a respected science journal, *Scientific American,* which targeted a popular audience consisting of the expanding college-educated population. Lewis distinguished between institutionalized structural inequality, which he saw as causing poverty in developing nations, and what he considered to be insignificant "leftover" U.S. poverty primarily caused by a persistence of the "culture of poverty." His argument for a "social work" solution to American poverty which aimed at changing people's values and behavior resonated with longtime U.S. discourses and reinforced dominant policy positions in the immediate postwar period.

At the end of the article, Lewis asks, "What is the future of the culture of poverty?" Then distinguishing between developing nations which may require structural change through revolution and "countries in which [poverty] represents a relatively small segment of the population," he supports the classic treatment of individuals through behavior change by endorsing individual moral uplift and psychiatric and social work treatment (Lewis 1996:404).[5]

Lewis's unquestioning belief in U.S. social mobility was characteristic of this era of technological optimism. However, it totally ignored uneven capitalist development in the United States and was oblivious to the structured inequality of women and people of color who faced a discriminatory labor market. In line with long-standing U.S. ideology, he called female-headed households "broken families," accepted the return to a patriarchal family as a solution to poverty, and characterized people in the "culture" as having "weak ego structures."

Poverty became an explicitly racial issue with the widely read *The Negro Family: The Case for National Action,* Daniel Patrick Moynihan's 1965 report on black "ghetto" poverty to President Johnson (Moynihan 1965). Moynihan, both a social scientist and a politician, made heavy use of the "culture of poverty" concept as he focused attention on a moralist/behavioral explanation for poverty which he blamed on the aftermath of slavery. He was misleading about both the prevalence and deviance of the single-mother-headed household in this population. It was the Moynihan report that legitimized the focus in welfare debates on controlling black women's conjugal relations, reproduction, and family "pathology" (Mink 1995).

As an outcome of these ideas, many programs in the War on Poverty were aimed at reforming individual behavioral deficits using professional expertise. For example, Head Start was based on the assumption that education failed because poor mothers could not intellectually stimulate their children to prepare them for school.[6] Assumptions about dysfunctional families and inadequate parenting implied that poor parents might be doing more harm than good.[7] Most programs still intact today aim at behavioral change.

Yet the proposed War on Poverty also included redistributive proposals such as the negative income tax. Although the negative income tax was never successfully legislated, some redistributive programs did come into being, for example, progressive jobs programs which met definitions of "fair work." Nancy Rose defines such work as "government job creation and related employment and training programs—that respect the dignity of the individual, involve voluntary participation, labor market wages and often develop innovative projects [meaningful work]" (1995:3). One such program was the Comprehensive Educational and Training Act (CETA).[8] These job creation programs were subject to immediate attack and retrenchment (Morgen and Weigt 2001). In fact CETA was replaced by the Job Training Partnership Act in 1982. The new program excluded public sector work and heavily involved the private sector in public-private partnerships. The private sector was given the upper hand in making decisions about labor needs and working conditions.

Alternative Constructions of the Poor as Competent Strategists

At the same time, attempts to portray poor people as active strategists for a better life rather than as pathological and passive objects of state policy developed in rebuttal to Lewis's culturalist explanations of social "disorganization" and his psychological depiction of "weak ego structure." Anthropologists and others offered ethnographic portrayals that emphasized the impact of large-scale political and economic developments, such as the nature of the labor market, on the creation and reproduction of poverty (Liebow 1967; C. Valentine 1968; Leacock 1971; Eames and Goode 1973; Stack 1974; B. L. Valentine 1978; Katz 1989, 1993; Marks 1991). Much classic work on poverty across social scientific disciplines was created in this endeavor. It showed that the assumptions about the social and personal incompetence of the poor were themselves part of a historically formed U.S. ideology. Consumption patterns that seemed irrational were shown to be survival strategies (Stack 1974;

Eames and Goode 1973). Poor people's behaviors in the labor market were not self-destructive but actually rational choices vis-à-vis dangerous and dirty dead-end jobs (Liebow 1967; B. L. Valentine 1978). Family networks and household composition among the poor were not "broken" or "dysfunctional" but rather functional and unnecessarily pathologized simply because they differed from those idealized among policymakers and the white middle class.

Since family structure was so critically linked to issues of morality and values by Lewis and Moynihan, it was especially important to show that conjugal bonds and structures were more a response to the material conditions of poverty than a cause of such conditions. Many have demonstrated a long historical relationship between high rates of black male unemployment, linked to discrimination and interrelated features of equal male and female labor force participation, more black women as primary wage earners, and more black single motherhood since women cannot count on consistent male employment and consequent economic assistance. Always having to work, black women created alternative extended family structures in which the consanguine bond between adult siblings was stronger than the conjugal bond (Stack 1974; Aschenbrenner 1975).

As Leith Mullings (1995) and Gwendolyn Mink (1995) point out, black mothers' reproduction has always been viewed as problematic. Mullings connects this to a culture of stratified reproduction in the United States, which was first defined by Faye Ginsburg and Rayna Rapp as a framework in which "some people are empowered to nurture and reproduce while others are disempowered" (1995:3). As the poor were increasingly represented in public discourse by black single mothers, they became increasingly imaged as hypersexualized, lazy, and immoral welfare cheats (Katz 1989) and denied the very virtues of motherhood which had given white women symbolic value in the reproduction of national culture.

The attempts to represent poor single mothers as competent strategists, however, inadvertently left intact two erroneous images of U.S. poverty. Lewis's concept was based on research in Mexico and Puerto Rico. Latin Americanists familiar with the squatter housing movements in urban centers attacked Lewis's formulation that the poor were parochial and self-isolated from mainstream collective political action. Yet critics in the United States studied ghetto communities as if they were bounded entities unaffected by the policies of the state or the movements for civil rights or welfare rights, thus denying their political engagement. Furthermore, the bulk of urban ethnography was in black communities, thereby following the widespread popular assumption reinforced by Moynihan that poverty was a black problem (Hyatt 1995).

As we will see below, later research did address the nature of political agency among the poor, particularly poor women.

Globalization and Neoliberalism

As the major shocks of globalization were felt in the 1970s in the aftermath of a series of international agreements concerning the freeing up of exchanges of financial capital, information, and commodities,[9] capital suffered a crisis of decline in profits and productivity. Suddenly, discourses about globalism shifted attention from individual morality to the structural imperatives of global markets to justify changes in the relationship between capital and labor. In the face of what was depicted as the natural, inevitable globalization of competition, arguments were made for flexible labor in order to restore efficiency and productivity.

This justified a move away from the former Fordist labor management relationships in which men were assumed to be breadwinners and were provided with family wages. A general attack on labor costs included downsizing firms, shifts from full-time stable employment to part-time temporary work, the weakening of union protections, and attacks on state regulation and taxation. Manufacturing jobs in the United States were destroyed and degraded as production moved to new offshore, Sunbelt, and suburban labor markets unfriendly to union organizing. Other manufacturers lowered labor costs through subcontracting production to smaller, less protected firms with exploitative labor practices.[10]

New jobs in the restructured economy were found in the expanding service economy which employed a two-tiered labor force: a core consisting of highly educated professionals and a tier of low-end unskilled or semiskilled workers in health care, food service, hospitality and tourism, retailing, and data input for the financial sector. The low end was characterized by low wages and flexible (high turnover) part-time and temporary work with no benefits.

Neoliberalism and Individual Autonomy

As global economic competition produced increased capital conglomeration and demands for flexible labor, a resurgence of liberal eighteenth-century ideas about the nature of human beings and their ideal relationship to the state and market fit well with the need for unregulated wage rates and working conditions. Discourses which associated the most enlightened society with sovereign individuals regarded unfettered freedom to participate in the market as the highest good. In the United States, this ideology was frequently justified through the Locke-based sacred texts of the Founding Fathers written for a nation of small farms and enterprises imagined in reaction to absolute monarchies. These ideas did not take into account the realities of power inequality in the hierarchical structure of the global political economy today. They also ignored the structural inequalities based on race and gender historically inscribed in the political economic structure.

Soon the New Economy was itself valorized as the narrative shifted from gloom about deindustrialization to optimism about high technology information systems which would save the U.S. economy. Forms of self-employment such as entrepreneurship and consultancies were extolled. The New Economy would allow people to become "liberated" workers as the increasing loss of work security was newly configured as virtuous "freedom." Workers would be autonomous agents constantly reinventing themselves to take advantage of unlimited new opportunities in a continually expanding economy.

There were major consequences for women stemming from the way in which markets were venerated. Only paid labor which produced market commodities was valued. Individual responsibility, highly vaunted, was associated not with the connectedness or caretaking associated with women's work in social reproduction but with the autonomy and self-sufficiency linked to contracts of market exchange. A major assault on state social policies began on the grounds that they supposedly stifled individual motivation and the incentive to work. Individuals damaged by state dependency needed to be cured through programs restoring self-respect and self-esteem, transforming them into autonomous individuals (Cruikshank 1996).

At the same time, ironically, shifts in the labor market had created a major contradiction between the discursive construction of the ideal family with a male provider and female caretaker and the material realities of two income households. The end of Fordism meant that more than one income was needed to support a family. This shift toward women's employment loosened conjugal interdependence as women across social classes and racial categories entered the labor force. This allowed women to become more independent of abusive husbands and other problem marriages. These processes produced different kinds of discourse and gender consciousness among different class and racial groups depending on their historical experience. As we saw above, black women had always worked and had often been primary earners as well as major caretakers, relying on female networks for support. Their dependency on men had long been constrained by a racialized labor market which led to frequent male unemployment and insecure low-wage work. In contrast, some white working-class women, while increasingly living in female-headed households and depending on female support, were still tied to models of the ideal patriarchal family structure which had been reinforced in the era of Fordist family wages. They focused on their role as mothers and were more ambivalent about working. At the same time, the women's movement engendered in other white working- and middle-class women multiple and contradictory discourses of freedom from patriarchal dependence, self-development through work and career, and the maintenance of maternal roles.

Race, Immigration, and Poverty

While the conflation of poverty and race developed in the 1960s was never completely redressed, later work which focused on white poverty (Fitchen 1991; Susser 1982; Kingfisher 1996; Halperin 1990) attempted to redress the conflated notion that poverty and blackness were the same.

At the same time, as racially different new immigrants from non-European nations in Latin America, Asia, and the Caribbean entered the United States as labor migrants after immigration policy changed in response to globalization,[11] new multicultural discourses drew attention to growing nonblack movements for economic and social inclusion. Between 1960 and 1996, 17,289,266 new immigrants entered the United States, including legal immigrants and undocumented visitors overstaying their visas. This does not include those workers who cross the border illegally (DeSipio and de la Garza 1998:17–18). The majority of new immigrants entered the low-wage labor market. They joined native-born minorities in being pathologized as parasitic and undeserving outsiders.[12] English language competence became the major focus of anti-immigrant demonization. While Asian-Americans were stereotyped as high academic achievers and viewed as a "model" minority in spite of the poverty of many Southeast Asian refugees, Latinos (largely Puerto Ricans in the east and Mexicans in the west) were often lumped with blacks in the underclass.

Defunding the Safety Net

As we saw with progressive jobs programs, attempts to retrench the War on Poverty began immediately after programs were put in place as global pressures on profit and productivity mounted in the 1970s. There was an accelerating withdrawal of funds from antipoverty programs egged on by increasing conservative antistate allegations of the spread of dependency and bureaucratic inefficiency. At this juncture, the poor and their public support systems became internal scapegoats for any unresolved problems in the state and market system—the pressures of global competition, "high" taxes, the state deficit, and so on.[13]

Reduction in benefits or failure to upgrade benefits in response to inflation made it impossible for single mothers on welfare to make ends meet. In response, they were increasingly forced to depend on banned work in the underground economy which left them vulnerable to both sanctions and an image as welfare cheats (Susser and Kreniske 1987; Edin and Lein 1997).

During the Reagan era a new outcry linked dependency and its associated "personal *ir*responsibility" to old concerns with the virtue of poor women in a discourse of "family values" which focused on the need to control women's sexuality. The right argued that it was dependency on the state rather than poverty that was the evil destroying people's lives. The poor, largely configured as black women, were seen as enslaved by state dependency which produced a loss of the work ethic and uncontrolled reproduction. They needed to be liberated from the state. One conservative called the War on Poverty programs the "liberal plantation" (Jack Kemp, quoted in Hyatt 2001:221).

The right argued that dependency threatened the family by encouraging promiscuity and out-of-wedlock births as a way to increase cash assistance. This emphasis on the threat to family values especially resonated in this time of moral panic when Americans across classes were being affected by women's new roles as workers and by high rates of divorce.

These arguments were supported by a run of neoconservative books (Gilder 1991; Murray 1984; Mead 1992) using research often heavily funded by right-wing think tanks (Stefancic and Delgado 1996). This work used broad sweeping statistical correlations to try to prove a linear causal relationship between the overly active welfare state and permanent dependency as well as an increase in childbirth out of wedlock in spite of specific studies which showed otherwise. At the same time, the Reagan regime was busy producing changes in the tax structure which significantly redistributed wealth upward (Barlett and Steele 1994).

In the new environment of neoliberalism, the scene was set for focusing on the belief that only paid work would liberate poor women from the shackles of state dependency. This required demeaning poor women's unpaid contributions as mothers and making them autonomous self-governing agents. Shifting women from welfare to work became the rallying cry. While the emphasis was on "capacity building" for poor women, many critics pointed out that such reforms had significant labor market wage rate effects (Piven 1998) and conveniently provided cheap state-subsidized low-wage workers.

In a short time, antistate neoconservatives who had begun this campaign were joined by free market neoliberals in a much heralded New Consensus which was exemplified by Senator Daniel Patrick Moynihan, a major broker of the legislative compromise. As he stated, "conservatives have persuaded liberals that there is nothing wrong with obligating able-bodied adults to work. Liberals have persuaded conservatives that most adults want to work and need some help to do so" (quoted in Naples 1997:907).

Both sides accepted the belief, at least when it came to the poor, that personal autonomy and worth was linked to participation in the labor market and that society would do best if individuals were no longer dependent, except for brief moments, on the state. Members of the right, long subscribing to the benefits of unfettered markets, differed from neoliberals in their virulent distrust of the state and its bureaucracies (except for military defense) and their hypervalorization of patriarchal "family values." It was at their insistence that all federal welfare-to-work legislation contained contradictory pressures on women to return to an original and "desirable" form of dependency on men as opposed to the state (Fraser and Gordon 1994; Mink 1995).

Neoliberals, on the other hand, pushed for some role for state participation in supporting programs to liberate and reform the poor. While the right was adamantly against the state, neoliberals emphasized the reform of the state, by using privatization, the discipline of labor markets, and other market mechanisms to achieve more efficient and cost-effective distributions of resources in the putative new world of unlimited global opportunities.

The new bipartisan compromise depended on joining incompatible concerns with "family values" of neoconservative discourses to the free market interest in efficiency. The former promoted returning women to patriarchal dependence while the latter promoted autonomous (and cheap and subsidized) women workers. No attention was given to pre-existing structural inequities which negated the premise of individuals as equal actors on a level playing field. Similarly, the social impossibility of working single mothers supporting families without any sustained state obligation to support childcare was conveniently overlooked.

Perpetuating the Racial Moral Divide: The Underclass Debate

Creating the political will to break the social contract depended on increasingly harsh social configurations of "the poor" by elites, professionals, media pundits, and the public. Political discourse created representations of the cheating welfare queen and the horrors of "children having children." Journalistic treatments of women and children on welfare (Auletta 1983) still described their lives as distanced and culturally impenetrable to the middle class. Constructing the poor as deviant "others" dampened empathy and calls for social justice. Social scientists again reinforced such images through the "underclass" debate, which in many ways was a reprise of the culture of poverty discourse (Katz 1993). The work of sociologist William Julius Wilson (1980, 1987), based on demographic analysis, was designed to counter the neoconservative anti-welfare dependency arguments by linking black poverty to the economic structure, that is, the disappearance of good jobs. However, while Wilson made this linkage, his work, like Lewis's, left the causal link between behavioral pathology and poverty intact. He also reinforced the conflation of race and poverty by dealing only with black poor. Wilson asserted an "underclass" that, while produced by the loss of good jobs, was perpetuated by ghetto isolation and the spatial "concentration" of dysfunctional deficits such as unwed motherhood and reliance on the underground economy, crime, drugs, and violence.

According to Wilson, personal pathology was the inevitable result of both economic restructuring and the suburban flight of middle-class black role models. His proposed solutions did argue for job creation but they also required intervention in individual uplift and reform. In fact, Wilson scolds the left for giving the upper hand to neoconservative arguments by failing to come to grips with psychological pathologies of the black poor.[14] Wilson also downplayed the continuing significance of racism for blacks. In regard to gender, his preoccupation with unwed motherhood depicted women as passive target objects in need of help and his preferred solution to poverty was for men, once employed, to marry the mothers of their children born out-of-wedlock (Di Leonardo 1998; B. Williams 1992).

At the same time, several recent ethnographic accounts of streetwise male youth involved in drugs and violence have also perpetuated the underclass image of ghetto pathology. Books by Philippe Bourgois (1996) and Elijah Anderson (1999) graphically describe lives of crime, violence, and the abuse of women, concentrating on the most extreme behaviors of poor male youth and not on the variety that actually exists. Bourgois, in *In Search of Respect*, does try to explain these ways of life as partial responses to the actual labor market experiences of the youth, which produce an oppositional search for respect and meaning. Nonetheless, this nuanced and complex argument is not easy to popularize. The nuances have been lost in newspaper and radio coverage which emphasize lurid and sensationalized behavioral stereotypes. Anderson's *Code of the Street*, which more closely follows Wilson's arguments, has been similarly popularized and is titillating for a middle-class audience.[15] In depicting the strange antisocial "street codes" governing sexuality and violence, and contrasting them to those of "decent" ghetto families with middle-class values, Anderson develops a picture of hapless victims without agency caught in a timeless web of exotic, destructive, "ghetto-specific" behaviors. These are only vaguely linked to history and political economy.

The Family Support Act (1988)

The ultimate move toward a new construction of women as primarily workers with a corresponding downplaying of their social reproductive roles as caretakers was carried out in two stages. First the development of the Family Support Act of 1988 institutionalized the idea of moving women on welfare to work at the federal level while still recognizing their roles as mothers. It permitted a wide range of transition to work activities (job training, education, worklike community service or public works as options). Second came the passage of PRWORA in 1996, which provided much more draconian welfare-to-work programs that mandated paid work in the labor market within limited time periods and ended the entitlement aspect of welfare.

Nancy Naples (1997) has analyzed the congressional testimony for the Family Support Act between 1987 and 1988 as severely constrained by the limited set of acceptable frames for discussion created by the legislators' "new consensus." These frames focused on the transition from welfare to work and the restoration of patriarchal family values. Testimony given on issues outside the frame was ignored by techniques such as not asking any questions, diverting attention to a minor point in testimony, and making dismissive statements. Naples refers to an exchange in which a legislator, who was concerned about "external" issues such as what would happen to the children of working mothers without affordable childcare, was pressured to admit to the marginality of his concern.

It was especially ironic to use "family support" in the title of a law which argued that poor mothers should be workers first. This was particularly true since there was great societal ambivalence about mothers working in general in spite of increasing economic necessity. Race clearly played a role here. Poor (black) mothers were bad mothers and role models both in terms of instilling a work ethic and controlling their sexuality. Mink (1995) argues that the resentment felt by the increasing number of working women toward welfare mothers paid to stay home and take care of their children would not have existed without the racial "othering" which distanced the black mother. Without racial images, there would have been more willingness to imagine oneself in the same situation.

In this context any cogent argument about the way in which forcing women to work would contradict their childcare roles was allowed no discursive space. It was easy to ignore the contradiction in women's roles since there was an unspoken assumption that because poor (black) women were unfit mothers, their children would be better off without them. One witness, when asked about what would happen to children if their mothers were not successfully incorporated into the labor market, answered with a description of state foster care policies related to child neglect (Naples 1997:924–25). A famous remark made in 1994 by the Speaker of the House about the desirability of bringing back orphanages also represents this persistent underlying theme.

There was also a major disconnect between the labor market based argument for working women, in which women were constructed in economic terms as workers, and the avoidance of any view of the family as an economic entity. Families were only seen as symbolic repositories of morality. The discussion of family ignored children's survival needs. Male role models were suddenly morally critical to family success regardless of the fact that these were the same men demonized as lazy and antisocial in popular discourse and the social science literature. There was a major push to force irresponsible biological fathers to acknowledge paternity even though it was acknowledged that most could not add material support to the household because of their unemployment or low wages. As one witness testified, "Child support should be pursued even when cost benefits are not readily apparent as may be the case with teenage fathers and others only intermittently employed. This makes a strong statement about the primary responsibility of parents to care for their children. Public policy must encourage, and obligate, parents to assume this responsibility" (Naples 1997: 931). Absent was any recognition that state policies actually helped to reduce women's access to male income[16] and led to separation of men and women when homeless shelters and transitional housing rules placed men and sometimes older male children in different settings from women and children (Susser 1999).

Cultural panic over the epidemic of teenage pregnancies (in spite of data on their decline) promoted family caps which withheld child stipends from any children born out of wedlock in the future in order to discourage conception. This emphasis ignored research showing no relationship between being on welfare and having more children (Bane and Ellwood 1994). In general, statistical evidence was rejected as irrelevant. As one report from a Reagan White House working group on the family stated: "Statistical evidence does not prove those suppositions [that welfare benefits are an incentive to bear children]; and yet even the most casual observer of public assistance programs understands there is indeed some relationship between the availability of welfare and the inclination of many young women to bear fatherless children" (Watts and Astone 1997:415). In fact, almost no attention was given to testimony about the material implications of this legislation for the poor. No discussion occurred about the critical role that the strength of the economy would play in the success of any work-oriented program. While the labor needs of business put forth through the testimony of business organizations was considered a relevant structural fact, there were no other allusions to the economy. There was no acknowledgment, for instance, of the fact that proposals for women to do unpaid "worklike" tasks as "volunteers" or public works such as street-cleaning in exchange for benefits below minimum wage, might be a boon for employers in a tight labor market but would negatively affect wage rates and displacement rates for the working poor (Piven 1998). Union concerns that creating cheap labor without legal protection or grievance rights not only would affect new workers but would create a chilling effect on the conditions of work for the working poor fell on deaf ears. Testimony on the lack of careers in low-wage jobs also elicited no interest. The facts that low-wage jobs did not pay living wages and that women working in them would have to work more than one job and face difficult childcare and transportation logistics to survive were ignored.

The assumption that businesses, unlike poor women, would use state subsidies efficiently and wisely was implicit throughout. Any discussion of state intervention in the labor market to develop a full employment jobs program, raise the minimum wage, or strengthen or enforce labor rights was out of order in this antistate free market political space.

The ultimate result of constructing the poor as raced, incompetent actors placed all obligations to be reformed on poor women, not the welfare system or the low-wage labor market. No state responsibility was acknowledged for the childcare needed to raise citizens. The one person who raised the issues of unpaid childcare had to force her way to the microphone and was ignored. The gender and racial composition of legislators (white male) and witnesses (predominantly professional managerial class) was striking.[17]

Personal Responsibility and Work Opportunity Reconciliation Act

Representing the National Governors' Association, future president Bill Clinton had testified at the 1988 hearings in favor of workfare. As a neoliberal centrist, he had spoken in his first term of "ending welfare as we know it." In 1994, a large number of conservative congressmen were elected on the platform of a "Contract with America" developed by the House Speaker Newt Gingrich. Its central plank was to end welfare dependency.

Thus, it was not surprising when in 1996, the Personal Responsibility and Work Opportunity Reconciliation Act (PRWORA) was passed. At the signing ceremony, several black women recounted their success in finding jobs through earlier experimental welfare-to-work programs, symbolically underscoring the association of black women with welfare and lending an aura of "moral reclamation" to work programs which subjected women to the discipline of the labor market. The new law ended Aid to Families with Dependent Children (AFDC) and replaced it with Temporary Assistance for Needy Families (TANF). This legislation definitively rent the safety net by putting a five-year lifetime limit on the time in which a household could receive cash assistance and mandating immediate work-preparation activities and real work after two years of benefits.[18] This move signaled that the linkage between welfare and the protection of people from the depredations of volatile market forces was no longer recognized. The legislation and the rhetoric leading to it was a triumph in rendering the relation between poverty and the workings of the political economy totally invisible. Poverty was the fault of irresponsible behavior and welfare state dependency.

Poor women's roles as paid workers, first normalized in 1988, were now made central. At the same time their roles as mothers were greatly reduced in significance. While the Family Support Act exempted pregnant women and those with children under three years from work, only women with children aged one year or less were exempted from work requirements under PRWORA.

By devolving control to individual states, uniform federal guarantees of support were eliminated. Federal time limits were *maxima* and states were free to shorten eligibility.[19] The emphasis on *rapid* attachment to the work force encouraged states to put people to work before the two-year limit and made it difficult to use alternate routes to "self-sufficiency," like higher education.

The legislation itself continued to be contradictory in containing a neoliberal valorization of women's self-sufficiency in the market and a neoconservative valorization of dependency on patriarchal control of sexuality and reproduction.[20] The attempt to preserve family "morality" persisted as underage mothers were forced to live with their parents, thereby losing separate household benefits and overburdening a generation that had already raised children. Bonuses were given to states to reduce out-of-wedlock births and money was made available for abstinence programs and for programs to establish paternity for children born out of wedlock, again with no material benefit (Watts and Astone 1997). Twenty-one states (42 percent) implemented family caps (Hayward 1998).

Both the Family Support Act and the PRWORA presented another ironic contradiction because in the name of liberating women and providing the "freedom" and autonomy valued by neoliberal ideology, the nature of sanctions and surveillance increased. The law strengthened federal penalties against the states for not fulfilling quotas for mandates and sanctions. It also encouraged draconian sanctioning of recipients by states for having more children, missing training sessions or work, or allowing children to miss school.[21] These approaches could only be justified by constructing welfare recipients as so damaged and incapacitated that they needed to be denied basic rights in order to force their ethical reform into self-governing agents through any kind of work. In this way, they were clearly excluded from full citizenship. The fact that the 1996 laws also took away rights to Supplemental Security Income (SSI) and food stamps (and Medicaid for the first five years) from legal immigrants also shows the implicit exclusion from social citizenship which linked poor people constructed as immigrants, native-born minorities, and women.

In the years since 1996, the major welfare reform narrative has been about the extraordinary drop in the caseload of welfare recipients,[22] which is used as the major evaluative criterion of the reform. But why should the state be proud of getting women off welfare but not into career ladders or out of poverty? Many people attribute the disappearance of women from the welfare rolls to the current strength of the economy with its tight labor market and worry about the lack of attention to planning for inevitable downturns. Draconian sanctions have forced many women off the rolls. There is significant evidence that this caseload drop also reflects the fact that women on welfare were already working in exploitive jobs in the underground economy, since benefits could not support families, and/or are doubling up with other poor kin-related families. Little follow-up information exists on women once they are placed in their first jobs, but there are indications that job retention is low.[23] Evidence shows that women are having very difficult times with childcare and that being placed in suburban jobs has created extreme transportation problems for inner-city women, further interfering with family roles.

Particular forms of implementation engender additional unintended results. For example, in Philadelphia, an increase in mandated work from twenty hours to thirty in order to reach state quotas for work has resulted in many women having to work two jobs. A second job is necessary since employers are not willing to offer more than twenty hours to one worker. As a result, childcare scheduling difficulties and longer and more logistically complex work weeks and commutes all lead to more time away from family. There is also a striking inability to recruit women for special programs that deal with substance abuse or records of incarceration. Poor women have developed a strongly shared belief that the state is using these programs to locate "bad" mothers in order to remove children from their homes. This is certainly not an outrageous reaction since the Congressional Budget Office itself suggested that the continued federal funding of foster care programs might give states incentives to rely on these funds when household time limits on cash assistance run out. Poor women's experiences with the state make them sensitive to the transparent messages of the public discussions about orphanages and public talk about the increased need for foster care after the five-year limit on welfare began in 2001.

Welfare Reform and the Alternative Political Subject

In the 1970s, as discussed above, there developed through in-depth studies an alternative picture of poor women as competently developing family survival strategies. These were generally ignored in the public debate. In the decades since, new in-depth analysis of poor women's lives has demonstrated that their unpaid work consists of more than family nurturing. They also engage in heavy levels of work as community builders and political activists making demands for concessions by the state in this era when the state has withdrawn services from poor communities (Bookman and Morgen 1988; Susser 1982). Many had learned political organizing skills as participants in the civil rights and welfare rights movements (Piven and Cloward 1979) as well as the Community Action Program of the War on Poverty. For example, Nancy Naples (1991, 1998) has described how poor women employed through the Community Action Program did not become co-opted and depoliticized by the state which employed them but retained their earlier activist ideas and practice. Poor white women (Susser 1982), African-American women (Naples 1998; Stack 1996; Hyatt 1997, 2001), Latino women (Pardo 1998; Naples 1998), and multiracial alliances of women (Goode 1998, 2001) have moved beyond family to participate in collective social movements to make claims on the state. They seek concessions such as better schools (Goode 2001; Pardo 1998), city services (Susser 1982), strengthening the role of community organizations (Naples 1998; Pardo 1998; Stack 1996; Goode 2001) and tenant management in public housing (Hyatt 2001). Tenant management was created in response to activist claims made by women in public housing projects after they had been massively defunded in the 1970s. These analyses link this community work to "activist mothering" (Naples 1998), in which women see their tasks as extensions of their nurturing roles and rely on expanded informal networks to participate in collective action.

Yet welfare reform as it is currently structured has had three potentially depoliticizing effects on these women and on the critical political networks they have developed. First, the surveillance and sanction system forces women to spend more time in sessions with agents of the state. For example, the head of one school-based mothers' organization in Philadelphia complained to me that her coactivists spent so much time at appointments related to work and training, scheduled without consultation, that they could no longer attend the traditional group meetings at times when children were dropped off or picked up at school.

Secondly, in an attempt to privatize moral uplift, two masculinist structures were given significant roles: the private corporation and the Faith Based Organization (FBO). PRWORA encourages the principle of privatizing welfare-to-work programs through contracts between the state and private entities. Moreover, special actions were taken to remove former restrictions on contracts with churches based on the separation of church and state.

Catherine Kingfisher has shown that lower level social service workers who are street level bureaucrats can be structurally pressured to feel socially and morally distant from poor women clients in spite of shared class positions and life experiences (Kingfisher 2001). If this is so, representatives of masculinist corporations and church-based programs who are in many ways not only distant from poor women's experiences in terms of gender and class but threatened by their political subjectivity are likely to be willfully ignorant of their strengths. The formal hierarchical structures characteristic of their organizations diverge significantly from the informal, open-ended networks of activist mothers (Naples 1998:193.)

Barbara Ehrenreich (1997) has described the world of corporate welfare-to-work programs with large national corporations bidding for welfare-to-work contracts. Conglomerates like Lockheed and Unisys formerly supported by defense contracts during the Cold War now have contracts with state and local governments to provide training (but not jobs) for welfare recipients. These are the very corporations known for cost overruns and delays, and yet the implicit popular assumption remains that corporations are most efficient in managing resources.

At the same time, church-related programs or FBOs have become acclaimed as instruments of self-empowerment linked to social programs designed to reform individuals. These include welfare-to-work, rehabilitation from substance abuse, and homelessness programs. FBOs are seen as best able to spiritually reclaim people through the kind of emotional connection made through public exhortations and audience response. These often follow the tenets of self-help twelve-step programs which became popular in late twentieth-century America for reforming people thought to be unable to control themselves in regard to sex, gambling, anger, violence, or drug and alcohol abuse. For such groups, the image of poor women as morally flawed is common sense and any understanding of their competence and political subjectivity would interfere with the organizational mission. Often the corporate training providers hire trainers who use similar preaching/exhortation techniques.

Organizations across the political spectrum from the liberal Call to Renewal to the religious right push to give churches more public resources to confront poverty and other social ills. The use of religious organizations fits into the crescendo of calls to renew civil society and civic responsibility using organizations outside the state.[24] This talk advocates restoring civic engagement by having individuals act through voluntary organizations. The general valorization of any and all nongovernmental organizations (NGOs) leaves them unproblematized and unexamined in terms of whose interests they represent. Extolling activities like mentoring, which emphasize paternalistic individual uplift and an asymmetry between mentor and client, is contradictory to poor women's local political agency and involvement in protest and demand campaigns aimed at changing structures of power.

The patriarchal tenor of faith-based movements is demonstrated by the well-known national movement Promise Keepers, which is aimed at getting men to accept their responsibilities as family leaders and bread-winners. A woman journalist observing a meeting of FBOs, commented on the disconcerting fact that the podium speakers and participants were all men (Eisner 2000).

Even when this is not so, the demands of state and foundation supporters and competition for contracts and funds have professionalized and masculinized such organizations. In the case of one church-based program run by women clergy which I observed for three years, the board gradually changed from one dominated by women (local poor women service recipients and suburban church women) to one dominated by lawyers, bankers, and small businessmen. Talk shifted to accounting techniques, press releases, web pages, and videotape public relations. The token client women felt increasingly marginalized and stopped attending. The formalization of rules imposed by the new managerial-class board replaced the informal relationships between staff and participants and ultimately led to a long period of conflict and turnover in staff and participants.

The last depoliticizing process pertains to the effect the implementation of new welfare policy has on individual consciousness. Both the draconian application of sanctions to those who resist welfare-to-work programs and the now taken for granted belief that there are no limits on what a self-reformed individual can do work against resistance and political activism. Through the new type of training program, individuals are exposed to threats and shame referred to as "tough love," "demanding love," or "severe mercy."

For example, in one exemplary three-week job preparation program described in a segment of the CBS television program *60 Minutes*,[25] distinctions were made between good and bad participants depending on how quickly they accepted often demeaning jobs.[26] Special attention was given to one woman, who was described at graduation as having been "truly transformed" so that "she really had her future in her hands." She turned out to be a big disappointment, for after being sent to several jobs she soon left them. There were many shots of her being publicly shamed and humiliated by the head of the program with comparisons made to successful workers who had stayed in their jobs. The well-known TV interviewer asks her why she left since "the whole lesson here is that you have to swallow your pride and put up with a lot." The program participant replies, "You can only take as much as you can. I'm not going to get stepped on wherever I go."

Her defiant explanations of why she left each job alluded to problems with working conditions and abusive personal treatment by her bosses. The behavior could be read as her active resistance to dirty, dangerous, and dead-end jobs for which her bosses received not only material incentives but the symbolic capital for "saving" a former welfare worker.[27] Yet this meaning was suppressed by both the trainer who ridiculed the participant and the producer who edited the tape. It was ironic that in the name of self-empowerment this woman was being told to accept whatever work conditions she was placed in. The head of the program had the last word when he suggested that the participant, who had since left the program, would be back when her lifetime welfare limit was reached and she needed a broker to be accepted in the labor market.

Sanctions are based on the unquestioned faith that forcing people into low-end jobs will make them into good workers. This is echoed in the marketing ad for the Philadelphia welfare-to-work program which shows kids with their mothers saying: "Need a hard worker? Moms coming off welfare are motivated, responsible employees. They have to be. Hire one today" (Naymik, quoted in Hyatt 2001). The advertising agency head was quoted in a local paper as saying, "You can't hire a better worker than a welfare mother because working makes the difference between surviving and living on the street with kids. How much more serious can it be?" (Naymik 1998:17). Yet this assumption about the efficacy of force is rebutted by the work of Kathryn Edin and Laura Lein (1997) whose study shows that welfare recipients in work programs respond best to meaningful work which teaches them transferable skills and has a future, in other words, "fair work" (Rose 1995).

In the job preparation described on *60 Minutes*, the amount of praise successful participants received served to further reinforce the internalization of an ideology of self-governance leading to self-blame if one fails or harsh judgments of others if one succeeds. Women in this program respond like the women who witnessed Clinton's signing of PRWORA. They develop a narrative of moral self-reform seeing themselves as having heroically and permanently changed their lives. They separate themselves from the "bad" poor. The ability of such programs to generate the blame of oneself or other poor is disempowering and has a dampening effect on political subjectivity and collective action.

Katherine Newman (1999) finds that fast-food workers with no benefits and limited working hours, income, and mobility develop moral disdain for the nonworking poor rather than a critique of their working conditions. Donna Goldstein (2001) interviewed participants in a micro-enterprise program that provides participants little in the way of credit or marketing skills but expects them to develop enterprises. She found that participants all see themselves as successful because of their new subjectivity as independent entrepreneurs and ignore the lack of material improvements in their lives. Vin Lyon Callo (2001) found that guests in a homeless shelter predominantly buy into ideologies that link homelessness to individual inadequacies rather than political economy and apply blame to both themselves and others. However, he was able to develop some political space in the shelter over a two-year period for critical reflections on the housing market, labor market, and inequality and a renewed sense that collective challenges were possible. Incipient local campaigns were organized around these issues. While these actions were vulnerable to state pressures on shelter funding, they changed people's sense of what was thinkable and possible to do.

Taken together, the sanctions and surveillance of PRWORA disempower the collective actions of poor women by putting more pressures on their daily activities. The operations of corporate and faith-based programs subordinate women to powerful males and fail to recognize or build on their organizational strengths and social relations. This is not surprising since the existence of women's strength as interconnected conscious political subjects is threatening to the state and its corporate and church beneficiaries. Harsh sanctions and the overweening celebration of "successful" cases of welfare-to-work transitions strengthen the faith of many poor women in the power of the liberated self and reinforce the preexisting tendency to find moral flaws in oneself and others. This works against the development of a critical understanding of power.

In the final analysis, the racialized discourses of family morality in the new welfare reform continue to reinforce the image of the pathological black woman. Such a belief works in tandem with faith in individual reform within the imagined infinite expansion of the new global economy. It persists as a hedge against the failure of "tough love" and "severe mercy," as a necessary corollary of welfare-to-work, because it can be reinvigorated to explain failure when an economic downturn or the five-year limits hit. Right now there is no political space for introducing political economic understanding into national discussions. We must therefore turn our attention to more clearly understanding the processes which have disabled poor people's collective political agency and explore more fully the sites of intervention and the conditions under which poor women can build on their agency and activism.

Chapter 6
The Great Undoing

State Formation, Gender Politics, and Social Policy in Canada

Janine Brodie

For the past two decades, Canadians have been mired in complex and multiple processes of fundamental change. Among other things, the post-World War II consensus about the role of the state, the nature of citizenship, and popular understandings of the appropriate relationship among the public and the private and the collective and the individual have been incrementally and progressively recast into a model of governance which would have been inconceivable a half century ago. This tectonic shift in the epicenter of Canadian politics was not accomplished through constitutional change or through a massive remodeling of the institutions of government. Indeed, the structure and formal institutions of the Canadian state remain virtually identical to those of twenty years ago (Pal 2000:2). Instead, change has been accomplished largely, often insidiously, at the level of discourse and the way we come to understand the state, the public sphere, and our relationships with them.

As Canadians enter the twenty-first century, they, like their counterparts throughout the western world, have been ushered through a paradigmatic shift in the dominant philosophy of governance. The latter term is meant to capture the historically shifting and politically negotiated (and enforced) relationships among the three principle domains of a liberal-democratic polity—the state, civil society, and the market—as well as the ways in which citizens understand themselves, articulate their interests, exercise their rights and obligations, and mediate their differences (UNDP 1997:11). Philosophies of governance, if well conceived and widely supported, tend to have long shelf lives. For example, the consensus underlying the post war years, variously described as "the postwar compromise," "embedded liberalism," and "the welfare state," shaped Canada's political geography for thirty years. Since the early 1980s, it has been gradually and progressively replaced with a new set of assumptions of governance. This new philosophy of governance, neoliberalism, represents an amalgam of policy postures including decentralization, privatization, individualization, and the elevation of the market over the public sector.

Like all philosophies of governance, neoliberalism projects and sustains its own spaces of inclusion and exclusion and configurations of classed, racialized, and gendered social space. Philosophies of governance are saturated with temporality and relations of domination which are often hidden within ruling assumptions, public discussions, and policy documents. They are "commonsense" understandings of who we are and how we should govern ourselves. The fact that these seemingly universal and timeless understandings of the world shift precipitously from one era to another occupies little space in the public imagination. The universal, the timeless, the commonsensical, by definition, resist public debate and the exploration of alternative ways of thinking. As such, philosophies of governance act as templates which inform the terrain and activities of the state, shaping, among other things, the identification, content, and delivery of public goods. In the process, these "commonsense" ideas and discourses write a certain coherence and predictability into the chaos of politics as well as into value patterns and identity formation in civil society. Governing philosophies, in other words, help shape the patterns of political contestation and mobilization which governments must respond to during any era (Brodie 1997). This chapter focuses on changes in social policy during the past twenty years in order to trace how neoliberalism is reconfiguring the gender order in contemporary Canada. As this story unfolds, it will become increasingly apparent that gender exposes the many contradictions inherent in this new governing order, if not its Achilles' heel.

Governments, Governance, and Gender

The emergence of the neoliberal state in Canada and elsewhere has been marked by a growing income polarization between the rich and the poor (both within countries and between the North and the South), an acceleration and intensification of the feminization of poverty, and the marginalization of already marginalized groups, especially single mothers, persons with disabilities, and visible minority women, to the fringes of the labor market and of society. At the same time, the political muscle and tangible accomplishments of the second wave of Canadian feminism during the 1970s and 1980s have all but disappeared. In only a few years, gender and the equality agenda generally have been virtually erased from public discourse and public policy. This magical disappearing act does not signal a victory over gender-based inequality in

Canada. Indeed, almost every measure of economic and social well being demonstrates the opposite. Instead, the undoing of the gender equality policy agenda in Canada (indeed, all structurally-based equality claims) reflects the way in which the concepts of gender and group equality have been de/reconstructed within the neoliberal governing paradigm. This becomes apparent when this paradigm is contrasted with the assumptions underpinning the postwar welfare state.

Liberal Progressivism and the Welfare State

The period leading up to the formation of the welfare state in Canada very much parallels the experience of the past quarter century—years characterized by the breakdown of the logic of the prevailing philosophy of governance followed by various attempts to "reinvent" government. The Great Depression of the 1930s revealed the inadequacies of a classical laissez-faire philosophy of governance in an increasingly urbanized and industrialized society. Throughout the 1930s and 1940s, Canadians were offered a menu of different visions of a new governing order by a variety of ideology peddlers, including two new political parties, the Cooperative Commonwealth Federation (CCF, Fabian socialism) and the Social Credit (SC, right-wing populism). Eventually, a broad-based elite-mass consensus emerged around a new blueprint of governance which prescribed a radical realignment of the boundaries among the state, the market, civil society, and the home. This liberal-progressive conception of governance borrowed heavily from the insights of John Maynard Keynes and rested on a number of key pillars which gave unique form to the Canadian welfare state in the postwar years (Lipietz 1994:342). Unlike previous eras, this governing philosophy assumed that:

- economic activity would be collectively regulated in order to maximize stability and the collective welfare of all citizens;
- the state would provide social welfare for its citizens *as a right of citizenship*; and
- state practices would be guided by a commitment to formal equality among its citizens and impersonal procedures in implementation and regulation of public policy (Young 1990b:67).

The distribution of the benefits of the welfare state was to be calculable, impersonal, formal, and bureaucratic (Lipietz 1994:353). Citizens became bearers of social rights which, in turn, were linked to broader conceptions of progress, democracy, social planning, and equality. Liberal progressivism held out the promise of a better and more secure society to a polity recovering from the ravages of the Depression and world war.

Feminist interpretations of the welfare state have consistently pointed out that its liberal-progressivist discourse of universality, unconditionality, equality, and neutrality was decidedly gendered. Social citizenship rights were premised largely on full-time employment. This definition of citizen-worker, combined with the postwar construction of the appropriate gender order as male breadwinner and dependent wife and children, meant that men gained the *entitlements* of social citizenship. They could claim social security as a right. Women, in contrast, were cast as dependent citizens—dependent either on individual men, family, or state-funded and delivered social welfare which involved surveillance, conditionality, social stigma, and lower levels of compensation (Bakker 1994a; Young 1990b). In other words, social rights were neither universal nor unconditional but, instead, highly gendered, casting the male breadwinner as the social citizen and women as dependents or clients of the state. Feminist scholars have demonstrated that this particular articulation of the gender order through, among other vehicles, public policy and popular culture, excluded the experiences of working-class, unmarried, and minority women who rarely had the luxury of dependency. But, as Scott, Horne, and Thurston explain, the model of the dependent woman was central to the formation of public policy and promoted aggressively by public institutions and reformers alike (2000:35). In the eyes of the welfare state, women's political identity and destiny was filtered through the lens of the patriarchal family. Public policy included women under the umbrella of the state primarily as wives and mothers.

Although accurate and appropriate, this popular assessment of the gendered underpinning of the welfare state does not tell the whole story. Liberal-progressive discourse also provided for women and a nascent women's movement to pronounce themselves as something different from and more than dependents, wives, and mothers. This new governing philosophy, especially the priority it attached to social rights, equality, democracy, social planning, and progress, provided a different political space for women which was outside the confines of the home. Women were encouraged and, indeed, empowered by the state to make claims on the state as *citizens* who had been actively denied the promise of equality and progress, although all too frequently it was white middle-class women who had the loudest voice (Brodie 1995). Liberal progressivism, in other words, encouraged its own style of politics and of identity formation and mobilization among disadvantaged groups. This politics, as Carol Smart points out, was "dependent upon the identification of an interest group with a shared identity" that could be shown to have been "denied their full and proper legal and/or human rights." This kind of politics presumed the existence of a welfare state because it assumed immutable linkages among social rights, social equality, and social progress (Smart 1995:107). Liberal progressivism held out the promise that the many strains of structural and systemic disadvantage rooted in the postwar world could be minimized through social planning and public policy.

The second wave of the Canadian women's movement grew up beside and, in many ways, was shaped by the welfare state and its liberal-progressivist governing philosophy. Central to this relationship was the federal government's acquiescence in 1966 to the demands of a small group of influential women to appointment of a Royal Commission on the Status of Women (RCSW). Its mandate was to identify the major impediments to the achievement of gender equality in almost all walks of Canadian life and to recommend policy responses which would break down these barriers. Reporting in 1970, the RCSW made over 150 recommendations for federal government action. One unintended outcome of the royal commission was the consolidation of a growing and increasingly politicized women's movement, especially in English Canada, which fixed its eyes firmly on the federal state and its promise of planning and progress. In 1972, the National Action Committee on the Status of Women (NAC), second wave feminism's key frontline organization, was launched for the precise purpose of monitoring the federal government and pressuring it to implement the recommendations of the RCSW. In the process, feminist activists developed political acumen and policy expertise, particularly with respect to the gendered terrain of postwar social policy. Whether consciously or not, they prescribed to the liberal ideal that, armed with a solid argument and political pressure, the federal government would and could act to flatten structural disadvantage and realize the equality of genders and, potentially, of all disadvantaged groups.

The 1970s and early 1980s were empowering days for the women's movement. The goal of women's equality crept up the ladder of policy priorities, especially after the United Nations declared 1975 the International Year of Women. It was followed by the Decade of Women (1976–85) when governments of all countries were encouraged to put sexism and gender inequality squarely at the center of national and international policy agendas. These years saw the proliferation of strategic sites for women within the federal state—among them, the Women's Bureau in the Department of Labour, the Office of Equal Opportunity in the Public Service Commission, the Status of Women branch of the Privy Council Office, a minister responsible for the status of women within the federal cabinet, and, most important, the Women's Program in the citizenship branch of the Secretary of State. The placement of the latter was not accidental. It reflected the linkage drawn by liberal-progressivist discourse between democracy, equality, and inclusion. The Women's Program was specifically mandated to pursue "the development of a society in which the *full potential of women as citizens* is recognized and utilized" (Burt 1994:216). To this end, federal funding for the Women's Program mushroomed from a meager $223,000 in 1973 to a peak of $12.4 million in 1985.

The mid-1980s marked the apex of political influence for the second wave of the Canadian women's movement. In only a few short years, it had witnessed an exponential growth in the number of women in elective office, a proliferation of provincial and federal policy initiatives aimed at the elusive goal of gender equality, the entrenchment of a sexual equality clause in the new Charter of Rights and Freedoms, unprecedented attention from the major political parties both in speech and in platform, a televised federal leadership debate devoted exclusively to women's issues, and, in the early 1980s, the emergence of a gender gap which suggested that ordinary Canadian women were prepared to choose among political parties on the basis of what they were saying about and doing for women, especially in the social policy field. Throughout this period, indeed currently, pollsters found that women were much more likely than men to support social programs and an activist state.

Yet, these victories proved both vulnerable and short-lived. The mid-1980s also witnessed the election of the first overtly neoliberal government which promised, albeit with characteristic Canadian moderation, to chart the federal state along the path already carved by Margaret Thatcher and Ronald Reagan. Since the election of Brian Mulroney's Conservative government, Canadians have witnessed political parties of all stripes systematically undo the very foundations of the welfare state and replace it with a leaner and meaner neoliberal alternative. This transformation in governing philosophies is now essentially complete. What vestiges of the postwar welfare state that remain have been so undermined and altered that they would be unrecognizable to their creators. The proportion of federal spending currently directed to social programs is lower than in 1949, before the welfare state was set in place. The vast majority of Canada's unemployed no longer qualify for benefits while the federal government funnels the growing surpluses generated by the employee-funded program into general revenues. The gap between the rich and the poor has widened, the poor have grown poorer and are increasingly isolated in urban ghettos, and poverty is now more often the fate of a select groups of Canadians. "High risk" groups, in the federal government's current terminology, primarily consist of lone parent families, families headed by a disabled person, immigrants arriving during the past decade, Aboriginals, and senior women living alone (Canada Privy Council Office 1999). Deepening poverty and other measures of social exclusion are increasingly gendered at the same time as the goal of gender equality has been erased from public discourse and the formation of public policy. The next section of this chapter, which explores the foundational premises of neoliberal governance, fleshes out this paradox.

Performativity and the Neoliberal State

When Mulroney's Progressive Conservatives swept to power with an unprecedented majority in 1984, it was not immediately apparent that the major threat to the postwar equality agenda and social policy was less a formidable political opponent in government than the beginning of a process which would result in a paradigmatic shift in the prevailing philosophy of governance. From the mid-1980s onward, however, the women's movement, in coalition with other progressive groups, fought against the implementation of what they termed the "Mulroney" or "Tory" agenda. The women's movement was a frontline opponent of the Free Trade Agreement with the United States (FTA, 1988), the extension of this agreement to include Mexico (the North American Free Trade agreement, NAFTA, 1994), and two failed attempts to constitutionally recognize Quebec's unique position in the Canadian confederation and realize greater autonomy in areas of provincial jurisdiction (the Meech Lake Accord, 1987, and the Charlottetown Accord, 1992). In each case, the objections of the women's movement centered around both preserving the gains that had already been achieved and defending the power of the federal state to fund and shape social policy and enforce minimum national standards. Not surprisingly, the women's movement was increasingly reviled, by the federal government and neoliberal ideologues generally, as a selfish coalition of "special interests" that threatened Canadian consensus. At the time, journalists commonly joked that feminism had become the new "f-word" on Parliament Hill.

The collision between the federal government and the women's movement during the Mulroney years (1984–93) increasingly became centered on the federal government's growing embrace of the principle axioms of neoliberalism. In simple terms, this philosophy of governance emphasizes the importance of removing government from the economy, especially with respect to regulating business. Indeed, this fundamental tenet is encoded in NAFTA, which effectively exercises quasi-constitutional authority over the Canadian state and its electorate in important policy areas. Neoliberalism also downplays the importance of expending public funds to promote social well-being and equality agendas and it was precisely on this terrain that the government's repudiation of the women's movement centered. The dominant current of the second wave of the Canadian women's movement in the postwar years, responding to liberal-progessivist discourse and practice, consistently linked the achievement of women's equality to state intervention in the economy whether through social policy, the courts, or through the regulation of the private sector. Key feminist policy demands, constitutive elements of the postwar women's movement in Canada, such as universal and affordable childcare, income security for sole mothers and elderly women, affirmative action, and pay and employment equity, all called for more government, not less government. The undoing of the welfare state obviously threatened both the identity and the strategic agenda of the dominant current in the women's movement. These diametrically opposed worldviews leave little room for political compromise.

The governing philosophy of the neoliberal state has been termed *performativity* (Yeatman 1994). This term points to the increasing tendency for the state to fashion itself as a market player rather than as the embodiment of the public sphere, the source of public goods, the greater equalizer of structural inequalities, and the expression of democratic consensus. The neoliberal state increasingly rejects the fundamental assumption of liberal democracy that the provision of certain goods and services defies the logic of the market. Instead, the neoliberal state measures its performance by its capacity to commodify and displace the public either onto the market or onto the individual (hence, the term performativity). In the process, the very reason for the state and the distinction between the public and private is blurred and eroded. Public goods are privatized while the public sphere embraces as its governing logic market principles and measurements (Brodie 1997).

Performativity is a textbook case of institutional emulation—a process whereby one institution takes on the procedures and trappings of another. For example, a retailing chain might adopt an approach to personnel management which was initially developed by a manufacturing enterprise. Performativity, however, involves more than the transfer of certain practices from one sector of the economy to another. The term also points to the crossing of an institutional divide—a diffusion from the market concerned with private profit into the public sector concerned with social need, welfare, health, education, environment, and the general public good. In other words, performative discourse recommends the attrition of the realm of the public and, in so doing, contains and diverts political contestation. The idea of performativity marks the ascendancy of the market *over* the state and *inside* the state. This embrace of the logic of the market atrophies the public, closes political spaces, and further marginalizes the economically and socially marginalized who depend on the state to redress the most adverse consequences of the capitalist economy. A performative philosophy of governance engages with those who do not fit neatly into a market model in one of two ways: either they are treated as inadequate or dysfunctional market players or they are completely erased from the public agenda.

Performativity, being grounded in the assumptions and language of neoclassical economics and laissez-faire liberalism, also explicitly rejects the policy relevance of gender or any other systemic barrier to equality. These assumptions, revived from the distant past, depict the rational individual and the market player as the universal social actor. Yet, as feminist theorists have long argued, this actor can only be male within the context of a highly gendered social order. Moreover, neoclassical economics brackets out women's reproductive and caring labor because it has no market value. As Isabella Bakker reminds us, "markets operate without recognizing that the unpaid work of reproduction and maintenance of human resources contributes to the realization of formal market relations" (1994a:2). This labor is simply assumed in neoclassical economic models under the dubious phrase "other things being equal." But of course other things are never equal, a fact that should have rendered neoclassical economics suspect from the outset.

Liberalism, in turn, asks individuals to bracket out their particular social location such as those structured by gender, race, and class. This formula blinds us to the daily realities of living in gendered, raced, and classed bodies and to the fact that these bodies are treated differently and unequally across the entire spectrum of social relations. Within this barren discursive terrain, performativity sees only one social agent— one good citizen—the atomized market player who recognizes the limits and liabilities of state provision and embraces his/her obligation to work longer and harder to become self-reliant. As the federal government itself explains, "since the 1980s, the notion that individuals and families, rather than government, should have prime responsibility for their own economic security has gained widespread currency in Canada" (Canada HRDC 2000:3).

The government itself has been instrumental in planting this idea in the public's mind by undermining in voice and policy the very idea of collective provision and the economic viability of the welfare state. Michael Prince labels these kinds of messages as *dissuasion*—a discursive strategy that relies on language and symbols to alter attitudes and behavior in order to discourage reliance on government and the public purse (Prince 2000:167). In stark contrast to liberal progressivism, performativity provides little discursive or institutional space to make claims on the state on the basis of morality, fairness, collective difference, or structural inequality.

There is currently a school of state theorists, especially in the globalization literature, that argues that the undoing of the welfare state signals the death of the nation-state itself (Guehenno 1993). Clearly, globalization, as it is currently governed, does put exacting constraints on the once unchallenged notion of state sovereignty. However, it is probably more accurate to say that state power, structured by a performative governing philosophy, is being progressively redeployed from collective provision to the enforcement of the market model in virtually all aspects of daily life. The performativity philosophy of the neoliberal state rests on three fundamental pillars—privatization, decentralization, and individualization—all of which act simultaneously to intensify gender inequality and to erode the political relevance of gender.

Privatization

Privatization (and its ideological handmaiden, deregulation) is a key governing instrument of the neoliberal state which serves both to valorize market mechanisms over the public sector and to diminish the terrain of democratic accountability. Privatization rests on two contestable assumptions endemic to neoliberal governance. The first is that services and assets initially created or regulated in and through the public sector are better delivered and maintained through market mechanisms and the price system. The second is that the state crowds out private sector investment which both prevents corporations from succeeding in the new global economy and stops economic benefits from "trickling down" to ordinary Canadians.

Privatization first entered into the federal policy agenda in the early Mulroney years under the banner of "reprivatization"—a term which created the illusion that public goods and services were being returned to where they "naturally" belonged. In their nine years in office, the Conservatives privatized twenty-five Crown corporations and created none (Barlow and Campbell 1995:77). Somewhat paradoxically, for some of these years, one person wore two hats in the Mulroney cabinet—minister responsible for reprivatization and minister responsible for women. The election of the Chrétien government in 1993 intensified the drive toward privatization in federal policy circles. A 1994 Department of Finance document entitled *A New Framework for Economic Policy* declared that the reinvention of the federal government required it to "withdraw from those things that are no longer essential to the public interest or that can be better accomplished by provincial or local government" (quoted in Barlow and Campbell 1995:234). Yet, nowhere in this document is there an engaged discussion of what is essential to the public interest or who should decide this question. Canadians are simply expected to accept the erosion of the public sector, the attrition of government functions and bureaucracy, and the alleged benefits of privatization as a matter of faith. Most Canadians, however, remain skeptical. After twenty years of neoliberal governance, public opinion polls have consistently demonstrated a wide gulf between elites and the public on the alleged benefits of neoliberalism (Graves 2000).

Privatization involves much more than simply removing things from one sector and placing them in another. It is a profoundly cultural process in which the thing moved is itself transformed into something quite different. Objects become differently understood and regulated. The deinstitutionalized (privatized) schizophrenic becomes a street person and is more often attended to by the police than by mental health professionals. Citizens become gender-neutral shareholders and are asked to assess their government in terms of its credit-ratings and fiscal bottom lines rather than how it promotes collective well-being and democratic decision-making. As more power and authority seeps from the state into the market, consumers rather than citizens are empowered. As Melanie White rightly points out, neoliberalism creates "citizen consumers." "It extends political agency to producers, consumers and entrepreneurs at the same time as it marginalizes the poor, the working poor and the otherwise disenfranchised" (White 1999:57). Of course, government downsizing, privatization, and deregulation all have gendered underpinnings as the examples of health care and pay equity demonstrate.

The crowning achievement of the Canadian welfare state was the implementation of a universal public health-care system in the mid-1960s. It also represents a formidable hurdle for a complete conversion to neoliberal performativity in Canada. Health care consumes a significant proportion of both provincial and federal expenditures. It also represents a potential gold mine for the private sector as the profit margins of American private health-care providers readily attests. At the same time, Canadians have made its abundantly clear to government that its obsession with the market does not and will not extend to public health care. No matter how often neoliberal politicians suggest to the Canadian public that the health-care system is an unsustainable drain on the public purse or that strains in the system could be ameliorated by creating a "complementary" system of public and private provision, the public response has been an unambiguous "no way." Survey data show that public health care is deeply embedded in Canadians' perceptions about who we are as a people. In 1996, for example, approximately four of five Canadians identified public health care as the most important symbol of Canadian identity. In 1999, fully 91 percent of Canadians identified health care as the top priority for the federal government. In contrast, only 64 percent endorsed the view, prominent in governmental and business circles, that tax reduction is a priority. As a prominent pollster concluded from these and other findings, "the public does not want to reduce government's role solely to that of accountant" (Graves 2000: 63–64).

Privatization nonetheless has crept into the public system incrementally and imperceptibly. The proportion of total health-care spending consumed by the private sector has steadily risen since the mid-1980s. Pharmaceuticals represent the largest conduit for private sector profit as both the public health-care system and the general public are victims of the notoriously oligopolistic practices of this industry. Systematic cuts to health care, however, have intensified the privatization of the health-care system in a number of ways, including:

- privatizing costs of health care by shifting the burden of payments onto individuals (for example, refusal to recognize an illness or treatment as insured by the public system);
- shifting the burden from public institutions to community-based organizations and private households (for example, cost-cutting has resulted in shorter hospital stays which, in turn, shifts the cost of patient recuperation to the home and most often to the unpaid caring work of women);
- privatizing care work from public health-care workers to the growing for-profit caring industry; and
- privatizing management practices within the health-care system by adopting systems developed for the private sector (for example, the "efficiency" of nursing staff is now measured in terms of time allocation per patient rather than in terms of quality of care, trust, and interpersonal contact) (Scott, Horne, and Thurston 2000:1).

Each of these privatizing gestures has disproportionately affected women insomuch as they are less able to buy drugs or for-profit services and more likely to assume the role of caregiver, either informally in the home and community or formally as health-care workers. With regard to the latter, a recent report indicates that nurses, more than any other profession in Canada, show signs of high job-related stress and burnout and frequently opt for employment in the United States where they are promised higher pay and greater autonomy in the workplace.

The negative impact of privatization on women also can be viewed from the perspective of privatizing employment opportunities which were once the purview of the public sector. The welfare state was of critical importance to women as an employer and as a regulator of gender relations and employment practices in the workplace. The federal government was and remains the largest single employer of women in Canada and, in the postwar years, took upon itself the task of being a leader in setting standards for women's employment. Government downsizing and the privatization of public sector jobs obviously closes career options for women, especially young minority women, in an era of persistently high un- and underemployment.

More important, the federal government has dramatically rejected the notion that it is and should be a different kind of employer with broader goals than a stark cost-benefit analysis would recommend. Women in the public service were and are overwhelmingly employed in clerical positions, but, in the 1970s and 1980s, the federal government took a number of steps to increase the representation of women in mid and upper management. Pay and employment equity were endorsed as government policy and private and quasi-private sector employers with strong financial ties to government were expected to comply with these practices or risk losing government contracts. These policies did see some women rise to the ranks of middle management. Nevertheless, the vast majority of women in the federal bureaucracy remained in low paying clerical positions, their wages frozen by successive restraint budgets.

In 1984 the public service union filed a complaint with the Canadian Human Rights Tribunal to achieve equal pay for work of equal value for 65,000 federal clerical workers. The case dragged through the decade as government and union lawyers argued about how to determine what was equal work and equal value. By 1998 the tribunal appeared to be ready to issue its long-awaited decision and Liberal prime minister Jean Chrétien pledged that his government would honor the outcome. However, after the Canadian Human Rights Tribunal sided with the union in July 1998, the federal government began to equivocate, arguing that the decision was wrongheaded, based on flawed methodology, and too expensive. The tribunal did not declare how much the federal government owed its former clerical workers, although estimates are in the range of three to five billion dollars. Not surprisingly, a notoriously neoliberal national press sided with the government. The *Ottawa Sun* pronounced that "equal pay for equal work has always been a mug's game" which punishes taxpayers (July 30, 1998), while Canada's national newspaper, the *Globe and Mail*, denounced the tribunal's decision because "trying to adjudicate fairness is the fundamental flaw" (August 1, 1998). The idea that the federal government, the elected voice of "the people," cannot afford to honor a decision of a human rights tribunal or be seen to be fair to its women employees underlines how successfully performative discourse within the state has displaced the postwar gender equality agenda. Meanwhile, the case drags on.

Decentralization

In its simplest terms, decentralization is a governing instrument that transfers power, responsibility, and accountability from a single center to smaller units. Some of these units are more easily identified than others and some may not be subject to direct democratic control. Decentralization is generally applauded on the grounds that it enhances democratic accountability and corrects for the worst bureaucratic excesses of the welfare state. This was the case advanced by equality-seeking groups in the 1960s and 1970s. Decentralization, they argued, allowed for more control in the design and delivery of social services and for more integrated community-based and administered programs. Presumably, too, local administrators would be more easily held accountable by the objects of social programs. This depiction of the benefits of decentralization, however, was premised on two assumptions which quickly lost validity in the 1990s. The first was that social programs would continue to be funded at adequate levels and the second was that local control would be democratic and inclusive.

The Canadian experience, however, is that the democratic potential of decentralization can be quickly offset by fiscal constraints. The rhetoric of decentralization, in fact, has masked a demolition derby—a scurry of fiscal off-loading onto newly designated "shock absorbers." The federal government, for example, recovered its fiscal bottom line in the mid-1990s both by cutting social spending and by off-loading the cost of social programs onto the provinces. Social spending as a percentage of federal expenditures has declined from in excess of 50 percent in the 1960s to 43 percent in 1985 to 30 percent in 1996 (Phillips 1996:379). At the same time, federal transfers to the provinces, which are earmarked for social programs, dropped by 35 percent—an estimated $5.4 billion. The costs to the provinces was compounded by changes to the contributor-based unemployment scheme which was renamed Employment Insurance (EI) in 1996. The plan was changed to count hours rather than weeks worked for eligibility while tightening other eligibility requirements. The immediate impact was to reduce those receiving EI by 20 percent. In the intervening years, the proportion of unemployed receiving EI benefits has dropped from 74 percent in 1989 to 36 percent in 1998. In that year, 41 percent of unemployed men received benefits compared to 30 percent of unemployed women. Many of those disqualified were forced onto provincial welfare rolls which increased provincial social welfare budgets significantly. The federal government, on the other hand, was busy diverting employee contributions into general revenues. In 2000, it is estimated that the federal government will pay out $12 billion in benefits to the unemployed and pocket $18 billion in premiums (LeBlanc 1999:A4).

To understand how the federal government was able to abandon responsibility for social policy, it is necessary to take a quick tour of the complicated map of fiscal federalism in Canada. When the basic programs for the Canadian welfare state were set in place in the 1950s and 1960s, policymakers confronted a fundamental constitutional obstacle. Put simply, the federal government had the capacity to fund social programs but the provinces had constitutional jurisdiction over the key fields of postsecondary education, health, and social welfare. To bypass this obstacle, the federal government agreed to pay half of all provincial expenditures in these fields so long as the provinces implemented programs which were faithful to federal guidelines and national standards. The federal government continued this arrangement until the late 1970s when it instituted per capita funding for education and health. Instead of receiving matching federal dollars for health and education, the provinces received a block fund which went into general revenues and potentially could be used for any reason. Not surprisingly, it was from this point onward that various provincial governments began to exact cuts first to universities and then to hospitals and redistribute these funds to other areas of provincial responsibility.

The funding of social welfare, however, remained tied to the matching dollar formula until 1995 when the federal government introduced the Canada Health and Social Transfer (CHST). Since the mid-1960s, social welfare was designed and administered through the Canada Assistance Plan (CAP) which obliged the federal government to pay half of all the provinces' expenditures on social assistance as well as related programs, most of which were heavily subscribed to by poor women. The legal mandate of CAP was to "help lesson, remove or prevent the causes and effects of poverty" and, under its terms, residents could make claims for social assistance solely on the basis of need (Pulkingham and Ternowetsky 1999). The provinces, in other words, could not turn the poor away or require that they perform some kind of work to receive social assistance. CAP's matching dollar formula also extended to special programs for disadvantaged groups, thus providing a "fiscal carrot" for the provinces to elaborate and expand the social safety net. Many of these specialized programs directly assisted poor women, among them, homemaker services for the elderly and disabled, family counseling, services for abused and special-needs children, rape crisis and women's shelters, and subsidized day care.

The introduction of the CHST has seen the cancellation of many of these programs and cutbacks to others. This outcome, if not intended, could have been anticipated. The CHST effectively transfers a diminishing amount of federal money to the provinces for postsecondary education, health, and social assistance in the form of a block grant. This grant goes directly into provincial revenue and can be used for any purpose from debt reduction, to roads, to tax cuts. Provincial governments thus have every incentive to shift money away from social welfare to programs and practices which are more popular with their backers and voters. Ontario, for example, has cut social assistance payments, reduced related services, introduced workfare, closed schools and hospitals, and cut taxes for the more affluent. The introduction of the CHST has, in effect, pressured the provinces to reduce social assistance rates, ended federal incentives to develop new or specialized income assistance plans or social services, negated the very idea of national standards in social policy, and forced the poor into a losing battle with better organized and resourced competing interests for government resources (Prince 2000:178).

By the end of the 1990s, the predictable effects of the neoliberal assault on social programs was clearly evident in the daily lives of Canadians and in official government statistics. The homeless and food banks have become a familiar part of the social fabric when only twenty years ago they would have been exceptional. The income gap between the rich and the poor has widened while the poor have become poorer. The poor are also more likely than a decade ago to be concentrated in urban ghettos. According to a report of the Canadian Council on Social Development released in 2000, the number of poor people living in cities increased by 34 percent between 1990 and 1995. One third of the children living in Montreal and Toronto are now classified as poor (*Globe and Mail*, April 17, 2000, A5). Moreover, poverty is increasingly the fate of a few identifiable groups. Women are more likely to be poor than men and visible minority women are more likely to be poor than the "invisible" majority of Canadian women. One quarter of the former group is classified as poor compared to 13 percent of the latter. The federal government has recently identified five groups which, the government suggests, are at "high risk" for a life of poverty—single mothers, disabled persons, recent immigrants (predominately persons of color), Aboriginal peoples, and elderly women living alone. This notion of "high risk" conjures up medical images which stigmatize and decontextualize poverty in the same way that, for example, medical officials talk of gay men as being a high risk group with respect to HIV infection or Aboriginal peoples as a high risk group with respect to alcoholism. Again, this contrasts sharply with liberal progressivism's underlying moral code that everyone is at risk and everyone is responsible for everyone else.

The rates of poverty among these groups are startling by any measure. In 1997, a full 43 percent of families headed either by lone parents (80 percent of whom are women), recent immigrants, or persons with disabilities were, according to official measures, poor, compared to 9 percent of other families (HRDC 2000:1). Single mothers and their children are especially vulnerable to poverty as the following statistics amply demonstrate:

- 61 percent of single mothers live in poverty;
- 83 percent of single mothers under the age of twenty-five live in poverty;
- 45 percent of all children living in poverty are in lone parent families; and
- 33 percent of social assistance recipients are single parents (Canada Privy Council Office 1999:27–29).

The experience of Canada and other advanced industrial countries that have embraced neoliberal governance is that wealth trickles down to some and not others. The growing gulf between the rich and the poor is partly attributable to changes in the global economy and the labor market, to the persistence of structural barriers rooted in class, race, and gender, and to the undoing of the welfare state. In Canada, the residualization of social policy and the abandonment of the idea of collective responsibility for the structurally disadvantaged has been intensified by decentralization and governing instruments which discourage even minimum public provision for the disadvantaged.

Critics of decentralization have argued persuasively that this governing mechanism may be inappropriate for social welfare provision. Bob Deacon, for example, contends that "the more states have the autonomy to determine what and how social needs might be met . . . the less the guarantee they will be met" (1997:19). Certainly, this has been the case in Canada since the introduction of the Canada Health and Social Transfer.

In 1998, the decentralization of social policy was reaffirmed and extended by the federal government and the provinces in the Social Union Framework Agreement (SUFA). This agreement effectively ensures that in the foreseeable future the federal government will not be permitted to use its spending power to establish national social programs or set minimum national standards. The agreement effectively prohibits the federal government from introducing new national social programs without the consent of the majority of the provinces. It is widely conceded that a national public daycare system was the first, but certainly not the last, casualty of the SUFA. At the same time, however, the provinces are demanding from the federal government restoration of social transfer to pre-CHST levels.

Individualization

At the heart of the new governing philosophy is a tidal shift away from notions of collective values and shared fate to those of family and individual responsibility. The central operating principle here is that it is up to families to look after their own and it is up to government to make sure that they do. In a sense, the affirmation of family and individual responsibility is simply another manifestation of privatization and decentralization. But it is also more than this. First, it is an attempt to recast both the individual and the citizen in the abstract and decontextualized language of neoclassical economics and classic liberalism. Individualism valorizes the rational economic actor and market relations which, as we know, have particularly insidious consequences for women, children, and other marginalized groups. Women are assumed to take up the slack in the new order, particularly with respect to caring activities (Bakker 1996). The rebirth of abstract individualism represents the systematic erasure of structural factors in the formation of social policy. The poor become responsible for their own plight while the state becomes preoccupied with using its powers to enforce the individualization of the social costs associated with neoliberal public management and economic globalization more generally. In the process, civil servants become less guardians of the public interest and well-being, and more policing agents. The social bureaucracy, for example, is now charged with finding the "abusers" of unemployment and social assistance programs rather than assisting those in need to realize a better life.

The Canadian experience is replete with examples of this shift in thinking about social policy. The new "active" welfare model, which informed the federal social policy review in 1994 and is now being implemented by the provinces, is premised on a human resources model that sees poverty as an individual defect rather than as a product of social structures which, by definition, create winners and losers. Instead, poverty is attributed to individual skill or motivational deficits which lead to dependence on the state. The idea that social assistance recipients are dependent on welfare carries with it a barrage of negative images which stigmatize the poor and make them appear to be personally to blame for their condition. Welfare dependency, similar to drug dependence, is a mark of individual weakness, irresponsibility, and immaturity and, most of all, is avoidable (Fraser and Gordon 1994).

The dependency metaphor recommends particular policy responses and not others. It raises the specter of the pathological and dysfunctional and thus invites technical intervention, surveillance, and discipline at the level of the individual. One obvious disciplinary measure is to cut welfare benefits to a level below minimum subsistence; another is to force welfare recipients to work for their benefits. The most populous province, Ontario, has adopted workfare and has passed legislation to ensure that workfare will not be subject to the minimum protections provided other workers by employment standards legislation. Workfare, snitch-lines, and extraordinary surveillance are all affronts to the basic civil rights of welfare recipients. Obviously, too, these disciplinary practices are focused on some groups more than others. The systemic bases of poverty in Canada mean that women, persons with disabilities, visible minorities, and Aboriginal people have become the primary objects of the individualization in social policy.

At the same time, neoliberal governments are busy crafting legislation which attempts to reconstruct the patriarchal nuclear family and its distinct lines of responsibility and power relations. Youth have been cut from welfare rolls under the assumption that they will be cared for by their families. Disregarding the reason why children leave home in the first place, among them, physical, emotional, and sexual abuse, the result is often street kids, juvenile prostitution, addiction, disease, crime, and despair. Women's shelters have been closed, thereby forcing abused women to stay in or return to abusive homes. Perhaps the most obvious example of the reconstruction of the patriarchal family is the federal government's new child support legislation designed to discipline the so-called deadbeat dad—the father who refuses to support the children he has left. Although long a reviled figure in feminist discourse, the deadbeat dad's centrality to the neoliberal state has been more recent. The federal government has passed legislation which standardizes child support payments and sets penalties for parents who fail to make them. While few would disagree with the intent of the legislation, it fails to address the realities of child poverty in Canada. The federal government's own research, for example, indicates that few separated fathers fit the stereotypical image of the deadbeat dad. A great many separated and divorced fathers recouple and remarry and simply do not have the income to support two families. This policy also marks single mothers who can or will name fathers (deserving) and those who cannot or will not (undeserving).

The single or sole mother provides a more vexing case for neoliberal policymakers because often she cannot be wedged into the hetero-patriarchal model of privatized social provision. Under the welfare state, single mothers were primarily seen as mothers who were unemployable, at least until their children entered school. These mothers are now framed in policy as potential employables who need surveillance and discipline in order to make them take personal responsibility for their children or find a man who will. To this end, the Ontario government has revived the "spouse in the house" rule, which dictates that single mothers lose their benefits when they live with a man. New Brunswick has gone a step further, denying benefits to a woman who moved in with another woman in order to save money. Officials argued that any living relationship between two adults would thereafter be treated as equivalent to a husband and wife relationship. There was no indication that this was a lesbian relationship and most provinces, to date, have excluded same-sex relationships from the zealous eye of the welfare caseworker. However, a 1999 Supreme Court decision which effectively extends the same legal recognition to same-sex couples as that already enjoyed by heterosexual common law relationships opens the door for provincial governments to download social costs on all families, gay or straight.

The idea that the single mother should take care of herself and her children at the same time as the government is systematically withdrawing support for her to do so would seem to be, at best, counterintuitive. However, neoliberal policymakers seem unconcerned about realities of sole parenting or the material conditions of women and children caught in the distortion of extreme poverty in a highly unbalanced gender order. Single mothers, as we have seen, are the poorest among the poor in Canada. Nevertheless, they have been erased in the poverty debate through the federal government's child poverty initiative which constructs children as deserving independent of their family or community condition. Poor children just float out there completely decontextualized from the circumstances that surround and shape them.

Drawing children out of the vagaries of poverty should be a priority of any community, small or large, but the federal government's recent initiatives send the clear message that only children are legitimate victims of poverty. To this end, the federal government has implemented the National Child Benefit (NCB) which tops up family incomes to a minimal standard regardless of the type of family or source of income (Jenson 2000). This benefit is administered through the tax system and bears no pretense about addressing the root causes of income polarization among Canadian families. The NCB provides income assistance to poor Canadians, but this assistance is contingent upon the presence of young children. The childless poor or the poor whose children have left the nest have been constructed as the "illegitimate" poor, the ones who have no good reason for making claims on the state.

Conclusion

In 2000 the federal government boasted that for eight consecutive years the United Nations named Canada the best country in the world to live by placing it first on the Human Development Index (HDI), which combines measures of life expectancy, education, and income. Policy-makers were less vocal about the fact that Canada ranked eighth on the gender empowerment index and slid to eighth on the human poverty index. The government was decidedly silent about the fact that Canada would have been lodged among developing nations if the HDI only took account of Canada's Aboriginal peoples (UNDP 2000). These, nevertheless, should be worrying trends for social policy-makers.

The past two decades have witnessed the reinvention of the Canadian state and the implementation of a new philosophy of governance. Neither of these processes can be divorced from gender (or race or class). In contrast to the era of the welfare state which spoke to and helped form an undifferentiated category of women and advanced a state-driven gender equality agenda, the politics of gender is far more complex under the neoliberal state. Poverty has become increasingly feminized but it is not borne by all Canadian women. There is also increasing income polarization among Canadian women themselves, enabling some Canadian women, usually white middle-class professionals, to buy caring work from other Canadian women who are marked by economic, racial, and ethnic disadvantage. Women and men who have benefited from the new economic and political order, moreover, are increasingly likely to interpret both their prosperity and others' poverty as a measure of the individual rather than as resulting from a fissure in the social fabric. The systematic erasure of structural considerations in popular understandings as well as in the formation of social policy has profound implications for the formation of political identities and alliances under the umbrella of the neoliberal state. Blinkered by the requisites of performativity, "the economic fates of citizens are uncoupled from one another and are now understood and governed as a function of their own particular levels of enterprise, skill, inventiveness, and flexibility" (Rose 1996b:339). This individualized and distorted vision of ourselves, our families, and our communities both erases recognition of the systemic underpinnings of gender inequality (as well as that of race and class) and intensifies its manifestations because systemic solutions to these inequalities are discounted as irrelevant. This is the fundamental paradox confronting all equality seeking groups in the new millennium. It is a paradox which, if left unchallenged, will continue to marginalize and stigmatize many "different" women and, ultimately, exact great costs to all.

Chapter 7
The Responsible Citizen

Creating a New British Welfare Contract

Ruth Lister

The United Kingdom has been described as the "chief European test-ing ground for new right theory" (Marquand 1991:329). In the area of welfare reform, in particular, it acted as a conduit for new right ideas as they traveled from the United States to Europe on the back of the wave of economic globalizing forces. Welfare reform has been identified by Prime Minister Tony Blair as central to the New Labour project, which, according to Stephen Driver and Luke Martell, can be understood as "an exercise in *post-Thatcherite* politics" (1998:1, emphasis in original), shaped by Thatcherism, yet also representing a reaction against it.

This chapter will explore the gendered implications of the British wel-fare reform agenda, with particular reference to lone mothers. It starts by tracing the material and discursive forces which underpin welfare re-form, first under the Conservatives and then under New Labour. It then explores the policy responses, which have had to negotiate long-standing tensions in the state's relationship to the family and in the construction of lone mothers as primarily mothers or paid workers. The most recent of these is the New Deal program, designed to encourage lone mothers to take up paid work.

Material Trends

New Labour promotes welfare reform as an essential response to change in the worlds of work and the family as well as to increased inequality and social exclusion. Its Green Paper on welfare reform highlights as key trends:

- a doubling of the number of divorces in England and Wales between 1971 and 1995 to 155,000 a year;

- the experience of marital breakup by one in four children born in the 1970s;
- an increase in the proportion of families headed by a lone parent from 8 percent in 1971 to 22 percent in 1995;
- a shift in the incidence of lone parenthood, as first divorce and then single motherhood have grown in significance.

Patterns of lone motherhood are shaped by factors such as social class, "race," and age (Rowlingson, McKay, and Berthoud 1998). Overall the incidence of lone motherhood is high compared with most other European countries, but lower than in the United States (Kiernan, Land, and Lewis 1998). What has been of particular concern to policymakers in the United Kingdom over the past decade has been not just the increase in the numbers of lone mothers but also the decrease in the proportion in paid work—from 47 to 42 percent between the late 1970s and early 1990s. One consequence was a politically sensitive growth in lone mothers' reliance on social assistance from 37 percent in 1979 to 79 percent in 1991 (Ford and Millar 1998).[1] Although it is starting to rise again (to 44 percent by 1998), lone mothers' labor market participation is low relative to that in most other industrialized countries (Bradshaw et al. 1996). It also contrasts with the growing labor market participation of mothers in two-parent families, which had reached 68 percent by 1998 (UK EOC 1999b). Male employment, on the other hand, has declined, in the face of diminishing job opportunities for unskilled male workers, reflecting global economic trends.

These global economic trends, in conjunction with domestic Conservative economic, fiscal, and social policies, led to a massive rise in poverty and inequality during the last two decades of the twentieth century. At the end of the Conservatives' period in office, nearly a quarter of the population was living on an income below 50 percent of the average after housing costs (generally used as an unofficial poverty line in the absence of an official line), compared with just under one in ten in 1979. For children, the proportion was just over a third compared with one in ten in 1979. Over the same period, the real incomes of the bottom tenth of the population fell by 9 percent in real terms compared with an increase of 70 percent for the top tenth and 44 percent overall. According to John Hills, "this inequality growth was exceptional internationally . . . with inequality increasing further and faster in the 1980s than in any comparable country." The result was that "overall income inequality was greater in the mid-1990s than at any time in the forty years from the late 1940s" (Hills 1998a:5).

Within these figures are hidden complex crosscutting social divisions including those of gender, "race," disability, and age. Overall, in 1996–

97, women's gross average weekly income was 53 percent of men's, compared with 35 percent in 1975 (UK EOC 1999a). Over this period, the "gender income gap" has "narrowed for all age groups up to male state retirement age and particularly for younger age groups" (UK EOC 1997:2). This partly reflects a narrowing of the hourly full-time pay gap from 71 percent in 1975 to 80 percent in 1998, although the weekly pay gap is wider and the disparity between part-time female earnings and full-time male earnings "has not altered significantly" (UK EOC 1999a:4). Thus, not all women are benefiting from the narrowing of the gender income gap, as inequalities widen within the female population between better-educated "successful" women and those either in part-time low paid work or living on benefit.[2] Lone mothers and female pensioners are overrepresented in the bottom fifth of the income distribution (UK ONS/EOC 1998), as are women (and men) in the main "minority ethnic" groups (UK DSS 1999).[3] A range of studies reveal the disproportionate risk and extent of poverty experienced by families headed by a lone mother (Ford and Millar 1998; MacDermott, Garnham, and Holtermann 1998).

Discursive Themes

The nature of the response to these material trends has been shaped by the ideological beliefs of the government in power. These can be discerned in the discursive themes which have framed debates about welfare reform.

"Welfare Dependency"

A key theme has been that of "welfare dependency" or a "dependency culture." Originating with new right thinkers in the United States, it was embraced with enthusiasm by the Tories in the second half of the 1980s as supporting their goal of promoting self-reliance and independence. Practically every welfare policy reform came wrapped in the rhetoric of reducing dependence on the benefits culture.

The language of "welfare dependency" lives on under New Labour. In its first annual report, for example, published in the name of the prime minister, it states that "welfare dependency for those who are able to work ruins lives and holds back our economic prospects" and that "the welfare state is failing too many people, leaving them in passive dependency rather than being helped towards independence" (Prime Minister 1998:21, 56). Benefits are frequently described pejoratively and divisively as "hand outs," as in the welfare reform Green Paper's dismissal of those who, it claims, "believe that poverty is relieved exclusively by cash hand outs" (UK DSS 1998:19). The welfare reform agenda has been summed up by the prime minister as "the end of a something-for-nothing welfare state" (*Daily Mail*, February 10, 1999). The idea that receipt of benefits creates a dependency culture has become part of the conventional wisdom, despite the lack of empirical evidence to support it. Little or no attention is paid to the obverse argument that receipt of benefits can combat private dependency within the family and can provide mothers in particular with an income which enhances their independence.

Often linked with the discourse of dependency is that of the "underclass." In his first speech as prime minister, Tony Blair declared that "there is a case not just in moral terms but in enlightened self-interest to act, to tackle what we all know exists—an underclass of people cut off from society's mainstream, without any sense of shared purpose" (Blair 1997a). Generally, though, politicians have grown rather more wary about using the language of the "underclass" and on other occasions Blair has, at least, put the term in quotes, signaling an element of distancing from the term itself. The media have been less circumspect and again it has become something of a conventional wisdom, despite the lack of supporting empirical evidence (Lister 1996), that there is a group of people at the bottom who, in the words of Blair, "are increasingly set apart, living in a culture that is becoming more and more alienated" (1997a).

The notion of an "underclass," like that of the "dependency culture," has been imported from the United States, although arguably it has shed some of its explicitly racialized connotations en route (Lister 1996; Silva 1996; but see Law 1996). Its primary exponent has been Charles Murray who has spoken and published widely on the subject in Britain, assisted by the Institute of Economic Affairs (IEA) Health and Welfare Unit (a neoliberal think tank) and the *Sunday Times*. The pathological nature of the discourse is highlighted by Murray's description of himself as "a visitor from a plague area come to see whether the disease is spreading" and to ask "how contagious is this disease?" (Murray 1996a: 42). For Murray, members of the "underclass" are distinguished by their behavior and in his writings he has placed increasing emphasis on illegitimacy and family breakdown. Lone mothers are thus located at the heart of the "underclass" (Edwards and Duncan 1997). They play a pivotal role both as symptoms of the "underclass" and as contributors to its formation (Cook 1997).

Lone Mothers as "Problem" or "Threat"

The convergence, during the first half of the 1990s, of growing concerns about lone motherhood and about the emergence of a threatening "underclass," spawning juvenile criminals, erupted in a "moral panic" fueled by government ministers and the media (Burghes and Roberts 1995). This created "a category of mothers that is not only deemed 'not good enough' at the raising of children but is also pinpointed as positively harmful to society" (Roseneil and Mann 1996:191). In a speech in 1990, billed by the media as a moral crusade, Margaret Thatcher warned that "seeing life without fathers not as the exception but as the rule . . . is a new kind of *threat* to our whole way of life, the long-term implications of which we can barely grasp" (Thatcher 1990:10, emphasis added). In this way, a discourse of lone mothers as a social threat took hold in the 1990s. They were cast as "a drain on public expenditure and as a threat to the stability and order associated with the traditional two-parent family" (Kiernan, Land, and Lewis 1998:2; see also Edwards and Duncan 1997, 1999; J. Lewis 1997). The discourse was strengthened by the publicity given to a paper by two ethical socialists, published by the IEA Health and Welfare Unit (Dennis and Erdos 1992). This attributed many of society's ills to the damaging impact on children of lone parenthood and, in particular, of the absence of fathers from their lives.

The media became increasingly hostile to lone mothers, their stance exemplified by a special *Sunday Times* pullout headlined "Wedded to Welfare" and "Do They Want to Marry a Man or the State?" (July 11, 1993; cited in Roseneil and Mann 1996; see also Atkinson, Oerton, and Burns 1998; Cowan 1998). Around this time also, the first signs of media racialization of lone motherhood could be discerned, as the high rates of lone motherhood among African-Caribbean women were highlighted and linked to the welfare bill, even though black lone mothers are more likely than white to be in full-time paid work (Edwards and Duncan 1997; Song and Edwards 1997).

The vilification of lone mothers reached a crescendo at the 1993 Conservative Party conference, in the wake of calls from ministers for absent fathers to be forced back into the family home and for a more judgmental attitude toward lone parent families whose growth was blamed in part on the feminist movement. At the conference, ministers vied with each other in their moralizing attribution of a range of social ills to lone parent families. However, as it became clear that this orgy of lone mother-bashing was not resonating with the electorate and the government's promotion of "family values" was rather undermined by the personal indiscretions of a number of ministers, there was something of a retreat from this moralizing and hostile stance toward lone mothers.

The discourse of lone mothers as a social threat thus became somewhat more muted. While there are some slight echoes of it under New Labour, more dominant again is the longer standing discourse of lone mothers as a social problem. Here the emphasis is more on the disadvantages of poverty and unemployment associated with lone motherhood, rather than the perceived threat they constitute to society and the institution of "the family." Although the construction of the nature of the problem has shifted over time, the essentially problematic nature of lone parenthood has been a consistent theme in British social policy (Song 1996; Lewis 1998; Kiernan, Land, and Lewis 1998; Duncan and Edwards 1999). The influence of this social problem discourse has been much greater than in other European countries. In particular, in the Nordic countries lone parent families are not singled out as different from other families and their situation is more likely to be understood within a "lifestyle choice" discourse (Song 1996; Duncan and Edwards 1999).

Simon Duncan and Rosalind Edwards (1999) have analyzed how these different discourses shape the experiences of lone mothers themselves, identifying also a fourth discourse of "escaping patriarchy," in which women are no longer willing to be dependent upon and controlled by individual men. Although this has had little purchase on national policy debates (except that it represents the obverse of elements of the social threat discourse), they found in their study that it was vocalized by some lone mothers themselves. As one white working-class mother said to them, despite the lack of money and loneliness associated with lone motherhood, "I enjoy the freedom. If we want to all go out somewhere we can all go out, rather than when we get back he's coming home and he wants his tea. It's just an easy feeling" (Duncan and Edwards 1999:52). Duncan and Edwards emphasize the importance of local as well as dominant national discourses in framing lone mothers' own understandings of their situation. Thus, they discovered that, despite the dominance in political and media debate of a combination of social threat and social problem discourses, in particular neighborhoods alternative discourses of lone motherhood as a lifestyle choice or a positive decision to live independently of a man were also able to flourish.

"The Family"

The dominant discourses around lone motherhood have to be understood in the context of wider discourses around "the family" and "family breakdown." As Mary McIntosh has observed, "one of the most fascinating things about the attempt to demonize lone mothers is the assumptions it reveals about married motherhood and the family" (1996:149). It is also symptomatic of a particular response to changes in family patterns and structures (Fox Harding 1996).

Jane Millar identifies three reactions to family change under the headings of: "family reactionaries," who abhor the breakdown of the family and want to restore traditional family structures; "family pragmatists," who accept the changes as irreversible and therefore argue for the adaptation of policies in response; and "family libertarians," most commonly associated with feminism, who "positively welcome these changes as a sign of increasing freedom and autonomy for people to live in ways that they choose." The last view has, she suggests, "been increasingly crowded out of political and policy debates" (Millar 1998:123, 124). While the last two tend to be couched in the language of "families," the first adopts that of "the family" which "is not a neutral descriptive category but a morally loaded concept embodying an ideal image or model of relationships to be strived for and supported" (Chester 1986:28).

Under the Conservatives, it was very much a discourse of "the family" and its breakdown which underpinned the stance of both government and right-wing commentators toward lone mothers. Enveloped in this discourse were fears about the collapse of the institution of marriage, female sexual and economic autonomy, and male irresponsibility and redundancy (J. Lewis 1997). Conservative preoccupation with "the family" surfaced at intervals during the 1980s, having been prominent in the run-up to the 1979 election when the two main parties vied with each other in their claims to be "the party of the [traditional] family." It was not, though, until toward the end of Margaret Thatcher's reign that she really focused on the issue. Her memoirs revealed her growing belief that strengthening "the traditional family" was the only way to get to the root of crime and other social problems. She told the 1988 Conservative Women's Conference that "family breakdown . . . strikes at the very heart of society; therefore policies must be directed at strengthening the family."

A similar message was being promulgated by the right-wing think tanks, most vociferously the IEA Health and Welfare Unit which had as its central project "to restore the ideal of the two parent family" (Green 1993: viii), as "the traditional family of man, wife and children is being replaced by the mother-child-state unit" (Green 1995: iv). The IEA's position was articulated most clearly in one of a series of papers, *The Family: Is It Just Another Lifestyle Choice?*:

our free and reasonably successful society will be able to remain free and stable only when each generation moves into its maturity and its civic responsibilities when it has effectively internalized those values which make for freedom and stability. The only institution which can provide the time, the attention, the love and the care for doing that is not just "the family," but a stable two-parent mutually complementary nuclear family. The fewer of such families that we have, the less we will have of either freedom or stability. (Davies 1993:7)

The same year, 1993, witnessed a crescendo of public concern about the state of the family and juvenile crime in the wake of the murder of a two-year-old boy, James Bulger, by two ten-year-old boys (Roseneil and Mann 1996). Skillfully responding to the public mood, Tony Blair, then Shadow Home Secretary, declared that Labour would be "tough on crime, and tough on the causes of crime" (*The Guardian,* February 22, 1993).

"The family" has figured prominently in Blair's utterances as, first, leader of the Labour Party and, then, prime minister. While distancing himself from "Victorian hypocrisy about sex, women's employment or sexuality" (1997b) and "a nostalgic version of family life in the Fifties" (Blair 1998), it is, in other ways, a traditional two-parent family model which is Blair's touchstone, as reflected in his tendency to talk about "the family" rather than "families." In a major speech shortly before becoming prime minister, he identified "the family" as one of seven pillars of "the decent society." He promised that "we are going to buttress and consolidate and nourish the institution without which any social morality is impossible—the family. . . . We regard the family and the way in which children are brought up in the home as the bedrock on which many of our policies, especially on law and order and education, are founded. . . . So our social policy will revolve around the family. . . . We are the family party as well as the national party" (Blair 1997c).

Subsequently, Blair has attempted to chart a "third way," "between those who simply didn't care about the family and those who want to turn the clock back to a time before women went out to work" (Blair 1998:13). This has been translated into a Green Paper which, perhaps somewhat surprisingly, is entitled *Supporting Families* (as opposed to "the family").[4] In his foreword to the Green Paper, the Home Secretary, Jack Straw, declares that "family life is the foundation on which our communities, our society and our country are built. Families are central to this government's vision of a modern and decent country" (Straw 1998). The Green Paper itself treads a delicate tightrope. On the one hand, it falls over backward not to be seen as moralizing. On the other hand, the suspicion lurks that its commitment "to strengthening family life" is a commitment to shoring up the two-parent family. Thus, there is an uneasy tension between its acknowledgment that "many lone parents and unmarried couples raise their children every bit as successfully as married parents" and one of its central aims which is "to strengthen the institution of marriage" (U.K. Home Office 1998:4).

This same tension can be found in the government's attempts to defuse a political battle around the repeal of section 28 of the Local Government Act, which forbids local councils from "promoting" homosexuality in schools. In its place the government put forward a legal duty on teachers to teach "the significance of marriage and stable relationships as key building blocks of community and society."

The Third Way of Responsibility, Inclusion, and Opportunity

New Labour's discourse on "the family" is reinforced by that of "responsibility," which is central to New Labour thinking (Lister 1998). The responsibility of parents, absent and present, to care emotionally and materially for their children, to support their education, and to keep them out of trouble is a leitmotif running through a range of policies. It echoes the new statement of values in the Labour Party's constitution which sets as its ideal a community "where the rights we enjoy reflect the duties we owe." Blair has explicitly set out to reorient the Party's conceptualization of citizenship, emphasizing the centrality of obligation and responsibility to the New Labour project and distancing himself from "early Left thinking" in which the "language of responsibility [was] spoken far less fluently than that of rights" (Blair 1995). It is an expression of what David Marquand (1996) has described as a "new kind of moral collectivism" on the center-left. As such, it reflects the influences of both popular communitarianism and Christian Socialism.

New Labour's discourse of responsibility intertwines with those of inclusion and opportunity (RIO for short). In place of the former Labour commitment to greater equality, New Labour talks the language of equality of opportunity and social inclusion/exclusion (Lister 1997, 2002). Equality and redistribution through the tax-benefit system are rejected as "Old Labour," incompatible with a managerialist modernizing narrative which drives policy statements (Andrews 1999). The "new politics" which Labour is forging has been labeled "the third way," beyond "Old Left" and "New Right," and described by Blair as "a project built on unshakeable values, and a firm commitment to modernization—to shape the future by embracing change not seeking to defy it" (Blair 1998:20). Nowhere is this more the case than with regard to globalization: a key example of third way policies given by Blair is "the embracing of globalization as inevitable and also desirable" so that policy needs to equip people to respond to it (*The Guardian*, May 15, 1998). The narrative of modernization and change, which is couched in an apolitical discourse of inevitability, represents a "site of significant continuities" with the New Right (Clarke and Newman 1998; Finlayson 1998).

Policy Responses

Another site of significant continuity is that of the stance taken toward taxation and public spending. Despite the partial rehabilitation of public expenditure as a positive tool of government under New Labour, its welfare policies are framed by the low tax, low public spending ideological paradigm established by the Thatcher government. "Tax and spend" is no longer what Labour is about. Although the retreat from public spending, in fact, began under the 1974–79 Labour government in the face of the demands of the International Monetary Fund, and the Conservatives were not very successful in their aim of cutting welfare spending overall (Hills 1998b), the 1980s did represent something of an ideological watershed. Most notably, low income tax has now become an indisputable policy goal, reflected not only in Labour's pledge not to increase income tax rates (including the top rate which is low by European standards), but also a cut in the basic tax rate. This provides the backdrop for the more specific policy responses to the "problem" of lone mothers developed over the past couple of decades.

These policy responses had to negotiate a number of long-standing tensions. First, policy has shifted over the years from constructing lone mothers primarily as paid workers, expected to support their children themselves, to constructing them primarily as mothers whose first responsibility is to look after their children at home, with no requirement to be available for work as a condition of receiving social assistance (J. Lewis 1998). Jane Lewis (1997) has suggested that in this dichotomous treatment of lone mothers as *either* workers *or* mothers, Britain, like the United States, is typical of countries in which welfare policy is dominated by a strong "male-breadwinner" logic (see also Millar 1996a, b). Increasingly in such countries the pendulum is swinging (in some cases back) to treating lone mothers as workers. The Scandinavian countries, in contrast, have for some time tended to assume that all adults will participate in the labor market, so no distinction is made between parents in lone and two parent families.

Duncan and Edwards have investigated how lone mothers themselves perceive their responsibilities. Using the notion of "gendered moral rationalities," defined as "collective and social understandings about what is the proper relationship between motherhood and paid work," they identify three main orientations: "primarily mother, mother/worker integral, and primarily worker" (Duncan and Edwards 1999:3, 119). In their study, lone mothers who subscribed to the "primarily mother" orientation prioritized the benefits of looking after their children themselves over the financial rewards from paid work, even where they said they would ideally like to have a job. The "mother/worker integral" ori-

entation, subscribed to mainly by black lone mothers, meant that the
financial rewards from and the example set through paid work were defined as part of their moral responsibilities to their children. As one
black mother put it, "I've got great dreams for myself and my children.
By me working and trying to keep the household as stable as I can, I
think my children may see a better life for themselves than I saw when I
was growing up" (Duncan and Edwards 1999:116). Under the "primary
worker" orientation, lone mothers' primary identity was as workers and
their needs and those of their children were seen as separate. While, as
with any ideal types, not all lone mothers fit neatly into the categories,
the authors note how the typology's grounding in the lone mothers' own
responses serves to challenge the mother versus worker dichotomy with
which policymakers have tended to operate (see also van Drenth, Knijn,
and Lewis 1999).

Underlying this dichotomy has been a contradiction in the state's
stance toward lone mothers which "has been Janus-faced in often con-
demning lone motherhood and yet giving lone mothers the means to
subsistence" (Kiernan, Land, and Lewis 1998:277). This reflects a tension between wanting to discourage lone motherhood on the one hand,
and a concern to protect the children of lone mothers from poverty on
the other.

Perhaps the most fundamental tension lies in the state's relationship
to the family, reflecting the traditional split between the public and the
private, which has been particularly marked in Britain relative to other
European countries. Until now, there has been no formal family policy,
reflecting the liberal view that government should interfere in the "private" sphere of the family only when absolutely necessary and that parents should be responsible for their children (Hantrais and Letablier
1996). In practice, though, as Lorraine Fox Harding points out, it has
been far from "a *laissez-faire* model which does not attempt to mould
family life at all" (1996:186), for even without a formal family policy,
government policies have promoted particular family models.

The Conservatives: Shifting the Boundaries of Responsibility

The dilemma raised by the state's relationship to "the family" was particularly acute for the Conservatives. As Margaret Thatcher acknowledged in her memoirs, there is a difficulty in squaring an ideological
commitment to reducing the role of the state with intervention designed
to influence family life. A growing tension also emerged between the
Thatcherite commitment to a free enterprise society and a concern
among some Conservatives about the destructive impact of such a society on families and communities. More specifically in relation to lone

mothers, the Conservative government was torn between the continued power of traditional thinking, which accorded primacy to mothers' place in the home, and its espousal of the strand in neoliberal policy which prioritized reducing "welfare dependency."

Its response was, in effect, to attempt to sidestep these dilemmas through the introduction of the Child Support Act (CSA), combined with some minor social security reforms designed to increase the incentive to take paid work.[5] This policy stance represented both a shift in the balance of responsibility for the maintenance of lone parent families from the state to "absent parents" and an attempt to reduce "welfare dependency" by encouraging lone mothers to combine their child support with earnings. The intention was to increase the amount of maintenance paid (including a contribution to the maintenance of the caring parent) and to enforce it more effectively. Thus, in terms of the three possible sources of income available to lone mothers—the labor market, absent fathers, and the state—there was a clear attempt to reduce the role of the last in favor of the first two (J. Lewis 1997). This represented a relocation of "dependency" from the public sphere of the state to the respective private spheres of the (divided) family and the market.

The policy, which represented an unusual degree of parliamentary consensus around the objective of enforcing paternal financial responsibility, was described by a parliamentary committee as "the most far-reaching social reform to be made for 40 years" (Social Security Committee 1993:v). Very quickly, though, it also became one of the most discredited pieces of social reform.[6] As the director of the independent Family Policy Studies Centre observes, "no policy initiative affecting families has excited more public and political hostility, or more media attention than the Child Support Act. . . . From its inception, organized opposition to the Child Support Act has highlighted the success of aggrieved men in dominating the policy agenda, whereas lone parents and their organizations have tended to find themselves sidelined in the debate" (Roberts 1998:5). The aggrieved men achieved a number of policy and legislative changes remarkably quickly. (It was not until the election of a new Labour government that the balance was redressed somewhat in the favor of lone mothers, who, finally, are to be allowed to keep some of the child support rather than have it all set against their entitlement to social assistance. This is part of a package of Labour reforms to the CSA designed to make it more effective in meeting its objectives.)

The CSA was presented as being in the interests of children. However, the evidence from research and from voluntary organizations indicates that its impact on lone mothers and their children living on social assistance has been damaging more often than helpful. In one small study of the CSA's impact, the majority of lone parent families had not gained and a minority were financially worse off, in part because of a reduction in the informal help the former partner gave the family (Clarke, Craig, and Glendinning 1996). A requirement for those on benefit to name the absent parent, unless this would cause "harm or distress," has been the source of considerable anxiety and resentment. In another small study, one mother commented that "I would rather give up the money than go through the aggravation with him. I can't cope with it" (Daniel and Burgess n.d.:24–25). The authors comment that "perhaps the most striking aspect of the responses on this issue, however, is the overwhelming impression that the tone of the legislation and the threat of a benefit penalty in particular, is unnecessarily punitive" (26).

The same punitive impulse can be discerned in two other policy changes. One was a tightening up in homelessness legislation, designed in part to restrict lone mothers' access to public housing. The vilification of lone mothers, described above, had partly focused on teenage girls who allegedly get pregnant in order to jump the housing queue.[7] According to Norman Ginsburg, "the issue of teenage single mothers has been used as a wedge to soften up public opinion for undermining the rights to social housing of all homeless families in priority need" (1996:145; see also Cowan 1998). Ginsburg cites the 1995 White Paper *Our Future Homes*, which states that allocation schemes for social housing "should balance specific housing needs against the need to support married couples who take a responsible approach to family life" (U.K. Department of Environment 1995:36).

Right-wing pressure to remove "discrimination" against married couples with children likewise resulted in proposals to phase out, from 1996, the modest additional help received by lone parents through the social assistance and child benefit schemes. This help had been given in recognition of the extra costs lone parent families were believed to incur and of their greater vulnerability to poverty. In the name of "equity" between lone and two-parent families, the real incomes of some of the poorest families were to be reduced.

New Labour: "Reforming Welfare Around the Work Ethic"

One of the first decisions made by the new Labour government was to continue with the Tories' planned legislation to abolish altogether for new claimants this additional help. The justification given for doing so shifted uneasily between the financial consequences of having accepted the Conservatives' public spending totals for the first two years in office, the labor market opportunities being opened up to lone parents, and the need for equity between different family types. The measures were pushed through in the face of fierce opposition both outside and inside Parliament, which shook the government.[8]

Consequently, the 1998 budget attempted to repair some of the damage through a number of improvements in benefits for families generally (both in and out of work), designed to ensure that the great majority of lone parents affected by the cuts would end up no worse off (at the same time fueling the suspicion that the underlying agenda was one of support for the traditional two-parent family rather than affordability). These improvements included an above-inflation increase in the universal child benefit to be paid for by a reduction in the married couple's tax allowance, a policy which antipoverty campaigners and feminists had long been calling for.

The budget also confirmed the replacement of family credit (a means-tested in-work benefit for families with children paid to mothers) with a significantly more generous working families tax credit (influenced by the U.S. model and incorporating also a childcare credit) paid, in most cases, through the wage packet. In the face of opposition to the transfer of resources this would involve from mothers to fathers in many cases (Goode, Callender, and Lister 1998), the government compromised by allowing parents in one-earner two parent families to opt to receive the credit as a cash benefit. Subsequently, it has accepted the case for paying benefits for children to the caring parent, by proposing a longer term plan for an integrated child tax credit, paid to the caring parent (in or out of work) on top of the universal child benefit. This will be complemented by a working tax credit for low paid adults paid through the wage packet.

These tax credits are examples of a number of measures, including the introduction of a national statutory minimum wage (which has had a particular impact on low female wages) designed "to make work pay." Work, or rather paid work, lies at the heart of the New Labour trinity of responsibility, inclusion, and opportunity and is regarded as the most effective antidote to "welfare dependency." The mantra of "reforming welfare around the work ethic" is frequently intoned to promote the central thrust of social policy. "Welfare dependency" is to be reduced through a series of New Deal "welfare-to-work" schemes. The New Deal for lone parents was initially geared to providing lone parents with school-age children with advice and assistance in seeking paid work. Following the 2000 budget, it will also embrace training and a ladder of supported paid work options from a few hours while on benefit to full-time work. The options are all voluntary. However, following a number of pilot schemes, eventually virtually all lone parents (together with other claimants) will be required to attend a series of interviews with a personal adviser to discuss their job prospects as a condition of receiving benefit.

In the face of evidence that lack of affordable and suitable quality childcare constitutes a major barrier to the employment of those lone mothers who want paid employment, the government has launched an ambitious childcare strategy. Presented as integral to economic policy, it comprises both childcare provision and "family-friendly" employment provisions. For all the strategy's limitations, including those of resources, it does mark an important symbolic step in its acknowledgment that childcare is, at least partially, a public responsibility. As such, it has been widely welcomed.

Support for the New Deal itself has been more qualified. On the one hand, many have welcomed a genuine attempt to assist those lone mothers who want paid work; they welcome a policy shift which could strengthen lone mothers' long-term labor market position, provided that they do not simply get stuck in the kind of dead-end jobs all too often open to them.[9] On the other hand, in many eyes, the New Deal has been compromised by its association with the lone parent benefit cuts, a preoccupation with reducing "welfare dependency," and a perceived devaluing of the unpaid work of caring for children, as paid work is constructed as *the* citizenship obligation. Some consider that the pendulum is swinging too far in the direction of treating lone mothers as workers rather than mothers, thereby discounting the value of care to citizenship.

Attention has also been drawn to a tension between the government's preoccupation with paid work as the test of citizenship and its emphasis on parental responsibility for the behavior of young people and encouragement of parental (read *mothers'*) involvement in schools.[10] A small study in London found that "the desire to fulfill the demands of the schools and the parental involvement discourse, together with the deficit discourses around lone mothering, particularly of sons," was one of a number of factors discouraging lone mothers from taking up paid employment (Standing 1999:488).

By early 2000, about 133,000 lone parents had attended an interview. Nearly half of these were outside the target group (because of the presence of young children); the rest represented only about 15 percent of those invited to interview. Overall, just under a third had found a job: "not a bad outcome," observes Jane Millar, "compared with other similar schemes elsewhere" (Millar 2000:4).

The officially funded evaluation study of the pilot schemes found that only about one in five of lone parents approached became full participants in the program. The study concluded, however, that the pilot schemes had "a small positive effect on the number of lone parents moving off income support. After 18 months the number of lone parents on income support was estimated to be 3.3 per cent lower than it would have been in the absence of the programme" (Hales et al. 2000a:2). It was estimated that 80 percent of participants who found jobs would have done so anyway; the program was mainly "geared towards lone parents who were work-ready" (2). Nevertheless, two out of three participants felt that they had benefited from the program and over a quarter of those who had found jobs said that their personal adviser had given them significant help in achieving this. Particularly important was the personal adviser's role in "boosting confidence and encouraging a positive attitude" (9).

The main barriers faced by the "work-ready" were childcare, followed by lack of qualifications and work experience (Hales et al. 2000b). An earlier interim report on the pilot study emphasized that even the attempts of "'effective' advisers to assist lone parents into work were often thwarted by the insuperable barriers which lone parents regularly faced" (Finch et al. 1999). Those who had moved into paid work reported considerable levels of anxiety, especially in relation to financial insecurity during the transition to work and the care of ill children. Although not all their fears were realized, "appreciable minorities faced problems of the cost of living and transitional problems" (Hales et al. 2000b:16). Half said that they were better off financially but nearly a quarter said that they were worse off.

The New Deal is the centerpiece of "a new contract for welfare" which has been articulated in a series of government documents around the theme of "work for those who can, security for those who cannot." While many elements of the overall approach have received broad support, there have been two main sources of criticism. First, the aim of "work for those who can" is being pursued primarily through supply-side measures to improve employability rather than demand-side measures to enhance job opportunities. The latter have largely been abandoned in the face of the constraints believed to be imposed by globalizing economic forces and of the priority given to low inflation. Thus while social policy prioritizes reducing worklessness, economic policy does not. Although the overall unemployment rate has come down significantly, a serious jobs gap remains in many cities, often in areas where lone parents are concentrated with other workless groups (Turok and Webster 1998; Turok and Edge 1999).

Second, the pursuit of the aim of "security for those who cannot" work is constrained by an antipathy toward encouraging "welfare dependency" through improved social security benefits. Although a number of carefully targeted improvements have been implemented (including for children on social assistance), the government has ignored calls for a general review of the adequacy of benefit levels in the face of considerable evidence of their failure to meet the needs of recipients and the absence of any official public review since they were set after the war. At the same time, there appears to be an incremental drift toward greater reliance on means-testing and private provision and away from more universalistic provision. For all the talk of "modernization," calls for a modernized and more inclusive social insurance system, better attuned to the employment patterns and needs of women, have so far been largely ignored.[11] This is despite a commitment to "mainstreaming" women's perspectives in policymaking, concretized in the establishment of a Women's Unit and a (part-time) Minister for Women.[12]

Conclusion

It has been suggested that lone mothers represent a "litmus test . . . of gendered social rights" (Hobson 1994:171). In the United Kingdom lone mothers have provided a lightning conductor for a number of political concerns centering on family "breakdown," gendered labor market trends, "welfare dependency," and welfare spending. They have been at the center of policies designed to shift responsibility for family welfare from the state to individual families and to promote paid work as the best source of welfare and as a primary responsibility of citizenship. As the pendulum shifts between treating lone mothers as a threat or a problem and treating them as workers or mothers, what has remained constant is their disproportionate vulnerability to poverty as lone parents and as women.

Chapter 8
Paradoxes in "Paradise"

The Changing Politics of Women, Welfare, and Work in Australia

Susan L. Robertson

Paradise?

In his 1976 Boyer Lecture noted Australian historian Manning Clark observed:

> In the nineteenth century, Australians enjoyed the reputation of being in the vanguard of human progress; they were often the pioneers in the introduction of bourgeois democracy, and rather boastful about it. By contrast, in the twentieth century Australians seemed to have missed the boat carrying humanity into the future. . . . We had the institutions and the values to promote the use of parts of our country as quarries for foreign powers, but neither the institutions, nor the inclination, nor the belief to make our country a paradise for our people.

If there was, indeed, some kind of paradise to be had in twentieth-century Australia it was *a workingman's paradise*—the wage earners' welfare state—that rested on the bedrock of capitalism. It was, too, a paradise that depended on the creation and labor of an "other," a dependent and less worthy angel, Eve. Smoothed over and legitimized by bourgeois democracy, welfare statism, and the ideological seductiveness of "the lucky country," the social relations of patriarchy and capitalism in this far-off garden shaped the historic path of progress of Australia over the course of the twentieth century and with it the different experiences of its peoples. That many did not share in this "luck" —females, non-English-speaking migrants, and aboriginals—was rarely brought into view. However, in the workingman's welfare state in Australia, class, gender, and race interwove and cut across each other in a complex tapestry of social rights, responsibilities, obligations, and negations.

In the name of progress, the bowels of the red Australian earth were farmed, quarried, and commodified by settlers, colonial empires, and

international capital, while its soils were stained with the blood of indigenous peoples (and settlers) in the battle over land (Buckley and Wheelwright 1988:3). And, as the curtain fell on a "short but violent twentieth century" (Hobsbawm 1994), a new discourse on human progress
and welfare reform was being pioneered, framed by the metadiscourses
of globalization and neoliberalism. Together, these underpin the emergence of a new social settlement and a new social contract. This discursive frame legitimates a set of political strategies that have, as their object, new sites for quarrying. This occurs through privileging the market
as the means of—or at least the model for—coordinating *all* economic
and social affairs; the expansion of workfare for its citizens; the reconstruction of individual identities premised upon individualism, competitivism, and consumption; and the "degendering" and "regendering" of
women around the reconstruction of the family ethic and work ethic.

While the metadiscourses of globalization and neoliberalism, along
with a litany of practices in the area of "welfare reform," are familiar to
those who study similar processes in other contexts, I want to argue that
the historical specificity of Australia—as a *workingman's welfare state* dependent on a tradition of laborism[1]—shaped in turn the nature of both
the discursive framing and the available political strategies that could be
pursued by the state as the process of welfare restructuring got under-
way in the early 1980s. And, though issues of women's welfare had made
a brief appearance in the 1970s, welfare reform throughout the 1980s
and 1990s was framed by the combined rhetoric and practices of the Accord between organized (male) labor (the Australian Council of Trade
Unions, ACTU) and the Australian Labour Party (ALP) who held office
from 1983 to 1996 *and* the program of labor market and industrial relations restructuring driven by neoliberal assumptions.[2] These processes
began with the ALP and continued—albeit in more intensified form—
with the election of the Liberal/National Coalition in 1996. Over both
these periods, the discourses of "employability," "responsibility," "productivity," and workplace "flexibility," as the state pursued a complex
process of recommodification, worked to occlude considerations of gender and difference in Australian society, thereby masking the profoundly
gendered effects of the state's program of welfare reform. Over both
these periods transformations in the structure of the labor market and
the industrial relations regime made the conditions of work for a large
number of women in the secondary labor market more insecure and also
more intensified. At the heart of this chapter, then, is an exploration of
the dual process of occlusion and intensification of the gendered nature
of the state's welfare reforms that have had particular consequences for
sole mothers.

Central to this exploration of a new social contract and gender regime in Australia is an elaboration of the paradoxical nature of the Accord for labor in general, and women in particular. The first paradox is that despite the ALP's historic affiliation with the labor movement and its opposition to corporate capital, the Accord became a vehicle through which the state and corporate capital exacted fundamental changes in the structure of labor markets, the industrial relations regime, and the social wage. The end result was that the Labour Party symbolically closed a period of Australia's history, earning "managerial credentials at the expense of emptying out the labour tradition, even while constantly appealing to it" (Beilhartz 1994:4). A second paradox is that, despite the rhetoric of choice, flexibility, and employability that promised to open up new opportunities for women in the labor market, the structure and processes of the Accord excluded women's voices and their interests, thereby contributing to the development and consolidation of a neoliberal welfare state and gender regime which has intensified gender, class, and racial divisions.

Disarray in Paradise

By the late 1970s, all signs in Australia pointed to disarray in the workingman's paradise: high unemployment, negative growth, growing social welfare payouts, and inflation. The long postwar boom that had characterized the development of the Keynesian welfare state settlement was over and the Australian state was engaged in a search for a solution to the political and economic crisis. An anxious period emerged in Australia, destabilized by the uncertainties underlying economic globalization and fears of becoming a "banana republic" (Kelly 1992). The specter of the "banana republic" was seen at the time in Australia as a warning that the country's underlying institutions and ideas required dramatic revision. The public's fears were mobilized in growing pressure for the remaking of the Australian political tradition and signaled the end of what Paul Kelly describes as a unique "Australian Settlement that was embodied in five key ideas—protection, regulation, introspection, arbitration and commodity reliance" (1992:197). Kelly's failure to identify institutionalized patriarchy as central to the Australian settlement over the course of the century is a notable though not surprising omission; the hegemony of the workingman's wage, institutionalized in each of these five key ideas, had created the conditions for the invisibility of women in this settlement—conditions that I would argue continue into the twenty-first century.

By the early 1980s, Australia found itself drawn into the global economy. At the same time, there was increasing pressure for a program of economic and public sector reform with arguments which followed maxims about the crisis of "ungovernable democracies," "overloaded" states, unruly unions, and "welfare dependency." Solutions were invariably aimed at moving some of the coordination functions away from states and bureaucracies to economies and markets (Pusey 1991). Competitivism and marketization—the twin strategies of neoliberalism— were promoted as solutions to the problems of globalization. However, how states have taken up neoliberal solutions to problems of government and governance has varied largely as a result of the differing political traditions and arrangements between the state, capital, labor, and civil society. Robert Cox (1987) usefully distinguishes between two forms of liberal states: *hyperliberal* and *competitive progressive* states. Cox defines hyperliberalism as a form of liberalism where governments use confrontational strategies to remove the internal obstacles to economic liberalism; for instance, the "New Zealand experiment" and Thatcherism in England. On the other hand, *competitive progressivism* is a consensus-based process of adjustment, typified in various forms of corporatism. This can be exemplified in, for example, tripartite corporatism in Japan and Germany, or bipartite corporatism in Australia. The distinction between the two forms is particularly useful in the case of Australia, as it identifies and makes explicit two periods in the process of restructuring. The nature of the political struggles and the strategies of the state in the two phases have been different. In the first phase, a strategy of competitive progressivism was used to erase difference and neutralize dissent by incorporating organized (male) labor voices into the processes of government and governance, while at the same time promoting the competitive state project. In the second phase, with many of the institutions emptied of the "labour tradition" (Beilhartz 1994) and old practices disembedded, a more assertive and confrontational form of neoliberal discourse and practice was then able to emerge to consolidate a new neoliberal welfare state in Australia.

Before turning to a closer examination of the restructuring of the welfare state in Australia over the period in question, I want to comment briefly upon the nature of welfare states themselves. There are numerous definitions and conceptions of the welfare state—some broad, some narrow. My intention is to take a broad view and, following Gary Teeple (1995:15), conceptualize welfare states as sets of institutionalized responses where the state has intervened with a range of social policies and programs to manage class conflict and provide for a range of social needs not accommodated by the capitalist mode of production. Teeple identifies interventions as occurring in four key areas: (1) *the production and reproduction of classes and their preparation for the labor market*, for example, education, health; (2) *the labor market*, for example, wages, hours of work, training, immigration; (3) *production*, for example, industrial relations; and (4) *unproductive and after-productive life,* for example, pensions, social assistance. Clearly societies differ in the pattern, intensity and weighting of these interventions over time. And, while all four aspects are important to understanding the nature of the welfare state in Australia, its history has created a pattern of welfare provision that differentiates it from others. These two key aspects of welfare intervention in Australia—the labor market and production—have been historically shaped by an accord between the state, capital, and organized labor, or laborism, giving rise to a particular form of institutionalized patriarchy and capitalism, the *workingman's welfare state.*[3] Privileging labor market and production also explains why women, children, and others on the margins of the workforce have benefited less than one would expect. However, an analysis of the welfare state in Australia focused upon the pattern of benefits or education and health provisions, with little reference to the way they are framed by interventions in the labor market and production, will tend to overlook significant determinants of the Australian welfare state both historically and in the contemporary period.

The *Male* Wage Earners' Welfare State—Demanding Dependence

Francis Castles (1985) has argued that throughout most of this century, Australia was a *wage earners' welfare state.* In practice this that meant income stability was guaranteed through high male employment (maintained through tariff protections and control over immigration), and high wages for males were negotiated by the labor movement through the arbitration courts.[4] This particular form of the welfare state in Australia emerged in the 1890s (Wiseman 1998); its foundations articulated in the establishment of state and federal conciliation and arbitration commissions as a means of mediating the conflict between capital and labor. The principle of the "living" or "family wage" was formulated as a demand for an ethical wages policy based on family need (Beilhartz, Considine, and Watts 1992:76). Within this framework, the *value* of women's labor in the home and workforce was simultaneously essential and denied. The workingman's paradise was premised upon women's reproductive role and their unpaid labor, buoyed by the construction of women as necessarily different from, and therefore dependent upon, men.[5] Dependence on men was demanded and waged labor valorized.

However, by the early 1970s, challenges to the state's welfare regime—arising from the women's movement and strategic advocacy groups[6] and also from the election of the Australian Labour Party in 1972—brought about a shift in electoral politics toward a social democratic agenda. This watershed in social policymaking directed at women was marked by a series of important reforms in both welfare and wages policy.[7] In 1973 (the same year as in New Zealand), the Labour government introduced the supporting mother's benefit, based on the assumption that a woman who cared full-time for her children should not be forced into the workforce because of the absence of a breadwinner. More important, the language of the legislation was cleaned up so that the moral overtones of the legislation, carried in words like "good character" and "not deserving," were repealed (Levi and Singleton 1991:648). With the extension of the supporting parent's benefit to men in 1977, "mothering" by men (at least legislatively) was also endorsed. During this period there were also important gains in the area of wage parity. In 1972 the Federal Arbitration Commission rescinded the legislation determining male and female categories and in 1974 increased female wages to approximately 80 percent of male wages. However, secure paid employment was increasingly being eroded by major changes taking place in the organization of work and the distribution of paid work arising from fundamental changes in Australia's relationship to the global and regional economies. The fiscal crisis of the state and the political turmoil that followed resulted in more pragmatic politics within the Labour Party on its return to power in 1983 (Beilhartz 1994).

Remaking the State's Social Contract

In the remainder of this chapter I want to focus on two linked but distinct phases in the restructuring of the welfare state in Australia and in particular on the way in which the rise of the discourses of flexibility, choice, responsibility, and employability were progressively mobilized both as a diagnosis of the "problem" of single parenthood and, at the same time, as its essential solution. The first phase, "competitive progressivism," epitomized by the Accord between organized labor and the Australian Labour Party and directed at workplace and worker flexibility, was fundamentally paradoxical in its outcomes for large segments of labor, particularly women. The second "hyperliberal" phase followed the election of the Liberal/National Coalition in 1996. This phase is typified by the state's more confrontational stance to industrial relations reform and systematic promotion of the discourses of the market, choice, responsibility, and Victorian family values. Over these two phases, the problem of single parenthood was progressively focused upon and associated with escalating government welfare expenditure, growing poverty, a disregard for the welfare of the child, and the loss of moral values (Reekie 1996:328). And, while aspects of the nature of the social problem might have some basis in "reality," the significance of the cultural construction of social problems like single parenthood is that it has the capacity to generate a series of related but highly contested political meanings. In other words, how a social problem, like single parenthood, is conceptualized and how it might be changed depend on the terms in which it is discussed at any given moment in time. In that sense they are historically specific discursive relations which must be located within a historically specific social formation.

Competitive Progressivism and the Accord—Whose Trojan Horse?

Following the election of the Hawke Labour government in 1983 Australia, a new restructuring agenda emerged, centered around the development of an internationally competitive economy and "rescaling" the state's social welfare commitments. A key political strategy by Labour was the Accord. Though hailed as a temporary moment of social democracy because of the way the union movement participated in the process of restructuring, it has more recently been argued that the Accord locked the union movement into policies it could not control and which fundamentally opposed its interests (Hampson 1996). In short, the Accord unleashed a process that had serious consequences for its citizens, particularly women.

A series of movements can be distilled in the life of the Accord, each incarnation—from Mark 1 (1983) to Mark 8 (1996)[8] (Hampson 1996)—presenting the union leadership with new strategic dilemmas and questions. However, participation in and the process of the Accord were from the start profoundly gendered, leading Shaun Carney (1988) to declare it a "suit-led recovery" by the "pinstripe proletariat." As the Accord entered each new phase of negotiation, women found their work and welfare interests still at the margins. This was hardly surprising since corporatist arrangements are negotiated by unions on behalf of workers and the unemployed and depend heavily on labor arbitration as a major mechanism for change (Levi and Singleton 1991:639). Margaret Levi and Sara Singleton (1991) note that, while trade unions have from time to time initiated policies that positively affect women, issues of concern to women are rarely on the agenda. Nonetheless, as we shall see, key initiatives in the area of childcare and welfare benefits were successfully pressed forward from the Labour left. However these were framed by the new discourses of employability and responsibility. Employability, however, meant employment in paid rather than unpaid work. The discourse thus constructs unpaid work in the home as the activity of those who are both unskilled and irresponsible citizens and whose right to full citizenship status must be secured through laboring in the paid labor force.

Discord in the Accord—From Welfare to Workfare

As early as 1984, the ACTU was dissatisfied with the Accord. However, its response was to retreat into policy development rather than to wage more politically damaging battles. The main milestone in this process was *Australia Reconstructed* (ACTU/TDC 1987)—embracing both interventions in investment policy and sweeping changes to the industrial relations system. It was "a political cat among the pigeons" (Hampson 1996:60), for if the ACTU opposed the policy changes embraced, it opposed the Accord. If it opposed the Accord, it risked Labour's loss at the election. The end result was that the ACTU endorsed the government's reform agenda of internationalizing the economy and promoting workplace and industrial relations restructuring. This agenda was given considerable edge with the 1987 stock market crash; attention turned to attracting overseas investment funds and the reorganization and management of local labor. This involved new approaches to the organization of work and extracting more work from existing labor and meant not only creating the conditions for attracting Japanese investment funds but promoting Japanese methods of work organization, such as flexible or lean production techniques (Hampson 1998). These initiatives were dependent upon restructuring both the labor market and the industrial relations regime. Both had gender implications. In particular, these initiatives entailed encouraging those not in the labor market, such as social welfare beneficiaries, to train and be available for counseling and work as part of the state's "clever country" strategy—an orientation Peter Saunders characterizes as an "active society" approach to social security (1994:21).

Though the ALP had made considerable mileage in sweeping electoral gestures, such as "no child will live in poverty in Australia" and generous promises of childcare,[9] the social welfare benefit system had, until 1986, been largely ignored. This was despite increasing evidence that both rates of poverty and social security payments had increased (Saunders 1994:143). Indeed, prior to 1985, the only significant change was the introduction of the Family Income Supplement in 1983; a system which provided support to low-income working families with children (21). However, over the course of the 1980s, though the real incomes of almost the entire population in Australia rose, the gap had also widened between the rich and the poor, casting serious doubts on the trickle-down theory of the economic rationalists.

Following growing pressure from within and outside government over the provision and cost of social welfare,[10] and cognizant of the need to secure an electoral victory with the female vote, the ALP committed itself to reviewing the system of social security. To that end the minister for social security, Brian Howe, appointed respected feminist left academic Bettina Cass to head up a comprehensive review of social policies in 1986 (Australian DSS Social Security Review 1986). Cass argued that such a review would need to take account of the considerable economic, social, and demographic changes that had occurred in Australian society since the 1970s. With the state now focused on administrative efficiency, budgetary constraint, eligibility, and the active/responsible/clever society, the state's social welfare provisions were reoriented toward the labor market and beneficiaries toward actively seeking work. The unemployment benefit was reconstituted as a Job Search Allowance (1991), and a Newstart program was introduced designed to encourage entry to the labor market for those who had been out of the labor market for more than twelve months. For the unemployed, it meant that more stringent conditions were attached to eligibility. The unemployed were also compelled to undertake retraining and to demonstrate they were actively involved in searching for work to continue receiving the allowances. For employers, incentives were provided to hire those who had been out of the labor market for some time.

From 1987 onward, the Social Security Review resulted in significant change in the social security system in Australia. The Family Income Supplement (1983) was expanded and replaced with what was now titled Family Allowance Supplement. However, the shift in the discursive frame—from *income* to *allowance*—signaled a move from entitlement to an income to a right to an allowance in exchange for particular obligations and responsibilities. In the policy rounds that followed, the government reversed the process of extending eligibility to those on benefits, by cracking down on "ineligibles" or "cheats," many of whom were women. Levi and Singleton (1991:642–43) argue that this was widely viewed at the time by social welfare lobby groups, including the Australian Council for Social Services (ACOSS), as important in order to get more generously targeted benefits to the more disadvantaged groups through the system. Up until this point, payment had continued for pensions as long as there was no reason to doubt eligibility. Now new procedures required claimants to establish their entitlements. Since the early 1970s sole parents, as a population, had almost doubled from 8.7 percent of all families with dependent children in 1975 (of which 70.9 percent were in receipt of income support) to 15.7 percent in 1990 (of which 73.9 percent received income support). In 1990 the outlay in income support for sole parents was 2.33 billion; only 22 percent less than was spent on unemployment benefits (Lambert 1994:77). These figures were also used by conservative social scientists to argue that welfare benefits created distortions in the market and encouraged welfare recipients like sole mothers to seek dependency upon the state.[11] Ignored was the fact that benefit dependency upon the state related entirely to the level of economic activity of the nation and the rate of unemployment (Lambert 1994:91).

The problem of sole parenthood attracted the attention of an increasing number of political commentators, professionals, experts, and academics in Australia. The voices which resonated emanated largely from "conservative" social scientists such as Alan Tapper (1990), Charles Murray (1994), and Peter Swan and Mikhail Bernstam (1986). In these accounts, single parenthood is contrasted negatively with two-parent families. In Swan and Bernstam's account (1986), for example, single mothers are constructed as "brides of the state." They argue that, in the restricted youth labor market between 1960 to 1980, single motherhood became an alternative occupation for women. This then perpetuated their dependence on male protection (cf. Swan, cited by Reekie 1996:334–35). What was required was more flexible work and labor markets enabling young women to enter the world of work rather than to construct a future dependent upon state benefits.

However, these discourses on "the problem" of sole mothers ignored the fact that the proportion of male sole parents claiming benefits had risen dramatically in the 1980s—by more than 300 percent—though from a low base of 9.7 percent to 34.7 percent (Lambert 1994:82). They also disregarded the fact that indigenous sole parents constituted 34 percent of indigenous families with children (in comparison with the 18 percent of the Australian population in general in 1991) and that the custodial parent was more likely to be male than female (Daley and Smith 1998:51).[12] Finally, such views tend to promote an image of sole mothers as dependent in perpetuity. However, as Suzanne Lambert (1994) observes, net of transfers to other pensions, the mean duration of dependence for sole mothers is three years while the median is fourteen months. These "facts" were strategically ignored; instead, key interest groups and spokespersons for an array of conservative and neoliberal think tanks promoted the specter of a burgeoning number of willful women damaging a future generation of children through "choosing" to live without the fathers of their children as brides of the state for as long as they could (Reekie 1996).[13] A cacophony of voices emerged, driven by a contradictory set of workfare and moral expectations focused on "the problem" of single parenthood. Solo-parent families were constructed as "father absent" families and, as such, "decayed" or "nonintact," with the children in those families more likely to be involved in criminal behavior, sexual precocity, and drugs. Further, according to Tapper, the state, by subsidizing sole mothers, discriminated against two-parent families and those who stayed together. This was viewed as unjust and inequitable (cf. Tapper 1990, written at the invitation of the Australian Institute of Public Policy). The discursive logic worked something like this: Those most in need of work were those who were dependent on the state. Those who were most dependent on the state were single parents whose children were more likely to be living in poverty. Single parents were most likely to be single mothers, hence single mothers should enhance their employability and enter the workforce as a solution to their children's poverty. The slide toward the individualization of the problem and its solution is carried through the registers of choice and responsibility. Single mothers can "choose" to enter the workforce. Single mothers are also "responsible," like any other citizen, for their own welfare and the welfare of their children, and that welfare is secured through training and work.

The focus on employability and work as the solution to poverty makes two assumptions: that wages are adequate and that childcare is available and affordable. Both wages and childcare availability have been inadequate, though for some women this has been minimized by entry into the skilled professions. For most women, however, the structure of the labor market and wages have been, and continue to be, profoundly inequitable. In spite of this, the state has adopted an indifferent stance toward the gendered consequences of the restructuring of the labor market, in the process making gender invisible. One of the most obvious ways in which this occurred was when sole mothers were bought into the discourse through being constructed as "parent" rather than "mother," though the overwhelming proportion of sole parents (and beneficiaries) are female (rather than male).

Three key policy and program initiatives can be identified. The first of the policy initiatives, the introduction of the controversial Child Support Scheme (1988) to collect child support from noncustodial parents, was an attempt by the state to not only increase overall revenue and shift the burden of financing to the community (Castles and Shirley 1996:98) but also to promote among noncustodial parents a notion of responsibility for child support and spousal maintenance. While dependent upon the Child Support Scheme being able to obtain maintenance/alimony payments from noncustodial parents, the Department of Social Security acknowledged a 50 percent increase in the number of sole parent pensioners declaring income support from maintenance payments (Lambert 1994). While figures support an improvement, the fact remains that the majority of sole parents are still without any maintenance/alimony support, and where this support is forthcoming, it is more likely to be for women who are already slightly better off (Lambert 1994:86). The second initiative, the Sole Parent Pension of 1989, combined the previous supporting parent benefit and the widow's pension. However, where mothers had remained eligible as long as they had a student or child under twenty-five years of age, the pension was now canceled when the youngest turned sixteen. To be eligible, the parent must be living outside a marital or de facto relationship and have low income and assets. That is, eligibility for sole mothers still rests on family status, continuing the rule that a woman is a man's responsibility and that, even if the relationship is a de facto one, it assumes a man in the household will provide economic support for the woman and children in that household. The implicit moralism of this position, as well as the surveillance of eligibility such a position entails, captures the fundamental and continuing contradiction experienced by sole mothers: their dependence on privatizing male protection is demanded, but their dependence on the protection of the patriarchal state is either denied or highly managed. The third initiative, Jobs, Education and Training (JET), introduced in 1989, was directed at sole parents in an attempt to integrate income support and labor market programs. The program provided to sole parent pensioners voluntary counseling on the availability of education, training, and employment, as well access to around twelve weeks of childcare.

However, despite what appears to be a more generous approach to welfare expenditure for sole mothers, the conditions for eligibility—as well as the discursive shifts to employability and responsibility—have (aside from the provision of childcare) systematically denied gender differences. Sole mothers are more likely than sole fathers to experience inequalities in the labor market because of the history of occupational segregation and lower wages. Sole mothers, because of their dependence on state benefits, are by far the most significant group of low-income individuals. Relative to their male counterparts, sole mothers are more than twice as likely to be welfare recipients, the average amount of time they spend as welfare dependents is higher, and they have on average more children to support (Lambert 1994:79). The increase in sole parenthood and the increasing incidence of poverty and welfare dependency among sole parents highlights the importance of the issues for women. Aside from the aged, sole parents are the fastest growing demographic group in the population. However, by the same token, those dependent upon benefits has declined since 1986 (Lambert 1994:82), while the duration of dependence has increased.

In reviewing this period in Australia, Francis Castles and Ian Shirley observe that, "the record has been one of modest adjustments to the existing system, with changes to income testing arrangements to facilitate easier entry into the labor force and increases in the real level of most benefits" (1996:104–5). While this is the case, it does not make clear that the combination of changes in the labor market and industrial relations regimes in Australia over this period has been so dramatic as to curtail opportunities for women in the low end of the employment market. This came about as employers sought on the one hand to avoid the conditions imposed by the award structure (overtime, sick leave, holiday pay, and so forth) and on the other to restructure work-places to promote greater flexibility at the level of the firm. The uneasy and untidy compromise between a dual system of restructured awards and enterprise bargaining that emerged was placed under further pres-sure with the government's Industrial Relations Reform Act 1994 which enabled nonunion workers to form their own bargaining units. Eager to explore other ways of increasing wages, disenchanted and alienated workers looked to other mechanisms—including enterprise bargaining and individual workplace agreements—to achieve their aims. However, as we shall see, these approaches appear to create further disparities for female workers, particularly those on the margins and working in highly feminized occupations. Added to this is the fact that the problems of workplace entry have been compounded for sole mothers who now find it increasingly difficult to either afford or negotiate the conditions for adequate childcare.

Less Than She Bargained For

Because of the way it was managed through the ALP/ACTU Accord, one of the outcomes of the restructuring of the welfare state in Aus-tralia is that, rhetorically and structurally, issues of gender equality and the plight of sole mothers slipped from view. This tendency was exac-erbated with the election of the Howard Liberal/National Coalition in 1996. Rather than signaling a new direction in welfare policy, the Coali-tion has intensified the process of neoliberal informed restructuring that had, paradoxically, begun with the Accord. The continuities can be seen in the comments made by Pru Goward, executive director of the Office of the Status of Women, appointed in 1996 by the Coalition govern-ment. Goward has argued that gender inequalities are more likely to be resolved through the application of market principles and by em-bracing globalization. She goes on: "The intense competition of post-industrialism pays little attention to issues of gender. Thank goodness. Like justice, global economics is blind . . . and works best when it is non-discriminatory" (cited in Pocock 1998:581). Goward rejects the so-called "feminist model" of dealing with discrimination against women as a form of "protectionism." Instead she appeals to the market, human capital theory, and family values (Goward 1997:56) as the best means of redress-ing women's disadvantage. While at one level I agree with Goward that globalization and neoliberalism pay little "direct" attention to gender as a question of equity, the underlying assumptions of neoliberalism are profoundly gendered. I also want to suggest that the state's silence on such strategies and their implication for women—a politics of omission (Offe 1996)—are nonetheless strategies pursued by the state. The internationalization of the economy and the introduction of markets as the primary means for coordinating social life are not neutral devices with indifferent effects. Rather, ideas such as labor market flexibility and individual choice are sought by capital and promoted by states in a complex process of recommodification and social control and are profoundly gendered in their consequences.

Goward (1997) also argues that recent reforms in childcare provision, family-friendly policies that reward previously unpaid domestic labor, and a move toward enterprise bargaining and individual workplace contracts provide new flexibility and choice for women in their lives. In her words, these reforms enable women to work "smarter" (Goward 1997: 57). Smart work here appears to mean interiorizing the discourses of the clever country where the exchanges between the state and the citizen are mediated by the contractual obligations of laboring. The emphasis upon work as the mechanism for the distribution of income for all citizens (even those with dependents), rather than benefits distributed by the state on the basis of need, represents a significant shift in the nature of the social contract between the state and all its citizens. This assumes that work is a more equitable means of distribution. Further, work as a mechanism for redistribution assumes all citizens are equally treated in their ability to access work and negotiate pay, conditions, and so on. There is now growing evidence that the decades of restructuring have changed patterns of work and unevenly affected the employment opportunities for most women, the bulk of whom work in the secondary labor market. Like other economies, Australia has experienced a serious decline in the proportion of workers in full-time employment—from 75 percent in 1973 to 63.2 percent in 1998 (Pocock 1998). These shifts reflect a decline in full-time work opportunities as a result of wider processes of employment restructuring, a decline in manufacturing and manual jobs, and the rise of nonmanual and service positions. The decline in full-time employment opportunities has been intensified since the election of the Liberal/National Coalition to government. Drawing on Australian Bureau of Statistics (ABS) data (catalog 6254.0), John Burgess and his colleagues (1998) observe that since the Coalition parties came to office, over 100,000 federal public sector jobs have disappeared due to cuts in expenditure and contracting-out policies.

The changing pattern of participation in work has also continued so that by 1998, male levels of participation had declined to 72.8 percent (from 79.3 percent in 1978) while female rates had increased to 53.9 (from 43.8 in 1978 [ABS catalogs 6204.0, 6203.0, 6101.0]). However, though the overall number of women participating in work has increased as a consequence of the desire for economic independence and discursive and practical shifts in welfare state provision, labor market growth has tended to be in *casual* and *part-time*, not full-time work. While part-time work increased by over 300 percent (Pocock, 1998), full-time employment rose by only 20 percent. In terms of the overall labor market, since 1978 there has been a net increase of 2.4 million jobs of which over 50 percent have been part-time, and in that time the labor force has grown by 2.7 million (Burgess et al. 1998). In short, the disjuncture between these two figures reflects the high level of unemployment spread unevenly over the community.

The distinction between casual and part-time work is important. Casual work refers to temporary arrangements between the employer and employee with a minimal employment contract. Iain Campbell's research (cited in Pocock 1998:586–87) suggests that in 1996 there were 1.84 million casual workers in Australia. Around 53 percent of this number were women. Further, while around one-third were *long-term full-time* (but casual) employees doing the core work of the organization, the other two-thirds were part-time. Though casual workers attract an additional loading on their rate of pay (around 20 percent), intended to compensate for the loss of holiday pay, sick leave, and permanency, casual workers still earn less than part-timers (around 90 percent). Part-time work arrangements, on the other hand, are more formal and have until more recently been protected by the system of award wages.

Barbara Pocock (1998) argues that award regulation of the conditions of permanent employment has encouraged employers to circumvent such provisions by increasing their employment through the pool of flexible casual labor. This increases the numerical and fiscal flexibility of the firm while minimizing the costs associated with permanent employees. Given that women are more likely to be in the casual and part-time labor market, they are more likely to be working under conditions that limit their ability to bargain individually. This is largely because they have few protections and their "casual" status excludes them from being represented in negotiations over enterprise agreements. And, while neoliberals argue that the rise of part-time work can be interpreted as the desire by workers for more flexible work arrangements (because they happen to be women), Burgess and his colleagues (1998:105) report that the percentage of part-time workers who want more hours has nearly doubled over the past twenty years. They argue that this indicates that the structural changes toward casualization, and hence precarious employment, have been forced upon the workforce. Already, Australia has one of the biggest casual workforces in the Organization for Economic Cooperation and Development (OECD); around 20 percent of the workforce compared to 5–7 percent in Britain (Campbell and Burgess 1997, cited in Burgess et al. 1998). Rather than facilitating flexibility for female workers in managing work and home responsibilities, part-time work is increasing with irregular, unpredictable, and unsociable hours (Lee and Strachan 1998). This enables the employer to schedule work around peaks in trading activity (and not pay overtime or premium rates of pay) and in the process reduce the wages, while generating new burdens for sole mothers who must negotiate nonstandard childcare hours over un-predictable periods of employment.

Entry to the labor market for sole mothers is dependent upon the availability of sufficiently well paid work and affordable childcare, includ-ing after-school care. Cuts in funding to the more generous childcare provisions under Labour were signaled by the Keating government in 1995, but since the election in 1996 of the Coalition government there have been significant changes to childcare. Though the Coalition is at pains to present itself as "family friendly" and keen to support families with dependent children in whatever their "choice" of work and child-care arrangements, there is a considerable distance between rhetoric and reality. In summarizing the changes in childcare policy under the Coalition, Julie Lee and Glenda Strachan (1998:99) observe that the ele-ment of universal access to assistance for childcare costs has been re-moved while the real price of childcare has increased. More important, the Coalition has shifted its policy emphasis away from community part-nership to reliance on the market. This assumes that, with some equity concerns addressed through income supplementation, the interplay of market forces will deliver optimum childcare. However, Lee and Stra-chan argue that a "user-pays" principle, if used to determine provision, will "increase inequalities between families where women in full-time and/or professional occupations can afford formal childcare and women in less advantaged labour market positions will be compelled to resort to informal services and/or withdraw from the labour market" (1998:99).

It could be argued that the "family friendliness" of the Coalition's childcare and workfare policies only extends as far as the family itself equates to a Victorian image of the family; that is, one shaped by the paternalist discourse of worker protection/female dependence that has typified Australia's welfare history. In relation to the former, the intro-duction of the Family Tax Initiative Part B provides a nonworking spouse with a child under five years of age with an extra rebate of $500, provided the partner in work receives less than $65,000. While it can be argued that women who stay at home ought to be compensated for their labor, this level of rebate can hardly be viewed as adequate compensation for laboring at home.

A further and equally important feature of the state's approach to childcare policy is the view that childcare can be negotiated by individual workers in an individual workplace agreement or as part of enterprise bargaining. According to the Department of Industrial Relations, this enables productivity and equity to be pursued simultaneously, where women can tailor their working time and other workplace arrangements to accommodate family commitments (Australia DIR 1992). Despite this focus, evidence to date suggests that there is little inclusion of clauses which deal with any aspect of childcare in enterprise agreements. Lee and Strachan (1998:95) report that in 1998, only around 2.6 percent of Federal awards and agreements discussed childcare, that these were split between public and private sector employment, and that the majority of the clauses refer to the fact that the childcare matters will be looked at *in the future.* This evidence is corroborated by Paul Boreham and his colleagues (1996) in a study of enterprise bargaining agreements and gender. Their findings are particularly pertinent for sole mothers for they look at the relationship between types of sectors and childcare clauses in enterprise agreements. One finding is that enterprise bargaining is not being used to secure work arrangements designed to enhance gender equity. A second finding is that highly feminized organizations are only marginally more likely to have equity provisions and favorable working time flexibility for women workers. Third, the degree of feminization of a workplace is strongly related to the degree of exclusion from decision-making. Fourth, women are more likely than men to be employed in organizations where employees are given little or no say in the major workplace decisions that affect them. If, as we can assume, sole mothers are more likely to be employed in highly feminized jobs, they are less likely to be in a situation where they can participate in negotiating either conditions of work, including childcare, or remuneration. As Boreham and his colleagues note:

To the extent that enterprise bargaining shifts the setting of pay and conditions to the workplace level, the degree to which the interests of different groups are represented in negotiations is likely to become a key determinant of the presence or absence of particular conditions of work. To the extent that women's interests appear to be marginalised in such negotiations . . . this shift can only lead to a reduced likelihood that their interests will be furthered by enterprise bargaining. (1996:65)

Moving the negotiation of childcare arrangements to the workplace assumes only those who work need to access childcare; by implication, those who do not work have no need for childcare. This means that sole mothers out of the workplace will have limited opportunities for relief from childcare. However, documenting the precise nature of the consequences of these policies for sole mothers—in the context of a policy of workfare—has been thwarted by the federal government's reluctance to undertake a detailed analysis. This led to the United Nations Committee on the Elimination of Discrimination Against Women (UNCEDAW) criticizing Australia in its 1997 report for retreating from the role it played in gender issues internationally and for the erosion of women's policy structures at home (Pocock 1998).

Conclusion

In this chapter I have argued that the Accord in Australia has been fundamentally paradoxical in its consequences for women—in particular sole mothers—and raises important questions about the way in which corporatism, as a form of neoliberal statism, contributed to the emergence of a new gender regime in Australia. As we have seen, corporatist arrangements operate on the basis of consensus. However, consensus is developed by marginalizing particular voices and solutions; in this case, women and their welfare and workplace concerns. Corporatism in Australia, a form of competitive progressivism, involved peak interest groups (corporate capital, peak labor groups) in the negotiation of economic policy with the state. However, such arrangements, though they might be viewed by labor as a potential Trojan horse, are typically compromised because of important differences in power and interests between labor, the state, and capital. This is exacerbated when liberal economic policies are promoted by the state, for as Ian Hampson (1996:70) observes: "Economic liberalism is fundamentally opposed to organized labor's interests. If economic liberalism is hegemonic, unions should not involve themselves in it." Corporatist arrangements are also likely to be gendered. Thus, to the extent that corporatism continues the privileging of peak "economic" interest groups (unlike social movements) and male labor, it promotes the interests of the economically (male) powerful (including the labor aristocracy) and perpetuates a particular type of social class and gender regime.

The gender regime of the welfare state in Australia has, historically, been shaped by state interventions in the labor market and productive sector—both spheres that have privileged male labor and depended upon constructing women as less worthy and dependent upon a male wage. This not only privileged a notion of family headed by a male but in fact denied other family arrangements, including those headed up by mothers. The relationship of sole mothers to the state and labor market, over the course of the twentieth century, had been mediated by juridical and institutionalized patriarchy. Though the 1970s represented a watershed in welfare policy, where new opportunities for women were created, including the repeal of the "immoral" and "undeserving poor" aspects of the state's legislation, one of the outcomes of the restructuring over the last two decades is that gender—and with it the plight of sole mothers—has slipped from view. That is, the discourses of employability, flexibility, responsibility, and choice following enterprise bargaining and the restructuring of labor markets were presumed, ipso facto, to create real opportunities for women that were previously not available. Indeed, the very existence of these discourses has deflected all structural challenges. As I have argued, the reality is very different for many women. While these discourses have, as Anna Yeatman notes, "legitimized new self-regulated modes of employment, in the same measure they contribute to the delegitimizing of established legal and policy paternalistic discourses of worker protection" (1996:41). It is within this new more individualized and contractualized discursive and practical frame that sole mothers find themselves multiply jeopardized. In the labor market they have been further peripheralized and marginalized, while in the household their labor is neither compensated for nor augmented by the state. At the same time, sole mothers are increasingly publicly scrutinized by segments of the population for their "caring" responsibilities. If the consequences of welfare restructuring—informed by globalization and neo-liberalism—can be "litmused" through the effects on sole mothers, then, unlike Goward (cited in Pocock 1998), we would have to argue that such processes are anything but neutral. It might be argued that if the poor are expected to work, the state might reasonably be expected to create the conditions for a strengthening of the economy. However, since the legislation does not regulate the economy or provide for jobs, the basis of the new social contract between the state and its citizens is both unequal and likely to collapse as the contradictions become more and more untenable.

Chapter 9
Neoliberalism and
Tino Rangatiratanga

Welfare State Restructuring in Aotearoa/New Zealand

Wendy Larner

The "New Zealand experiment" has been touted internationally as an exemplary case of neoliberalism and market-oriented restructuring. In the decade following the 1984 election the country saw a remarkable succession of reform-minded politicians and policymakers. During the 1980s, economic reforms, initiated by a social democratic Labour government, included corporatization, deregulation, and the privatization of many state sector activities. In the 1990s, under a more conservative National government, social policy and the welfare state became the central targets of reformers. Domestically, these policy changes have been highly controversial. Cuts in social spending and a shift to "user pays" are interpreted as a major assault on the "cradle to grave" welfare state. Local analysts are highly pessimistic about the consequences of welfare state restructuring, identifying continued high levels of unemployment and increased social polarization. Maori and Pacific Island women,[1] in particular, have borne the brunt of the processes associated with welfare state restructuring, with the consequence that poverty is now more strongly racialized and gendered in Aotearoa/New Zealand.

Disconcertingly, the new prominence of neoliberalism and market-oriented restructuring in a welfare state society is not anomalous. High profile governments in Australia, Britain, and the United States, among others, have implemented political programs premised on economic liberalization and social policy reform. In this regard, it is useful to begin this chapter by observing that in New Zealand most analysts focus on aspects of welfare state restructuring that reflect experiences elsewhere. The emphasis is on cuts in benefit levels and the increased targeting of social assistance. It is argued that welfare reform is driven predominantly by fiscal concerns (Boston, Dalziel, and St. John 1999), although some commentators identify a shift from economic to moral argumentation in recent years (Kingfisher 1999; Peters 1997). These emphases reflect the fact that welfare state restructuring in Aotearoa/New Zealand is usually unequivocally attributed to a shift in governmental aspirations from social democracy to neoliberalism.

There has, however, been another major influence on the changing relationships between state, communities, and citizens in Aotearoa/New Zealand during the last two decades, namely, increased recognition of the claims of indigenous Maori *iwi* (tribal groups). Dispossessed of much of their land in the late nineteenth century, Maori have struggled for 150 years to have their experience of social and economic injustice recognized by New Zealand governments. During the 1980s there finally appeared to be some progress. The fourth Labour government gave retrospective power to the Waitangi Tribunal,[2] thereby opening up the land claims process and the possibility to address long-standing grievances. During the same period there were significant attempts to institutionalize equity and biculturalism in major institutions and organizations. The aim was to overcome historical social and economic disparities between Maori and non-Maori and to advance *tino rangatiratanga* (self-determination).

This chapter analyzes the specificity of welfare state restructuring in Aotearoa/New Zealand through a discussion of both neoliberalism and *tino rangatiratanga*. In the first half of the chapter I show that while these two political processes emerge from quite different social locations, each represents significant challenges to the postwar welfare state. Neoliberalism has undermined the policy goals of full employment and state responsibility for social well-being. It involves a new emphasis on market provisioning and self-responsibility. *Tino rangatiratanga* has significantly eroded the integrationist tendencies of postwar welfare state policies. It is characterized by calls for Maori autonomy and self-determination. My argument is that the discourse of welfare state restructuring in Aotearoa/New Zealand is shaped by both neoliberal claims about the market and individualism and Maori claims for positive development and economic self-sufficiency.

In the second half of the chapter I explore the gendered and racialized consequences of welfare state restructuring, arguing that profound contradictions emerge from the articulation of neoliberalism and *tino rangatiratanga*. On the one hand, changes associated with market-oriented restructuring, particularly a sustained rise in levels of unemployment, have disproportionately affected Maori and Pacific Island workers. On the other hand, as equity issues have received more attention and land claims have been settled, there have been improvements in educational achievement and labor market distribution for some Maori men and women. Class differences among Maori are being overlaid by new patterns of gender and ethnic difference associated with the globalization of the domestic economy and the changing composition of migration flows. Ultimately, however, neoliberalism has undermined aspirations for *tino rangatiratanga* with the consequence that women's poverty in Aotearoa/New Zealand has become more strongly racialized. The tensions associated with the reconfiguration of class, gender, and race relations are most pronounced in the case of sole mothers.

The "New Zealand Experiment"

In their two terms, the fourth Labour government (1984–1990) passed more legislation per year than any New Zealand government previously (Sharp 1994). Market liberalization in the financial, agricultural, and manufacturing sectors was accompanied by dramatic state sector restructuring. Initially nine corporations were established as "state owned enterprises," accounting for billions of dollars of assets and the employment of over 60,000 people. Among the government departments affected were some of New Zealand's largest employers, including the Post Office, Forestry Service, and State Coal Mines. The model was subsequently widely replicated, then many of the newly formed companies were either partially or fully privatized. By 1996 twenty-six separate asset sales had been concluded, accounting for over $13 billion (New Zealand Treasury 1997). Because many of the former government enterprises were sold to multinational companies, one consequence of state sector restructuring was the internationalization of the domestic economy.

A second set of changes initiated during the 1980s involved steps toward the liberalization of immigration flows. In 1986 a business migration scheme was introduced, with the intent of attracting wealthy entrepreneurs and their capital to New Zealand. In 1991 there was a further shift in emphasis, with the introduction of a new migration policy based on a points system emphasizing educational qualifications and work experience. The traditional source bias toward Britain was removed with the assumption that new migration patterns would involve a much more diverse range of countries. The new migration policy was also premised on an overall increase in levels of migration with the intention being to achieve an annual net migration gain of 20,000 people. The rationale for the changes in migration policies and programs was explicitly economic; new migrants would bring the capital, skills, and expertise needed in New Zealand's restructured economy. Thus not only was capital internationalized during the 1980s, so too was the labor market.

Economic reform was succeeded by social reform. In the early 1990s the National government marked its return to office with severe cuts to social spending, and benefit levels were reduced substantially. These spending cuts were justified on the grounds that they would "increase the 'rewards' for moving from welfare to work" (Finance Minister Ruth Richardson, quoted in Kelsey 1993:83). They were followed by the introduction of targeting and user-pays principles into the areas of health, housing, and education. Social program reforms were introduced in conjunction with new industrial relations legislation designed to deregulate the labor market. Under the Employment Contracts Act (1991) the principle of collectivism as the basis for industrial relations was replaced with the notion of an individual employment contract, in which the primary parties are the individual employees and their employers. Both sets of initiatives were portrayed as component parts of a policy program that would recreate the conditions for strong and sustainable economic growth.

Further liberalization of both foreign investment and immigration flows also characterized this period. Major regional initiatives, including the active promotion of investment opportunities through the visits of politicians, trade seminars, and the appointment of foreign direct investment counselors to embassies in Japan, Singapore, and Los Angeles resulted in record levels of inward investment. Likewise, immigration policies targeted people with high level technical and professional skills. By the year ended January 1995, net immigration gains were running at record levels and Auckland—New Zealand's largest city—was suffering major infrastructural problems. The composition of migration flows also changed dramatically during this period, with migration from "nontraditional" source countries, particularly in Asia, becoming much more significant (Lidgard, Bedford, and Goodwin 1998).

The introduction of a new political system, based on a mixed member version of proportional representation, slowed the economic reform process during the mid-1990s. At the same time, there was growing public awareness, both locally and internationally, of the social costs associated with market-oriented restructuring. Consequently, while social policy reemerged as a central theme in the political debates of the late 1990s, this most recent period has been characterized by short-lived, politically expedient initiatives and often subsequent public rejection. A high profile referendum on a compulsory retirement scheme was defeated, although it did contribute to debate over intergenerational transfers. Other initiatives included a proposed code of social and family responsibility released as a public discussion document and subsequently mothballed (see Larner 2000 for more detail). This controversial attempt to specify the rights and responsibilities of beneficiaries was accompanied by a televised "dob-in-a-bludger" campaign that encouraged

New Zealanders to report benefit fraud, the introduction of a "Community Wage" workfare scheme, and more stringent work testing.

While there is considerable cynicism about the motivation for these initiatives, there is also growing recognition that a return to the postwar welfare state, even if desirable, is now highly unlikely. Despite the election of a new, nominally social democratic Labour government in 1999, it is becoming clear that the conceptual foundations of the postwar welfare state in Aotearoa/New Zealand have been fundamentally eroded. Rather than the focus of state activity being a relatively closed national economy and the primary policy goal being the promotion of full employment, economic policies and programs are now designed to articulate domestic activities into global economic flows (Larner 1998). Integral to this shift is the redefinition of New Zealanders as "human resources" with the potential capacities of skill, ingenuity, and innovation. Moreover, whereas Keynesian welfarism was premised on the resident national population, organized into two-parent households with the male breadwinner and assumption of lifetime employment, under neoliberalism participation in paid work for both men and women is understood to be the primary basis for social inclusion, with a diminished welfare state responsible only for residual support.

Tino Rangatiratanga

The other significant influence on welfare state restructuring in Aotearoa/New Zealand has been the increased recognition by the state and many Pakeha of the political claims of Maori.[3] While a new generation of Maori activists had restimulated the debate over land alienation in the 1970s, it was only in the mid-1980s that the state responded in any significant way.[4] One of the first initiatives of the fourth Labour government was Hui Taumata, a Maori economic summit. This was accompanied by the launch of a "Decade of Maori Development." The impetus for these initiatives was found in long held aspirations for Maori economic self-sufficiency. Participants also stressed the significance of the Treaty of Waitangi in any future attempts to address Maori needs. Both themes were to prove central to subsequent developments.

In 1985 the Treaty of Waitangi Amendment Act granted retrospective powers to the Waitangi Tribunal, allowing investigation of treaty grievances back to 1840. This was part of a raft of social justice initiatives launched by the fourth Labour government in response to long-standing claims from their various political constituencies. Others included the establishment of a Ministry of Women's Affairs, the introduction of nuclear-free legislation, and new environment and human rights initiatives. Jane Kelsey (1991:109) argues convincingly that the treaty policy of the fourth Labour government was an attempt to pacify Maori demands without disrupting the basis for existing state power. Certainly, to this day, the powers of the Waitangi Tribunal remain recommendatory. However, the tribunal has also become a major public forum for the expression of both past and present injustices, and the claims process has raised the consciousness of both Maori and Pakeha in relation to the loss of land and resources.

Greater emphasis on the Treaty of Waitangi was accompanied by attempts to develop biculturalism in major organizations and institutions. One of the first government departments to be affected was the Department of Social Welfare, which was accused of institutional racism in the *Puao-te-ata-tu* report of 1986.[5] The solution proposed was that Maori play a larger role in developing policies and programs in the area of social welfare. One significant initiative, which constituted part of the department's response, was the Matua Whangai program in which "at risk" Maori children were left in the care of *whanau* (extended family) rather than taken into foster care. While the program was poorly resourced, and subject to criticism as a result, it marked a turning point in Maori-state relations. The new agenda would be to facilitate greater Maori control over resources and increase independence from the state in an attempt to generate Maori solutions to Maori social problems.

From 1986 to 1990 the fourth Labour government actively used the Treaty of Waitangi as a basis for government policy and administration (Fleras and Elliot 1992). At the same time a number of programs that had been pioneered by Maori (sometimes known as "flax-roots" initiatives) were picked up by the state. Notable among these were the *kohanga reo* and *kura kaupapa* Maori educational programs.[6] The Maori Language Act of 1987 declared Maori an official language and conferred the right to speak Maori in any legal proceedings. Significant inroads were also made in education, health, broadcasting, penal services, employment, and social service delivery. In 1988 the Labour government established two explicit policy principles: to increase the responsiveness of mainstream agencies to Maori and to devolve government functions to tribal authorities on the grounds that Maori were better placed to provide services to their own people than the state (New Zealand Government 1988).

In 1990, following the election of the National government, there was a change of orientation. *Ka Awatea*, a report sponsored by the new Minister of Maori Affairs, Winston Peters, proposed the mainstreaming of Maori policy and a new monitoring role for the Ministry of Maori Development, now known as Te Puni Kokiri. Despite Peters's abrupt departure from the National government thereafter, aspects of the mainstreaming approach were adopted and continue to influence current policy directions. There is criticism that too often the result has been to develop sectoral approaches then add a Maori view (M. Durie 1998). The provision of integrated services has also proved difficult in a public sector characterized by narrowly specified accountabilities (Waitangi Tribunal 1998). At the same time, however, the policy/purchaser/provider split has offered Maori opportunities to become directly involved in service delivery, and group targeting has made arguments for culturally specific service delivery easier to make (Cheyne, O'Brien, and Belgrave 1997).

The claims process also changed during the 1990s. In December 1994 the National government announced its intention to attempt to settle all claims fully and finally within a $1 billion financial limit which was to become known as the "fiscal envelope." Settlement was to be achieved through direct negotiation with individual *iwi* and would take place over a ten-year period. The fiscal envelope proposal met with widespread opposition, not only because of the arbitrary financial limit placed on the claims, but also because of the inadequate consultation that led up to the proposal. The credibility of Te Puni Kokiri was also sorely tested, as the government had charged the ministry with the task of presenting the unpopular proposal to Maori throughout the country (see Gardiner 1996). However, while the "fiscal envelope" itself was formally dropped in 1996, direct negotiations with *iwi* continued, resulting in major settlements with Tainui and Ngai Tahu, among others.

There are convincing arguments that these initiatives are attempts to coopt Maori and to legitimate what remains fundamentally a Pakeha state (see, for example, Kelsey 1991). However, while Maori aspirations remain a "struggle without end" (Walker 1990), as a leading commentator recently observed, "efforts to address disparities between Maori and non-Maori through more direct involvement in the delivery of social policy programs has been a major accomplishment in a state which, until a decade or more ago, refused to accept that culture was important or to recognise any good reason why Pakeha providers could not adequately meet Maori needs" (Durie 1998:89–90). In this context it can be argued that, just as the neoliberal reform program has eroded the presuppositions of the postwar welfare state, so too have claims for *tino rangatiratanga*. No longer are New Zealanders treated as if they were culturally and ethnically homogeneous, and the rights of Maori as *tangata te whenua* (people of the land) are widely acknowledged. The processes associated with the pursuit for *tino rangatiratanga* thus represent a qualitative shift away from the assimilationist and integrationist assumptions of earlier state forms.

The Discourse of Restructuring

The discourse of welfare state restructuring in Aotearoa/New Zealand, as elsewhere, has involved a move away from state provisioning to market provisioning, and a new emphasis on communities and families as the basis for social well-being. Notions of choice, economic self-sufficiency, and individual empowerment underpin this shift. My claim is that this is not simply a top-down discourse driven by neoliberal ideologues. In Aotearoa/New Zealand there is an unexpected articulation between the aspirations of neoliberals and some Maori that shape the specificity of welfare state restructuring. As Mason Durie has observed: "Positive Maori development, with its focus on tribal responsibilities for health, education, welfare, economic progress, and greater autonomy, fitted quite comfortably with the free market philosophy of a minimal state, non-government provision of services, economic self-sufficiency and privatization" (1998:11). This is not to suggest that the discourses of neoliberalism and *tino rangatiratanga* can be reduced to each other, nor is it to deny neoliberal hegemony. However it is to take seriously the idea that new welfare state arrangements emerge out of political struggle, rather than being simply imposed in a top-down manner. In Aotearoa/New Zealand demands from Maori for the right to deliver services in culturally appropriate forms constitute a very significant critique of the postwar welfare state. Moreover, as Elizabeth Rata (1997:11) argues, in the last two decades there has been a dialectical interaction between the state and Maori as both have attempted to reposition themselves in a wider global context. During this process neoliberals and some Maori found themselves in unexpected agreement on a key theme: namely, the dangers of continued dependency on the state. In this case, therefore, we see clearly that the claims of so-called "new social movements" are part of the discursive construction and reconstruction associated with welfare state restructuring (Brodie 1996a; Yeatman 1990).

Closer attention to the discourses of neoliberalism and *tino rangatiratanga* suggests both are dynamic. While most commentaries on neoliberalism in Aotearoa/New Zealand focus on continuities in the reform programs of the 1980s and 1990s, it is important to note that the Labour government shied away from welfare state reform, despite long-standing critiques from women, Maori, and beneficiary groups. Although there was a Royal Commission on Social Policy in 1988, "core" government services such as health, education, and social welfare were not part of Labour's liberalization program. Nor were there any major attempts to deregulate the labor market. In this regard, it can be argued that the fourth Labour government represents an early attempt to articulate neoliberalism and social democracy.

It was only in the early 1990s that the newly elected National government focused more specifically on the welfare state and social policy, while at the same time continuing with the economic liberalization program of their predecessors. In contrast to Labour's governmental project, it can be argued that their policies and programs represent an articulation of neoliberalism and neoconservatism. This articulation is exemplified in the recent proposal for a code of social and family responsibility. Whereas neoliberals see families as self-regulating sites of economic and social welfare (Brown 1995), the proposed code implied that state monitoring of familial relationships is necessary to ensure that family members fulfill their responsibilities to each other. As Barbara Cruikshank (2000:17) explains, "Neo-conservatives find themselves in the awkward position of calling for a strong state and authoritarian measures to produce a citizenry capable of existing under a liberal and limited state."

Just as the discourse of neoliberalism has shifted over the last two decades, so too has that of *tino rangatiratanga*. Rata (1997) suggests there have been two distinct phases in negotiations between the state and *iwi* (see also Sharp 1990:227–45). During the early 1980s attention was focused on the "bicultural project" in which the aim was to facilitate entry of Maori into key institutional locations. Rata argues that this process created structural sites within the state for some Maori. Certainly, by the 1990s virtually all government departments, many community organizations, and some large New Zealand companies had Maori advisers and Maori policy analysts. Rata claims these people subsequently fulfilled brokerage roles, thus allowing the second phase of change; "tribal economic development." In this second phase attention has shifted away from biculturalism and is now more focused on re-creating an economic base that will allow the generation of tribal wealth. She calls this second stage "tribal capitalism."

In conjunction with changing political agendas, the discourses surrounding Maori-Crown relations have also shifted. In their analysis of Waitangi Tribunal reports, Roger Maaka and Angie Fleras (1998) describe this shift as that from "contract to constitutionalism." They show that early tribunal reports assume Maori ceded sovereignty under the Treaty of Waitangi, and correspondingly represent *tino rangatiratanga* as involving tribal self-management along similar lines to local government. In contrast, more recent reports endorse the notion that Maori continue to have sovereignty by right of original occupancy. Claims for *tino rangatiratanga* are thus represented as "a dialogue between sovereigns," framed, in part, through concepts and categories derived from international law. Recent proposals for a "new constitutionalism" between Maori and the Crown can be situated in this context.

This later point highlights the fact that, despite strong local particularities, both discourses are also inflected by international influences. Neoliberal discourses have shifted from economic to moral argumentation, in part reflecting the growing influence of American interventions in local debates. Key events include the Business Roundtable sponsored visit of British academic David Green who mobilized influential right-wing critiques of the American welfare state in his call for the resurrection of "civil society." The prominence of American debates was also evident at "Beyond Dependency," a major conference sponsored by the Department of Social Welfare in 1996. The discourse of *tino rangatiratanga*, while generated out of the specificity of a particular political struggle, also has broader connotations. Mason Durie (1998:1), for example, stresses that the politics of Maori self-determination takes place "against the backdrop of a distinctive cultural identity, a changing national identity and a world-wide assertion by indigenous peoples of the rights to self-determination."

Finally, it is important to emphasize that these discourses articulate with each other. I have already alluded to the fact that the discourse of *tino rangatiratanga*, while creating space for more culturally sensitive and relevant policies and programs, has also been appropriated by neoliberal politicians to provide justification for devolution. But this is not a one-way process. Neoliberal conceptions have also been strategically deployed by Maori to advance their claims. For example, Brenda Tahi (1995) discusses how Te Ohu Whakatupu, the Maori Policy Unit of the Ministry of Women's Affairs, uses policy arguments about efficiency and effectiveness, rather than feminist analysis, to advance proposals that benefit Maori women. She cites the example of a program developed to encourage female Maori entrepreneurs on the grounds that Maori women are ideally positioned to contribute to the government's aspirations for an export-oriented, internationally competitive economy. In a more general discussion, Tania Rei (1998) shows that Maori women have a complex relationship with state institutions, and that their political activism has constantly involved the blending of Maori culture and Pakeha forms of organizational practice.

That said, there remain significant tensions between neoliberal claims for the free market and individualism and those for *tino rangatiratanga* premised on self-determination and cultural specificity. Contradictions between social understandings premised on the individual and those premised on communal forms of social life are the most obvious of these. Also evident are disjunctures between a worldview premised on a rigid separation of economic and social spheres, and one that insists social, cultural, and economic development are completely intertwined. Finally, as Anna Yeatman reminds us in her analysis of the relationship between "new social movements" and welfare state restructuring:

There is . . . a fundamental difference between the direction of their contribution and that of the neo-conservative, New Right and corporatist disestablishers of the ideal of social citizenship. Where the former are struggling towards the naming of new conditions and rhetoric of contemporary struggles for democratization, the latter represent a counter-revolution in relation to the revolutionary reforms which the ideal of social citizenship opened up. (1990:148)

In this context it will not be surprising to discover that the outcomes of welfare state restructuring in Aotearoa/New Zealand have been highly contradictory. Most notably, given the argument made thus far, one major effect of neoliberalism has been to undermine much of the progress made towards *tino rangatiratanga*. The consequences are particularly severe for Maori women, increasing numbers of whom have been forced to become reliant on the state for economic and social well-being at the very time the state is signaling its intention to withdraw support in the name of self-responsibility and independence. Before exploring this issue, however, it is useful to examine the implications of changing ideologies of work, identity, and gender for different groups of women in Aotearoa/New Zealand.

Ideologies of Work, Identity, and Gender

Feminist commentators on neoliberalism have begun to identify a significant shift in ideologies of work, identity, and gender. Government agencies now mobilize a degendered individual consumer-citizen in their programs and policies (Larner 1997; Probyn 1998). Access to the new "market citizenship" (Yeatman 1993) is primarily via labor force participation. Moreover, whereas Keynesian welfarism was premised on the model of the male breadwinner and female domestic worker, neoliberalism appears to constitute us all, both men and women, as potential paid workers. In the context of the shift to a gender neutral model of the citizen worker (Jenson 1999; O'Connor, Orloff, and Shaver 1999), it can be argued that neoliberal common sense incorporates some versions of (liberal) feminism (Fraser 1993).

However, new ideologies of work, identity, and gender articulate with long established forms of social inequality, resulting in new forms of convergence and divergence in women's experiences (see also Larner 1993, 1996). Given the new emphasis on women as potential paid workers, it is not surprising to discover that over the two decades there has been a steady increase in the labor force participation of New Zealand women.

Yet, just as the male breadwinner/female domestic worker model of the postwar welfare state predominantly reflected the experiences of middle-class Pakeha women, so too does the new model of gender relations. It is Pakeha women for whom full-time labor force participation has risen. These women have also begun to gain ground in certain historically male-dominated professional, administrative, and managerial occupations. In contrast, the reemergence of large-scale unemployment in the 1980s was accompanied by a marked decline in the full-time labor force participation of Maori and Pacific Island women.

These racially inflected patterns are explained by changing labor market opportunities. During the postwar period Maori and Pacific Island women had high levels of full-time labor force participation in comparison to other New Zealand women. They were also overrepresented in labor-intensive manufacturing occupations, reflecting a historical process in which a postwar manufacturing sector developed using Maori and Pacific Island workers to fill lower level labor market positions. Consequently, while the major outcome of economic restructuring in the 1980s was high levels of male unemployment, women from Maori and Pacific Island communities were also severely affected by job losses during this period. Indeed, the decline in women's full-time labor force participation rates in the late 1980s was almost entirely accounted for by these women. For example, between 1984 and 1994 labor force participation rates for Maori women declined by 8 percent, while that for non-Maori women increased by 2 percent (Love 1995:26). By the late 1990s Maori women had the lowest full-time labor force participation rate of any ethnic group and were far less likely to work part-time than other women (Te Puni Kokiri 1996:16).

Paradoxically, increased unemployment and declining labor force participation rates among Maori occurred at the same time as long-standing economic and social injustices finally began to be addressed by the state. Moreover, one consequence of the efforts to institutionalize biculturalism and settle land claims was some improvement in Maori educational achievements and labor market distributions (Te Puni Kokiri 1998). A new generation of Maori with tertiary education, armed with legal, analytical, and technical qualifications, have found their skills in considerable demand. Most notably, efforts to recruit Maori policy advisers and program leaders in government departments saw Maori representation in the public service increase steadily in the 1990s. By 1998 Maori accounted for 13.1 percent of the total public service workforce, compared to 9.1 percent in the labor force as a whole (State Services Commission 1998:6).

Despite the presence of the new Maori "technocrats" (E. Durie 1995:

19), long-standing labor force patterns persist. Not only do nearly one-third of Maori employed in the public service earn less than $30,000 per annum, Maori women remain underrepresented in higher public service income groups, with only 2.4 percent of Maori women earning over $60,000, compared to 5.2 percent of Maori men (State Services Commission 1998). Thus while the claims for *tino rangatiratanga* have meant economic benefits for some, the legacy of historical labor force inequalities continues. One consequence has been greater class differences among Maori, while an overall social and economic gap between Maori and non-Maori persists (Te Puni Kokiri 1998). As one commentator observed about the "Decade of Maori Development": "A trend which has emerged during this decade has been one of increasing social stratification of Maori. Some Maori are improving their social and economic status but the vast majority, under the current system, are destined to be at the very bottom of the economic scale in the foreseeable future" (Love 1995:25).

Increasing socioeconomic disparities among Maori articulate with a more general reconfiguration of patterns of gender inequality. Occupational mobility for some women has resulted in increased class differences among women. Those women who have access to market citizenship, either directly or indirectly, have the ability to buy themselves out of the traditional gender division of labor. Rather than juggling paid and unpaid work, they can opt for market provisioning of domestic services and childcare. High wage, dual income households increasingly eat out or rely on takeout food. Nannies, housecleaners, and gardeners have also become more common in New Zealand's major cities. In contrast, women who cannot afford such solutions now experience heightened versions of the "double burden," as the new emphasis on paid work means more women find themselves trying to cope with competing demands from employers, partners, and children.

Moreover, these trends are being overlaid by more complex patterns of cultural and ethnic difference associated with the globalization of the domestic economy and the changing composition of migration flows. New Zealand's major cities, Auckland in particular, have begun to more closely resemble the multiethnic "global cities" of the Pacific Rim than the culturally homogeneous society assumed by the architects of the postwar welfare state. There is growing evidence that women from "nontraditional" source countries are experiencing difficulties gaining access to the New Zealand labor market due to language problems, lack of recognition of overseas qualifications, and racial discrimination (Ho and Lidgard 1996). New migrants are also ineligible for social welfare benefits for two years after they first arrive in New Zealand. Consequently, many migrant women are forced to make alternative economic arrangements. Undocumented informal sector work and self-employment are two possible options for those women who find themselves excluded from the formal labor market.

New ideologies of work, identity, and gender thus have contradictory implications for women in Aotearoa/New Zealand. Postwar understandings premised on the male breadwinner/female domestic worker dichotomy have been considerably eroded, manifest in increased levels of male unemployment, the erosion of the family wage, and "feminization" of the labor force. A new conceptualization, premised on participation in paid work for both men and women, appears to be consolidating. However, this new emphasis on paid work for women has meant that tensions between the demands of paid and unpaid work have become more pronounced. Moreover, this new understanding articulates in complex ways with social inequalities premised on race/ethnicity. Maori and Pacific Island women are most likely to find themselves experiencing direct and indirect consequences of increased levels of poverty. This reconfiguration of class, gender, and race relations plays itself out most dramatically in the case of sole mothers.

Sole Mothers

It is well established that welfare state restructuring is associated with the feminization of poverty, and that sole mothers are at particular risk of declining living standards. In Aotearoa/New Zealand the vast majority of sole mothers are recipients of the Domestic Purposes Benefit (DPB). Introduced in 1973 to provide financial support for sole parents who were not in paid work, the benefit was designed to give women the freedom to leave unsatisfactory relationships while ensuring they did not suffer undue economic hardship. However, while the DPB may have succeeded in fulfilling the former aspiration, it was much less successful in the latter. The existence of few opportunities for relatively well paid work for women, combined with the lack of affordable childcare facilities, meant that most sole mothers in Aotearoa/New Zealand were forced to rely on the state until they reentered a relationship,[7] or until their children grew up. The consequence was relative poverty for many women. In this regard, it may be significant that it was in relation to the DPB that discussions of "welfare dependency" first began to surface (McClure 1998:186).

During the 1980s and 1990s the number of women on the DPB steadily increased, as did the average duration. While the increase mainly represented rising divorce rates and the breakup of de facto relationships, it was also partly a response to increased unemployment and declining male labor force participation, in that economic well-being could no longer be guaranteed by a relationship with a man. In this context, it often made more sense for sole mothers to opt for the security of a regular benefit, despite the relative poverty involved, than to enter a volatile labor market or an insecure future with a male partner (Shirley and Baker 1998). Moreover, given high levels of unemployment in Maori and Pacific Island communities, it is not surprising to find that these women became more highly represented among DPB recipients. Indeed, reflecting declining labor force participation and rising levels of unemployment, benefit receipt in general has become more strongly racialized in Aotearoa/New Zealand. Te Puni Kokiri (1998:18) recently estimated that 36 percent of Maori now rely on government benefits (excluding superannuation) as their main source of income.

In 1998, 32 percent of total applicants for the DPB identified as Maori, and 7 percent as Pacific Islanders (NZISS 1998). Current estimates suggest that 43 percent of Maori children now live in single-parent households, and only a third of these families are linked to *whanau* (M. Durie 1998). More generally, census data suggest that 28 percent of Maori do not appear to be affiliated to any *iwi* (Te Puni Kokiri 1996). Given that *tino rangatiratanga* is premised on the integrity of kin relationships, this point takes on particular significance. Most *whanau* have members across class boundaries, thus facilitating some redistribution of the benefits associated with "tribal capitalism." Both Ngai Tahu and Tainui, for example, have used settlement gains to provide educational opportunities for their members. Among those whose traditional kin relationships are unknown or eroded, the burden of responsibility rests on Maori women, both as primary caregivers and sole parents, to provide for themselves and their families (Te Puni Kokiri 1996:18).

At the same time as many Maori and Pacific Island women are coping with the direct and indirect consequences of high rates of unemployment and poverty, they also find themselves the targets of the new welfare-to-work programs designed to encourage financial independence and self-responsibility. The kinds of jobs available to sole mothers in the restructured domestic economy are most likely to be part-time and/or casual service sector jobs. Moreover, 61 percent of women on the DPB have no formal education qualifications (McClure 1998:249). For sole mothers the overwhelming consequence of benefit cuts and more stringent work testing has not been to facilitate their entry into paid work; rather, it has been renewed economic hardship.

Given this scenario, it is not surprising that the recent New Zealand Poverty Measurement Project found that while only 8.5 percent of Pakeha were poor, 27.3 percent of Maori and 35.8 percent of Pacific Islanders fell into this category, reflecting higher unemployment rates, lower incomes, and larger family sizes (Stephens 1999:254). Increased levels of poverty have been further exacerbated by sharp rent increases, particularly in Auckland. This is the combined consequence of an exponential property market, combined with the shift to market rentals for state-provided housing. For many low-income families, particularly those headed by sole mothers, the most feasible option is to share housing with extended families and/or friends. Correspondingly, there has been an upsurge in poverty related illnesses, particularly in South Auckland, that is directly attributed to poor housing and overcrowding (Murphy 1999; Stephens 1999).

Maori and Pacific Island women have thus borne the brunt of the processes associated with welfare state restructuring. Poverty has become more strongly racialized and gendered in Aotearoa/New Zealand. Only recently has this been explicitly acknowledged by those responsible for new governmental initiatives designed to target "welfare dependency." Moreover, there are now further attempts to tighten eligibility for the DPB, including work testing for those whose children are over the age of fourteen. Ultimately, the effect of more stringent work testing will be to force more sole mothers into a highly exploitative labor market. It seems likely that increasing numbers of women will find themselves in the paradoxical situation of being forced to juggle their own (unpaid) domestic work and childcare with paid work providing similar services to other women with higher incomes. Inevitably these new class differences among women will be strongly inflected by race/ethnicity.

Conclusion

The economic liberalization program of the fourth Labour government irreparably eroded the foundations of the postwar welfare state. Economic liberalization involved a significant shift away from Keynesian aspirations of protecting the national economy and promoting full employment. The consequence was a significant increase in overseas ownership and control of New Zealand based activities together with a sustained increase in levels of unemployment. Because Maori and Pacific Island workers had been historically overrepresented in labor-intensive manufacturing activities, these workers were most severely affected by economic restructuring. Thus the legacy of economic liberalization was that race/ethnicity became a salient division with regard to access to paid work.

During the same period, however, recognition of claims associated with *tino rangatiratanga* undermined assumptions of ethnic homogeneity that underpinned the postwar welfare state. Assimilationist and integrationist policies were replaced by those premised on cultural specificity, and claims for appropriate service delivery began to be recognized. Moreover, the move toward biculturalism in major institutions and organizations resulted in occupational mobility for some Maori. Ultimately, however, aspirations for *tino rangatiratanga* are being undermined by the consequences of neoliberalism. This can be most clearly seen in relation to the experiences of Maori women, many of whom find themselves excluded from the economic benefits associated with *tino rangatiratanga*, while at the same time forced to deal with the consequences of increased levels of poverty and disadvantage.

The analysis developed herein raises two sets of more general issues for feminist analysts of globalization, neoliberalism, and welfare state restructuring. First, not only do we need to consider more carefully specific national experiences of welfare state restructuring, it is also necessary to be sensitive to different experiences within and between social groups. Certainly, accounts that assume the homogeneity of "New Zealand women" as an analytical category, then assess their experiences against those of men using national data, require careful consideration in the context of increasing class differences among women and their inflection by race/ethnicity. Second, we are alerted to the ever-present danger of writing a "globalisation script" (Gibson-Graham 1996), which, in the case of Aotearoa/New Zealand, would portray Maori, workers, and women as the hapless victims of global capital and its local agents. This discussion of the contradictory relationships between neoliberalism and *tino rangatiratanga* shows that the claims of so-called "social movements" are integral to the discourse of welfare state restructuring.

Inevitably welfare state restructuring in Aotearoa/New Zealand will continue to be shaped not only by neoliberalism, but also by the demands of those who have been historically marginalized. Among Maori, for example, there are growing tensions not only between so-called "winner" and "loser" *iwi*, but also between *iwi*-based organizations and pan-Maori organizations delivering social services to largely disenfranchised urban communities (see Maaka 1994; Webb 1998). Moreover, new challenges are emerging from other constituencies. As a consequence of changing migration policies, Aotearoa/New Zealand is a much more ethnically and culturally diverse place than it has been historically. There is growing recognition of the need for culturally appropriate service delivery for Pacific Island communities and debates around the possibilities of multilingual, multicultural service delivery will only increase as other ethnic communities develop their political voices. In this context the complex race, gender, and class outcomes of welfare state restructuring in Aotearoa/New Zealand will continue to require careful attention.

Chapter 10
Where to Next?

Against and Beyond Neoliberalism

Catherine Kingfisher

This book has been a study of neoliberalism, both in and of itself at an abstract level, and in terms of its articulations with other cultural formations in specific contexts. On the one hand, it is clear from the case study chapters that the neoliberal project of welfare reform in the United States, Canada, Britain, Australia, and Aotearoa/New Zealand is deeply problematic for poor single mothers. On the other hand, the case study chapters also indicate that neoliberalism does not travel uncontested; rather, its movement across cultural space is marked by struggle and contradiction. These contradictions and struggles provide entry points for intervention—for making visible and articulating alternative possibilities. In this concluding chapter, I explore some of these points of entry for undermining and moving beyond the neoliberal project of welfare reform.

I begin by reiterating a point made earlier. In Part I, I argued that, given the currency of neoliberal approaches to personhood, state, and market, it behooves us to analyze neoliberalism as a cultural system and to track its movement across cultural space. These twinned foci have allowed for an analysis of neoliberalism that recognizes its force without assuming its hegemony. Too often, as J. K. Gibson-Graham points out in reference to analyses of capitalism as a unified, singular totality, "the project of understanding the beast . . . itself produce[s] a beast" (Gibson-Graham 1996:1; cf. S. Hall 1997). A similar point may be made in relation to analyses of neoliberalism, often understood in relationship to capitalism (here, for instance, the relationship between possessive individualism and the free market has been stressed). In response to its current purchase, we are required to analyze it in detail. But if we do so according to a particular fashion that is restricted to uncovering its essences—its fundamental features—we risk creating it as something that is perhaps more powerful and all-encompassing than it really is, ignoring in the process its contradictions, fractures, partialities, contingencies, and both dialectics with and determinations by other social forces. The point may be made by substituting the word *capitalism* in the following quotation with *neoliberalism* or *globalization*—or any of their various permutations, such as "global neoliberalism" (DeMartino 1999: 343) or "neoliberal market civilization" (Gill 1995:399):

If capitalism takes up the available social space, there's no room for anything else. If capitalism cannot coexist, there's no possibility of anything else. If capitalism is large, other things appear small and inconsequential. If capitalism functions as a unity, it cannot be partially or locally replaced. (Gibson-Graham 1996: 263)

In other words, if we think of global capitalism/neoliberalism as already hegemonic, as an unstoppable all-penetrating force, we fail to see other realities, other possibilities. This is not to argue against Marxist theory per se so much as against a particular reading or usage of Marxist theory. Nor is it to argue that the neoliberal constructions of personhood and market explored in this collection are not dominant. They are, insofar as they inform popular thinking and policymaking in relation to poor single mothers in the national contexts explored here. But this does not mean that they are the only discourses in circulation, or that all other discourses are doomed to always be in subsumption to neoliberalism. In other words, because the forms of hybridity explored in the case study chapters lean toward the assimilationist end of Nederveen Pieterse's (1995:56–57) continuum of hybridities, this does not preclude them from ever becoming more destabilizing. This is why it is crucial to frame the preliminary grammar of neoliberalism outlined in Chapters 2 and 3 in terms of Comaroff and Comaroff's (1992) definition of culture as *contingent* and *contradictory*, the particular form of which at any given moment is the outcome of historical struggle, and consequently transient and only "partially unified by temporary fixings of meaning" (Gibson-Graham 1996:11; see also Rosaldo 1989). Neoliberal culture is neither unitary nor immutable, and it is always in interaction with other cultural formations or discourses, for example, discourses of communitarianism, or of interdependence. Similarly, globalization has here been theorized as hybridization—a process rather than a state of being: "if globalization is understood in terms of simultaneous, complexly related processes in the realms of economy, politics, culture, technology and so forth," argues Tomlinson (1999:16), "we can see that it involves all sorts of contradictions, resistances and countervailing forces." Again, globalization is not simply a process of homogenization, of an even and total ascendancy of neoliberal culture; rather, it is a process characterized by "profound unevenness" (S. Hall 1997:33). The metaphor of conversation referred to in Chapter 4 here becomes one of multiple, ongoing, and overlapping conversations.

Contradictions and Alternatives

Temporary fixings of meanings and processes of hybridization indicate that the contradictions generated by/within any specific cultural formation provide openings for counterhegemonic projects. Dominant discourses always exist alongside alternative or oppositional discourses that offer different imaginings of social life and organization. With this framework in mind, we can revisit the discussions of globalization, neoliberalism and welfare reform contained in this collection with an eye to contradiction and disjuncture.

At the most general level, neoliberalism constructs a worldview in which possessive individuals, enabled by a minimalist state, go about the business of maximizing outcomes by means of the free exchange of goods and services in a capitalist free market economy. What is omitted from this worldview is significant. Most obvious is the erasure of reproductive labor. This erasure highlights a tension between women's roles as mothers versus (paid) workers that is particularly problematic for poor single mothers who must struggle to meet the needs of their children while simultaneously undertaking employment that is often underpaid, temporary, casualized, or otherwise inadequate to their financial needs. The neoliberal valorization of the free market also serves to obfuscate other forms of economic production, most notably household production (in the same way that, as Gibson-Graham [1996] indicates, many left analyses of capitalism do). As pointed out in Chapter 3, this neoliberal erasure of entire chunks of productive and reproductive activity makes for an unstable system (McDowell 1991:412) that is heading toward "a crisis in social reproduction" (Brodie 1994:58; see also Elson 1994).

Susan Robertson is clear on this point with regard to Australia, where neoliberal conceptions of person and market seem to have gained ascendancy without a great deal of struggle. The problems generated by the contradictions of neoliberal reform, according to Robertson, go beyond those experienced by poor single mothers. Insofar as welfare-to-work measures are not accompanied by the creation of jobs, or by the institutionalization of measures to improve low-income women's positions within the labor market (by means of, e.g., comparable worth legislation), "the basis of the new social contract between the state and its citizens is . . . likely to collapse as the contradictions become more and more untenable." Increases in not only the feminization of poverty, but also in child poverty and in crime, may fuel a level of political unrest that the system can no longer assuage or contain. Lister implies a similar possibility when she refers to the contradiction in Britain between social policy, which encourages employment and thus would require the generation of jobs; and economic policy, which, in relation to a global economy, is not as concerned with creating jobs as with coping with the forces of economic competition.

Other contributors to this collection also point to contradictions in the neoliberal project. In her chapter on the United States, for instance, Goode underscores the disjuncture between PRWORA's ostensible goal of individual autonomy and independence on the one hand, and increased state surveillance on the other. The marriage of these opposing positions and actions is possible only in a situation in which welfare recipients are constituted as not-quite persons who require state surveillance in order to become complete persons, despite the neoliberal distaste for the state. This contradiction is also evident in Aotearoa/New Zealand and Canada, where "the central operating principle . . . is that it is up to families to look after their own and it is up to government to make sure that they do" (Brodie, this volume).

In addition to contradictions within neoliberalism itself, Goode, Brodie, Lister, and Larner refer to a number of contradictions that arise in the course of the articulation of neoliberalism with other cultural formations. Most notable in the U.S. context is the articulation of neoliberal discourses of individuality and neoconservative discourses of the family. There are clear contradictions between, on the one hand, workfare programs that treat poor single mothers as autonomous individuals, and, on the other, legislation that works to encourage heterosexual nuclear family formation complete with female dependence. In Britain, the tensions generated by the articulation of neoliberal, neoconservative, and "modern" discourses of family formation are evidenced in Prime Minister Blair's flip-flopping references to "families" versus "the family." There are also tensions in Britain between the discourses of single motherhood and child poverty, resulting in conflict between government efforts to both discourage single motherhood and protect poor single mothers' children from poverty: while supporting poor single mothers provides an undesired de facto legitimation of their status as single mothers, failure to provide support would contribute to unacceptable increases in child poverty. Finally, Lister points to the problematics of worker-citizenship in the face of increasing government emphasis on parental as opposed to state responsibility for the well-being and education of the young. Goode points to the same contradiction as it is experienced by U.S. women who must hold down more than one job to meet workfare requirements, which in turn limits their participation in the community and family activities so valorized by American "family values."

The problems thrown up in the course of neoliberalism's articulation with other cultural formations serve to highlight alternative political discourses that may ultimately challenge neoliberal hegemony. Thus the reconstitutions of personhood, market, and state generated by neoliberalism may themselves engender new social movements and forms of consciousness, particularly as they interact with other, already existing ideas. Goode's chapter, which outlines alternative explanations of poverty in circulation in the United States, is instructive in this regard. Explanations that focus on political economy, and on the poor as competent strategists, stand in opposition to "culture of poverty" explanations that emphasize individual (culture-related) deficits. These alternative discourses of economics and poverty provide real challenges to neoliberal discourse, especially insofar as they have had some historical currency in the United States, particularly during the Depression/post-Depression era. They also dovetail with and provide the context within which what Goode refers to as "alternative political subjects" may come into being. While poor women's activist consciousness and practice is clearly compromised by PRWORA, it has a long history in the United States, and has the potential to be reinvigorated, as evidenced by, for example, the Welfare Mothers Organizing Center in Milwaukee, Wisconsin, and the Welfare Mom web site.

Lister refers to somewhat similar counterhegemonic sentiments in Britain, specifically as expressed by poor single mothers themselves. In an on-the-ground study of lone mothers' experiences, for example, Duncan and Edwards (1999, cited in Lister, this volume) found that some women viewed lone motherhood as positive, insofar as it provides independence from demanding men. A number of lone mothers also challenged the dichotomy of mother versus worker, which is perhaps the key dichotomy underlying welfare reform debates.

In Canada, liberal progressivism and feminism, while clearly compromised by neoliberalism, have not disappeared. As Brodie notes, in 1999 the Supreme Court extended the legal recognition awarded to heterosexual common law relationships to same-sex relationships. While Brodie's emphasis is on the appropriation of this in order to deny benefits to same-sex couples in New Brunswick, we can also read the decision as evidence that neoliberalism has not been completely successful in its efforts to erase liberal progressivism's moral code or feminist sensibilities.

Finally, the existence of *tino rangatiratanga* indicates that neoliberal hegemony is also incomplete in Aotearoa/New Zealand. *Tino rangatiratanga* is about autonomy and self-sufficiency, both valorized in neoliberal discourse. However, *tino rangatiratanga* takes a different stance toward these phenomena. Specifically, it emphasizes the communal over the individual, and the joining of the economic, cultural, and social over their distinction. Although the discourse of *tino rangatiratanga* contributed to the demise of Keynesianism in Aotearoa/New Zealand, it is also fundamentally different from the discourse of neoliberalism; and its currency, however weakened or compromised under a neoliberal regime, provides an alternative vision of what society could or should be like.

In sum, the chapters in this volume indicate both that neoliberalism itself contains contradictions that may lead (following a Marxist train of thought) to its own demise and that the articulation of neoliberalism with other discourses provides possibilities for alternative political thought and action. How these possibilities may be realized is the focus of the remainder of this chapter.

Practicalities: Above, Below, and at the Level of the Nation-State

"Think globally, act locally" has become a mainstay slogan of grassroots activist (particularly environmentalist) discourses and practices. Local action on issues related to welfare reform has certainly not been wanting in the countries discussed in this collection. For example, in addition to the U.S. groups mentioned above:

- In 1995 the Québec Federation of Women organized a Bread and Roses March Against Poverty that was successful in pressuring the government to increase the minimum wage and institute new legislation for child-support deductions.
- The National Association of Women and the Law is currently (as of December 2001) petitioning the Supreme Court of Canada in *Gosselin vs. Québec*, in which Louise Gosselin claims that the government of Québec's workfare stipulations violate her right to equality under the Canadian Charter of Rights and Freedoms.
- The Communities with a Conscious campaign, organized by the Auckland District Council of Social Services in Aotearoa/New Zealand, has received 110 pledges from organizations opposed to workfare. Pledging organizations range from Maori and women's groups to the more conventional branches of the Salvation Army.
- The Bristol Benefits Action Group in Britain is involved, on an ongoing basis, in actions designed to challenge Tony Blair's New Deal, including a 2000 protest that turned "employment zones" into "enjoyment zones."
- The Victoria Welfare Rights Unit in Australia works to both advocate on behalf of the poor and provide individual beneficiaries with information and support.

These examples, representing just the tip of the iceberg, indicate that local action is alive and well. In addition, however, I want to signal the importance of thinking in terms of two alternative versions of "think globally, act locally": *think locally, act globally,* and *think and act locally and globally.* Specifically, I want to build on Jan Nederveen Pieterse's (1997: 87) claim that we need to create linkages, forge articulations, and combine "local empowerment and global reform."

Insofar as globalization has fundamentally altered the sovereignty of nation-states, "Membership in nation-states ceases to be the only ground for the realization of rights" (Sassen 1998:95). Globalization, in Sassen's words, has created "new operational and formal openings for the participation of nonstate actors and subjects" (1998:94). A variety of international human rights related legal codes and instruments serve to undermine state sovereignty over citizens by focusing on persons rather than on citizens (where citizenship is determined by nation-states but humanity/personhood is transnational, or universal). Thus, while "grounded in interstate agreements," and thus dependent on the nation-state, these codes and instruments are now "partly independent of the states themselves" (Sassen 1996a:92), allowing groups and, in some cases, individuals to operate above the head of the state.

The possibility of going above the level of the state is crucial. According to Paul Hunt (1996:10), "international standards and procedures relating to social rights have a special importance because most states lack national social rights norms and mechanisms." The International Covenant on Economic, Social, and Cultural Rights (ICESCR) and the Convention on the Elimination of All Forms of Discrimination Against Women (CEDAW) provide two examples of already existing resources available for the assertion of social rights. Several articles of the ICESCR are particularly relevant to welfare state restructuring. Most salient at a general level is article 11, which asserts that "The States to the present Covenant recognize the right of everyone to an adequate standard of living for himself [*sic*] and his family, including adequate food, clothing and housing, and to the continuous improvement in living conditions" (UNICESCR 1966). In addition to this general assertion, the ICESCR contains articles that speak directly to the rise of welfare-to-work schemes discussed in this volume. Article 6, for instance, states that:

1. The States Parties to the present Covenant recognize the right to work, which includes the right of everyone to the opportunity to gain his [*sic*] living by work which he freely chooses or accepts, and will take appropriate steps to safeguard this right.
2. The steps to be taken by a State Party to the present Covenant to achieve the full realization of this right shall include technical and vocational guid-

ance and training programmes, policies and techniques to achieve steady economic, social and cultural development and full and productive employment under conditions safeguarding fundamental political and economic freedoms to the individual. (UNICESCR 1966)

Workfare programs clearly violate the provision that work be freely chosen or accepted, while the implementation of welfare-to-work programs in the context of high unemployment flies in the face of "full and productive employment." In addition, article 7, which stipulates "favourable conditions of work," including "fair wages and equal remuneration for work of equal value without distinction of any kind, in particular women being guaranteed conditions of work not inferior to those enjoyed by men, with equal pay for equal work" (UNICESCR 1966), is also violated when workfare schemes are instituted under conditions of occupational segregation.[1]

While there is currently no mechanism in place for the Committee on Economic, Social, and Cultural Rights (CESCR) to hear complaints put forth by individuals, there are mechanisms in place for the participation of nongovernmental organizations (NGOs). NGO participation to date, however, has been minimal (Hunt 1996:23), thus signaling that the ICESCR is an as yet underutilized resource (see also Appadurai 2000). Canada, Britain, Australia and Aotearoa/New Zealand are all signatories to the ICESCR (the United States is the one exception). Welfare rights groups in any of these countries could thus potentially make use of this resource. It is a resource that could be used to buttress some of the developments Joanna Kerr (1996) claims are necessary to counteract the negative impacts of globalization, in particular, those related to labor organizing and the regulation of work standards. (However, while NGO participation in CESCR deliberations has been minimal, welfare rights groups have made appeals to international agreements. The Poor People's World Summit to End Poverty, held in New York in November 2000, for example, made reference to the Universal Declaration of Human Rights [UDHR], and in particular, for the present purposes, to article 25, which refers to the right to an adequate standard of living, including food, clothing, housing, medical care, and social services. Significantly, the summit, sponsored by the Poor People's Economic Human Rights Campaign and the International Campaign for Economic Justice and hosted by the Kensington Welfare Rights Union, had as a deliberate goal the establishment of global frameworks for collaborative action. They illustrate, perhaps, Gills's [2000:3] claim that "the paradox of neoliberal economic globalization is that it both weakens and simultaneously activates the social forces of resistance.")

Nancy Fraser's (1997) vision of a Universal Caregiver model of welfare dovetails with some of the articles of the ICESCR, indicating where counterhegemonic thinking may take advantage of already existing structures and resources. Fraser's model combines what she refers to as the Universal Breadwinner model, most popular in North America, which claims that the road to women's emancipation lies in women's engagement in paid labor; and the Caregiver Parity model, most popular in Europe, which assumes that the road to women's emancipation involves supporting informal carework, that is, unpaid domestic reproductive work, usually performed by women. Fraser evaluates these two models on the basis of seven criteria which combine emphases on equality and difference, the two standard feminist measuring sticks of gender equity. The seven criteria are the antipoverty principle, the antiexploitation principle, the income-equality principle, the leisure-time equality principle, the equality-of-respect principle, the antimarginalization principle, and the antiandrocentrism principle. When evaluated in terms of these principles, both the Universal Breadwinner and Caregiver Parity models fall short, with the Universal Breadwinner model suffering from "workerism," and the Caregiver Parity model suffering from "domestic privatism" (Fraser 1997:62). The Universal Caregiver model, in contrast, jettisons the worst while combining the best elements of both. Specifically, the model works to dismantle the "gendered opposition between breadwinning and caregiving" by making "women's current life-patterns the norm for everyone"; it entails men's participation in caregiving and the redesign of institutional life to "eliminate the difficulty and strain" of balancing paid labor with caregiving (Fraser 1997:61). Requiring nothing less than the deconstruction and reconstruction of the current gender order, the Universal Caregiver welfare state would look something like the following:

Unlike Caregiver Parity, its employment sector would not be divided into two different tracks; all jobs would be designed for workers who are caregivers, too; all would have a shorter workweek than full-time jobs have now; and all would have the support of employment-enabling services. Unlike Universal Breadwinner, however, employees would not be assumed to shift all carework to social services. Some informal carework would be publicly supported and integrated on a par with paid work in a single social-insurance system. Some would be performed in households by relatives and friends, but such households would not necessarily be heterosexual nuclear families. Other supported carework would be located outside households altogether—in civil society. In state-funded but locally organized institutions, childless adults, older people, and others without kin-based responsibilities would join parents and others in democratic, self-managed carework activities. (Fraser 1997:61)

Seemingly utopian, the Universal Caregiver model, and Fraser's normative principles for the evaluation of gender equity, fit the articles of the

ICESCR referred to above. While the ICESCR does not advocate the deconstruction of gender, compliance with the articles could be best met—perhaps *only* met, in their entirety—by such a deconstruction. And such a deconstruction would, in turn, point to the shortcomings of the ICESCR, for example, with regard to article 7, which constitutes work narrowly as paid employment (Hunt 1996:105).

A major strength of the ICESCR is that it leans in the direction of substantive, as opposed to simply formal, equality—in the direction of equality of outcome rather than an official "equality of opportunity" that ignores historical and structural differences between groups by assuming a level playing field (Hunt 1996:88–89). The Convention on the Elimination of all Forms of Discrimination Against Women, ratified by 140 states as of 1995, focuses even more directly on substantive equality, going so far as to recommend affirmative action programs as one means of accomplishing de facto equality (Hunt 1996:91–95). Robertson accordingly refers in her chapter to CEDAW's criticism of Australia in its 1997 report. The current claim of neoliberal pundits in Australia that work is "a more equitable means of distribution" than the state provides a kind of formal equality that in fact undermines substantive equality. Lister similarly points in her chapter to New Labour's emphasis on (formal) equality of opportunity, as opposed to an "Old Labour" emphasis on "equality and redistribution through the tax-benefit system."

Although not explicitly stated as such, the goal of Fraser's thought experiment is clearly substantive equality—the emphasis on which provides one mechanism for transcending the gender equality/difference impasse. The distinction between formal and substantive equality is clearly evident in the case of neoliberal welfare reform that treats women as possessive individuals. While women's self-possession is a positive thing, viewing poor single mothers as individuals is problematic when their carework is elided. Poor single mothers are *not* on a level playing field with others who do not have childcare responsibilities. To declare them as such and expect them to behave accordingly provides a very superficial form of formal equality that in fact works against the accomplishment of substantive equality. This underscores Fraser's point that it is not enough to treat women like men. Differences from men also have to be acknowledged—but in a way that does not lead to "domestic privatism."

ICESCR and CEDAW, then, provide foundations for a welfare system that is considerably more equitable than the welfare regimes analyzed in this collection, in terms of both where they have been and where they seem to be going. Again, they are *already existing* resources, and their existence indicates that there is some international will in the right direction. NGOs and grassroots activists can use these tools. Thus working "below" the level of the state is wedded to operating "above" it. The campaign against the Multilateral Agreement on Investment (MAI), in which the Internet was instrumental, provides a good example of successful below-and-above articulation (Drohan 1998). The Workfare-FIGHT web site, which provides links to organizations and events in over fourteen countries, serves as a potential mechanism for precisely this kind of below-and-above articulation in relation to welfare state restructuring.

Indeed, it is often the case that work below and above the level of the state is targeted, by necessity, *at* the state. Both ICESCR and CEDAW depend on individual states for implementation of their provisions. In the end, as Cecelia Lynch (1998:164) points out, "a return to the state is in all probability necessary to meet the dislocations and poverty generated by the latest round of globalization. For it is not the United Nations, nor in most cases local communities, that can or will provide the social safety net and guarantees to fair remuneration necessary and adequate to social welfare at the turn of the millennium." International instruments such as ICESCR and CEDAW provide launching points for such local/national action.

Furthermore, insofar as economic globalization requires the nation-state, so the nation-state has some say over economic forces. Thus we need to think globally and locally/nationally and act globally and locally/nationally. Pointing to multilateral environmental agreements, which, despite their less than remarkable actual effectiveness nevertheless "create a framework that legitimates both the international pursuit of a common good and the role of national states in that pursuit," Sassen (1996: 56–57) argues that:

> In the longer term, it is more likely that stronger legal regimes will develop globally if the global issues involved have a national regulatory counterpart. Even when such regulatory approaches use the market as a tool for compliance, they can strengthen both the rule of law (nationally and globally) and accountability. The participation of national states in new international legal regimes of this sort may contribute to the development of transnational frameworks aimed at promoting greater equity.

Unfortunately, while social and moral considerations relating to issues like poverty, exclusion, and compassion are weighty, by themselves they "probably do not provide a broad enough basis and coalition for [global] reform" (Nederveen Pieterse 1997:90). Certainly the cause of poor single mothers does not seem to hold as much purchase as do issues related to the environment or indigenous peoples—two areas often cited as success cases in discussions of transnational coalitions and social movements—because they do not hold the same popular appeal as do the environment or indigeneity. Rather, poor single mothers seem to have been vilified not only in policy arenas, but also in mainstream public discourse. The category of the deserving poor has been increasingly narrowed to include fewer and fewer groups of people. As Brodie points out in her chapter in this volume, children now comprise one of the last categories of the deserving poor in Canada—one of the last groups that is not deemed to be responsible for its own poverty. Poor single motherhood (or poor children *coupled* with, rather than in isolation from, their [primarily female] caretakers) thus provides a questionable basis for widespread political mobilization. Rather, according to Nederveen Pieterse, "the major grounds for global reform probably fall under the rubrics of threat and opportunity," under which financial threats must be included. He states that "[t]he neoliberal regime may be in the short-term interest of larger corporations but involves growing risks arising from market failure" (1997:90). Discursively tapping into these risks may provide another avenue for remedy if appeals on the basis of rights discourse prove less than effective. Again, Nederveen Pieterse: "The structure of rights which corporations require in order to operate globally must be devised to include social rights, *not merely on the grounds of social justice but also on the grounds of social productivity*" (90, emphasis added). In other words, the most useful and productive discourses for opponents of dominant discourses are the dominant discourses themselves, simply by virtue of their dominant (and therefore appealing) status. Larner underscores the importance of the strategic use of dominant discourses in her chapter in this volume, with particular reference to Te Ohu Whakatupu, the Maori Policy Unit of the Ministry of Women's Affairs, which has deployed discourses of efficiency and effectiveness, rather than of feminism or social justice, to advance its causes (see Tahi 1995; see also Kerr 1996). In this sense, it becomes potentially beneficial to "set forth a global politics of inclusion in which the language of the market meets with the aims of human and social development" (Nederveen Pieterse 1997:91).

Conclusions

Globalization as connectivity provides mechanisms for the travel of ideas across cultural space, but in the process of their movement traveling ideas are subject to transformation. This collection has explored the travel of neoliberal approaches to constructing the world and has outlined both striking parallels and points of difference in the processes of welfare state restructuring in the United States, Canada, Britain, Australia, and Aotearoa/New Zealand. The similarities are at first glance overwhelming, but, as I have tried to stress in this chapter, global corridors of flow provide openings for a variety of possibilities. Reflexivity as a key feature of globalization—that is, awareness of "the world as a whole" (R. Robertson 1992:8)—offers an additional resource. "Connectivity," as Tomlinson puts it, "furnishes people with a cultural resource that they lacked before its expansion: a cultural awareness which is, in various senses, 'global'. . . '[T]he global' increasingly exists as a cultural horizon within which we (to varying degrees) frame our existence." Such connectivity provides a potential basis for "new forms of cultural/political alliance and solidarity" (Tomlinson 1999:30). This collection represents one effort to increase awareness of global patterns and of responses to those patterns. And, as I have outlined in this chapter, structures and discourses already exist that may be appropriated, modified, or otherwise used to move beyond critiques of neoliberalism to the construction of positive alternative possibilities (Nederveen Pieterse 1997:82, 84).

Brodie points out in her chapter in this volume that philosophies of governance take on the aura of "common sense." In this regard they comprise invisible cultures (Philips 1993), whose members are unaware of their constructed nature and, therefore, of their taken-for-granted assumptions. The essence of "common sense" is not only that it is reasonable, but also that it is "natural," normal, and inevitable. The fact that a particular system of "common sense" is only one among a vast array of possibilities is erased. In exploring how neoliberal culture is constructed, the contributors to this volume have endeavored to denaturalize it, and in so doing create openings for recognizing already existing alternative visions of personhood, production, reproduction, value, community, and citizenship and for thinking about how to construct new ones. As such, this collection represents one intervention in neoliberal "common sense."

Notes

Chapter 1. Introduction: The Global Feminization of Poverty

1. This is not to argue that the shift to neoliberal governance is only or purely negative for all people, or that it has the same impact on all women everywhere. Neoliberal discourses and practices generate winners as well as losers and affect women of different classes, races, ethnicities, and nationalities differently. The focus here is specifically on those women who stand to lose, rather than gain, from this shift in governance.

2. It is in relation to poor women in particular that the identities of mother and dependent housewife take on negative salience. In relation to wealthier classes of women, these roles continue to be valorized, if not romanticized.

3. Structural adjustment refers to a range of economic reforms, including cuts in public sector expenditure, designed to reduce the role of the state in favor of the market (see Connelly 1996).

4. By *poor single mother* I am referring to women who qualify for public assistance on the basis of single parenthood and low income, with the recognition that the details of such qualification are contextually variable.

5. The distinction between discourse and practice is problematic, insofar as discourse is a form of practice. I use both terms here to signal that material phenomenon, e.g., poverty rates, and the implementation of specific poverty-related policies are situated within particular systems of knowledge and meaning, that is, discourses. As Norman Fairclough (1992:64) states, "Discourse contributes to the constitution of all those dimensions of social structure which directly or indirectly shape and constrain it: its own norms and conventions, as well as the relations, identities and institutions which lie behind them. Discourse is a practice not just of representing the world, but of signifying the world, constituting and constructing the world in meaning."

6. There is some debate concerning the statistical bases of claims regarding the feminization of poverty, particularly in relation to assertions that, for instance, "70 percent of the world's poor are women" (UNDP 1995:iii, cited in Marcoux 1997:1). While comprehensive data are clearly difficult to come by, the existence of debates about the exact nature of gender poverty ratios does not mean that the feminization of poverty is not a real phenomenon—it just means that we do not fully understand the nature of the problem. As Alain Marcoux states, "That the gender bias in poverty does not reach the very high levels some-

times attributed to it does not mean that the bias is not real or not growing. Indeed, it seems to be both, although very unequally across countries and places" (1997:5). Audrey Rowe claims in this regard that "the extent of poverty among women is underestimated" (1991:75).

7. Orloff states in this regard that "An accurate picture of the content and effects of state social provision should not begin from the premise of a gender-neutral citizenship. Rather, one must take account of the very real gender differences in productive and reproductive labor and access to civil and political rights and how these differences influence the ways in which men and women struggle for and claim benefits from the state as citizens" (1993:309).

8. As Orloff states, "relations of domination based on control of women's bodies in the family, the workplace, and public spaces undermine women's abilities to participate as 'independent individuals'—citizens—in the polity, which in turn affect their capacities to demand and utilize social rights" (Orloff 1993:309).

9. Child poverty has become a major rallying point for both governmental and nongovernmental organizations in many nation-states. It seems to me that while child poverty is an increasing problem clearly deserving of concerted and urgent attention, the current focus on child poverty is myopic insofar as it serves to separate poor children from the contexts within which they are poor and which generate their poverty. Any focus on child poverty that excludes consideration of who cares for children will necessarily lead to failure. This myopic and ultimately doomed approach to poverty reflects the fact that children are among the last of the "deserving" poor, a category within which their mothers are clearly no longer included. Janine Brodie (this volume) makes a similar point.

10. The problematic nature of the local/global binary is discussed in Chapter 4.

Chapter 2. Neoliberalism I: Discourses of Personhood and Welfare Reform

Earlier versions of portions of this chapter appeared in Kingfisher (1999, 2001) and Kingfisher and Goldsmith (2001).

1. The Comaroffs provide an overview of what they see as key themes of neoliberal culture in their Introduction to the *Public Culture* Special Issue on Neoliberalism and Capitalism at the Millennium (Comaroff and Comaroff 2000).

2. By "natural" Smith means two things: first, the masking of the social and historical as "natural" (e.g., liberal bourgeois society); and second, a particular construction of "nature" as opposed to "culture," "society," or "civilization."

3. Robert Bellah and his colleagues, for instance, refer to various traditions of western individualism, including not only modern individualism, but also biblical/Christian, republican, and mythic individualism (Bellah et al. 1985).

4. For Weber, according to Friedman (1994:215), "the emergence of the modern self-controlled individual with an internally driven goal orientation or perhaps 'achievement motivation' is a cornerstone of the 'spirit of capitalism' in which the Protestant Reformation played a crucial role."

5. La Fontaine states further: "The institutions which reflect the idea of the (individualist) person are established and maintained by a society organised on the rule of law, the state in which persons are citizens. In such a society all members, even rulers are, ideally, subject to the law. As Weber pointed out long

ago, this principle is the defining characteristic of bureaucratic organisation. The main features of such structures are: a clear distinction between office and office-holder, and hence between an individual and his [*sic*] social role, and the allocation of authority on the basis of fitness for office, fitness being of course a quality of individuals. The equality of persons and competition for office are thus integral to the structure of Western society. Hierarchy and inequality are conceptualised as attributes of social roles; all individuals are equal as persons" (1985:137).

6. See also Shweder and Bourne (1984) who refer to egocentric versus socio-centric selves, and Marsella (1985), who distinguishes between individuated and unindividuated persons (see Spiro 1993 for further discussion of these binaries).

7. As Rouse (1995:358) states in reference to Mexican immigrants to the United States, "People may lose established identities, have difficulty in getting their claims to particular identities socially acknowledged, and find themselves obliged to operate, publicly at least, in terms of the identities ascribed to them by others." "From this perspective," he continues, "personhood is best understood in terms of people's chronic efforts to acquire and maintain possession of properties that they value."

8. Macpherson's pronoun usage ("his," "himself," "he") is, in fact, appropriate, in a specific rather than generic sense.

9. As Pateman summarizes it, "The patriarchal division between public and private is also a sexual division. Women, naturally lacking the capacities for public participation, remain within an association constituted by love, ties of blood, natural subjection and particularity, and in which they are governed by men. The public world of universal citizenship is an association of free and equal individuals, a sphere of property, rights and contract—and of men, who interact as formally equal citizens" (1989:183). "Sexual difference," in other words, "what it is to be a 'man' or 'woman,' and the construction of sexual difference as political difference, is central to civil society" (1988:16).

10. What constitutes workfare varies according to country. Most generally, workfare requires that welfare recipients engage in some form of recognized "work" (which does *not* include parenting) in exchange for their benefits. Activities designated as work may include formal discussions with welfare bureaucrats about future work plans or possibilities, education/training, active employment searches, volunteer work, or paid employment.

Chapter 3. Neoliberalism II: The Global Free Market

Earlier versions of portions of this chapter appeared in Kingfisher (1999, 2000) and Kingfisher and Goldsmith (2001).

1. See Gans (1972) who outlines the functions of poverty for the nonpoor.

2. Interest groups were no doubt pivotal in the formation of the welfare state, but it might be useful in this context to situate state responses to interest groups within the parameters of bipolarism.

3. Here I refer to the feminization of labor as a process that includes not only women's increased participation in paid labor, but also the "feminization" (e.g., casualization) of jobs held by men. See McDowell (1991) for detailed discussion.

4. Appadurai uses the suffix *scape* to index several features of landscapes. The first is their irregular shape. The second is that they "are not objectively given relations that look the same from every angle of vision but, rather . . . they are

deeply perspectival constructs" (1996a:33). Finally, the relationship among *scapes* "is deeply disjunctive and profoundly unpredictable because each of these landscapes is subject to its own constraints and incentives . . . at the same time as each acts as a constraint and a parameter for movements in the others" (1996a:35).

5. Ironically, however, the state plays a pivotal role in this process. See below and Part II.

6. Marx's analysis of capitalism as inherently expansive and Weber's analysis of bureaucratic rationalization as a culture spreading across Europe indicate that theories of what we now refer to as globalization are not new. In fact, not only have trade and other forms of exchange been taking place between various entities from time immemorial, but those entities, as they took the shape of nation-states, were integral to the continued process of globalization.

7. Sjolander also puts it well: "Globalization brings with it the internationalization of the state and the (globalized) diffusion of a neoliberal ideology, which increasingly constrains parties of the right and left to adopt similar political agendas, although their rhetoric may differ. States are relegated to the role of facilitators in the adaptation of the national economy to the new realities of emerging international economic structures, that is, to creating the policy environment, both nationally and internationally, which favours the globalization of production and service industries. Policy-makers blame difficult political choices on their lack of choice, citing the foreclosure of options born of the pressures of globalization" (1996:608–9).

8. These examples are taken from Kingfisher (1999) and Kingfisher and Goldsmith (2001).

9. I borrow from Peace (1998:7), who coined the phrase "poor bodies" "to keep the corporeality of 'the poor' clearly in mind."

10. Paradoxically, this internal/domestic differentiation may coexist with what is also deemed to be the inherent homogenization of globalism. See Chapter 4 for further discussion.

11. Here Sassen is referring not only to the political power of the state, but also to the political power of nonstate actors. See Chapter 10 for further discussion.

12. Other generators of global linkages cited by Robertson include the multiplication of interstate connections; the hegemony of the idea of the nation-state; and recognition that we are all part of humanity rather than members of groups fragmented along lines of gender, race, and so on. Robertson's emphasis on the centrality of the nation-state and the idea of humanity, however, needs to be juxtaposed with Hall's (1997) claims that just as the nation-state is under attack so it attempts to entrench itself further, and that globalization brings with it increasing fragmentation along lines of gender, race, etc. In this particular context, Robertson perhaps overemphasizes the idea of homogenization. See Chapter 4 for further discussion of homogeneity and heterogeneity.

13. This example is taken from Kingfisher (1999).

14. Ong (1999) is, in fact, one of Appadurai's critics. Here, however, I am using Ong and Appadurai as complementary, rather than as oppositional.

15. This is not to argue that gender has not been crucial in other eras of globalization. Mies (1986), for instance, discusses the centrality of gender to what she refers to as the old and new international divisions of labor. Hall (1997) similarly refers to the gendered nature of labor power in reference to what he views as older and newer forms, or eras, of globalization.

16. Although Sassen focuses her analysis on global cities, the case study chapters in Part II of this book are situated at the national level. Nor can we ignore

other territorialities of globalization, e.g., small towns and rural areas. My apologies, therefore, to Sassen for taking her work out of territorial context.

17. Sassen distinguishes between high finance services and low-value-added (female dominated) services. It is not clear whether Sjolander makes this distinction, although she seems to be referring for the most part to the latter.

18. The French Regulation School, best represented by the work of Aglietta (1979, 1982), analyzes regimes of accumulation not only in terms of strictly economic processes, but also in relation to state and social regulation of various spheres of life that contribute to the success of particular regimes.

19. The father representing capital, and the sons representing individual men/husbands.

20. Recognizing the conspiracy theory features of such an argument, one could speculate that welfare state restructuring is part and parcel of a strategy to make women more available as a source of cheap labor. Indeed, I make this point elsewhere in relation to the U.S. Family Support Act of 1988 (Kingfisher 1996). The problem, of course, is that the jobs are often not available. In a 1997 speech for instance, President Clinton claimed that approximately one million new jobs would have to be generated in the course of four years in order to make the 1996 welfare reform act successful (President Clinton, Sixth Annual Business Enterprise Awards Luncheon 1997).

21. In her discussion of the differential impact of poverty on girls and boys in the urban United States, Susser states: "Poor boys find themselves recruited into the illegal and frequently fatally attractive world of the drug trade in order to fulfill expectations of providing income for extremely needy households. In other words, from a young age, as fathers may disappear . . . boys in poor households are expected to and try to live up to the male role of provider, often in terms of leaving school and taking low-paying jobs (MacLeod 1987). Poor girls are more likely to be kept home busy with domestic tasks and channeled into schooling. They are less likely to be drawn into the competitive and dangerous territory of drug dealing and more likely to survive (Sharff 1987). As the rules change, and mothers receive even less support, the minimal protections currently experienced by girls from infancy may disappear, and girls will be drawn into some of the homicidal situations currently experienced by young boys" (Susser 1997:399).

22. Reprivatization refers institutionally to "initiatives aimed at dismantling or cutting back social-welfare services, selling off nationalized assets, and/or deregulating 'private' enterprise," and discursively to depoliticization (Fraser 1989:172).

23. This is not a position I am advocating, but rather reflects normative models of adulthood.

Chapter 4. Globalization as Hybridity

1. The metaphor of conversation suffers the same shortcoming, insofar as it posits separate parties to the conversation—unless, of course, we venture into the psychoanalytic territory of inner conversation with the self, in which one aspect of my self, say, the academic, converses with another, say, the mother—both of which are nevertheless still part of my self, and cannot be separated from each other. The problems of generalizing from the individual to social systems, however, are well known, so this is perhaps best left as food for thought.

2. See Collier and Yanagisako (1989) for an enlightening feminist anthropological attempt to grapple with the western penchant for binaries.

Chapter 5. From New Deal to Bad Deal: Racial and Political Implications of U.S. Welfare Reform

I am greatly indebted to Jeff Maskovsky and Susan Hyatt with whom I have been collaborating on several projects relating to poverty in the United States. Their insights and knowledge have been very important in the development of my thinking about these issues. However, they are not to blame for any fault with my arguments or conclusions. Thanks also to Catherine Kingfisher for her thoughtful and careful advice.

1. The law included sanctions to encourage states to put women to work as soon as possible. It limited the receipt of cash payments to two years at a time with a five-year lifetime limit and removed the exemption for pregnant women or mothers of handicapped children. It limited the standard exemption from work to mothers of infants only (one year or less), significantly lowering the former age limit.

2. Public education is an exception. Public education has been dominant in the United States but recent campaigns for privatization may change this. In the meantime, the number of people who have no health insurance keeps on rising.

3. ADC, which initially supported only children through their mothers, extended benefits to mothers in 1950 and to whole families in 1961, when it was renamed Aid to Families with Dependent Children.

4. For example, women's eligibility as mothers was monitored by social workers using state standards for "suitable homes." State workers also searched for instances of men in the household which made the household ineligible for aid.

5. Lewis's research career was oriented to the developing world. He was not really interested in U.S. social policy and paid very little attention to poverty in the United States.

6. Head Start provides intensive preschool preparation to children from "disadvantaged" homes.

7. In spite of the wrongheaded assumptions underlying Head Start legislation, the program, by giving children extra educational resources, has been extremely successful in relation to educational outcomes.

8. The Public Service Employment component of CETA was especially important in providing meaningful work. That, along with the Public Employment Program (1971–73) was the first public sector job creation effort since the New Deal (Morgen and Weigt 2001).

9. Institutions such as the World Bank and International Monetary Fund grew up as part of the implementation of the postwar Bretton Woods agreement and are now responsible for fiscal and monetary policy affecting the majority of developing nations.

10. These activities involve a variety of forms including legally recognized firms which violate labor laws, clandestine underground sweatshops, and those which rely on cottage industry or women's piecework at home.

11. In 1965, the passage of the first major immigration law since the anti-immigrant laws of the 1920s ushered in a new era of immigration. The new legislation removed the former quotas that had privileged immigrants from north-

ern Europe. The annual flows of new immigrants from all continents now equals those of the major waves in the late nineteenth and early twentieth centuries.

12. The most virulent nativism was displayed in the campaign for Proposition 187 in 1994 in California which severely impinged on the rights of immigrants to social services.

13. Sanford Schram (2000) argues that the poor replaced the Soviet bloc as an internal scapegoat in the post-Cold War era.

14. Wilson was doing his studies in the 1980s during the time when a major expansion of the drug economy was having strong destabilizing effects.

15. Both authors received prepublication publicity in magazines and radio interview shows, for example, Anderson (1996). These formats encouraged anecdotes about and descriptions of sexuality and violence.

16. Households with men were ineligible for most income support and for Medicaid (Stack 1974).

17. For example, of 246 witnesses, only one had experience as a welfare recipient and another was a single mother. Only five individuals would themselves be directly or indirectly affected by the new law. Most testimony came from the business community, public sector administrators, politicians, and advocates (Naples 1997: 917).

18. Defining work and work preparation was left up to each state.

19. Twenty states (40 percent) chose to have lifetime limits shorter than five years (Hayward 1998).

20. The new names for state welfare programs, from Wisconsin Works, Cal-WORKS, and Oregon's Jobs Plus to Tennessee's Families First and Colorado's welfare offices renamed Family Independence Centers, demonstrate an ambivalence over stressing work or family.

21. In addition, states varied in their rules regarding how many infractions and which kinds of infractions warranted removal from the welfare rolls. Some removed a whole family for one individual's violation while others only removed the person who had broken a rule. Some states dropped people for one violation while others allowed many. The fact that states had license to be more punitive than the federal mandates created some of the most unfair consequences of the new law.

22. The top fifteen states in terms of percentage reductions in the first year of the law range from Wyoming and Wisconsin (59 and 42 percent respectively) through five states with 30 to 35 percent reductions and eight with 25 to 29 percent reductions (U.S. Department of Health and Human Services 1999).

23. An analysis of state-specific studies shows that between 20 and 50 percent of those who initially found jobs lost them in less than a year (Brauner and Loprest 1999). Other studies found economic hardship (Coulton et al. 1999) and loss of health insurance (Jencks and Swingle 2000) among those employed.

24. For example, see the report *A Call to Civil Society* published by the Council on Civil Society in 1998 and the report of the National Commission on Civic Renewal of the same year.

25. The segment called "Project STRIVE" (Support and Training Result in Valuable Employment) was broadcast on *60 Minutes*, CBS, October 17, 1999.

26. The project was described as now undertaking presumably lucrative training contracts with cities all over the country to train others in their methods.

27. Incentives to employers vary in different states but make this labor very inexpensive. They often include both indirect (tax relief) as well as direct payment for wage subsidies.

Chapter 7. The Responsible Citizen:
Creating a New British Welfare Contract

1. The latest figures suggest a fall back to about three-fifths by the late 1990s.

2. The 1999 introduction of a minimum wage, even though at a lower rate than campaigned for by trade unions and others, has, however, improved the wages of the lowest paid female workers.

3. It should also be noted that women's poverty is underrecorded because the estimates of poverty are based on the income of the couple, thereby ignoring inequalities in the distribution of resources between partners as revealed by a number of studies.

4. This is the first time a government has published an official statement of family policy in the United Kingdom.

5. The Child Support Act replaced existing maintenance arrangements which were operated by the courts with a legally determined formula to be operated by an executive agency of government, the Child Support Agency. Following a White Paper in 1990, which set out the proposals, the act was implemented in 1993. For more information, see, for instance, Garnham and Knights (1994); Lister (1994); Clarke, Craig, and Glendinning (1996); Millar (1996a, b); Barnes, Day, and Cronin (1998).

6. This lack of support stands in contrast to that for the Australian scheme on which it was partially modeled, but, whereas in Australia there was a greater commitment to improving lone parent families' incomes, in Britain the primary motivation was to save money (Millar and Whiteford 1993; Millar 1996a, b).

7. Research suggests that this largely a myth (Kempson 1996:96).

8. For a critique of the debate around the cuts, see S. B. Smith (1999).

9. The House of Commons Select Committee on Education and Employment warned in its Seventh Report for 1998–99 of the dangers of lone parents moving into low paid, unskilled jobs with no prospect of progression. They therefore recommended that the New Deal for lone parents should place more emphasis on education and training to improve employability and less on quick job placement. The changes in the 2000 budget go some way to meeting these concerns but do not address the key problem for lone mothers who want to undertake education or training, namely childcare.

10. Legislation is now planned under which parents could face up to three months in jail for failing to make truanting children attend school (*The Guardian*, March 17, 2000).

11. See, for instance, the report of the Commission on Social Justice (1994) established by the late John Smith, when leader of the Labour Party.

12. The Women's Unit is typical of initiatives designed to cut across departmental boundaries. Other important examples are the Social Exclusion Unit, charged with producing "joined up solutions" to discrete problems of social exclusion and the Sure Start program, designed to target support on children's early years, especially in the areas of greatest need.

Chapter 8. Paradoxes in "Paradise": The Changing Politics
of Women, Welfare, and Work in Australia

1. Laborism refers to a consensus in Australian politics where economic and social development must rest upon the foundations of support from both orga-

nized labor and capital about the preeminence of wage labor and the second order or residual character of welfare as a source of income and social security. Thus, while laborism resisted the least palatable aspects of capitalism, it nonetheless accepted the fact of capitalism. Reforms and campaigns for social justice would take place within the framework of economic power embodied in the distribution and ownership of land, capital, and industrial technique (see Beilhartz, Considine, and Watts 1992).

2. The Accord was a bipartite agreement between the Australian Labour Party (ALP) and the Australian Council for Trade Unions (ACTU) that framed the process of government from 1983 to 1996.

3. Australia has always had a very low rate of social welfare expenditure. In a cross-national comparison of social welfare expenditure as a proportion of gross national product (GNP), in 1949–50 Australia was spending slightly more than half of the mean of 8.025. That is, its social welfare expenditures were on a par with the United States of America. Levi and Singleton (1991:635) argue that this proportion has not changed a great deal over the decades.

4. Known as the "New Protectionism"—combining protectionist trade policy with state mandated wage fixation.

5. Lack of support for women by the working-class labor movement becomes less puzzling when it is noted that the Australian Labour Party is the constituency of the labor movement and this is predominantly Irish Catholic. Hence, issues of importance to women were more likely to take a backseat to issues of importance to (male) workers.

6. For example, the Council on the Single Mother and Her Child, Parents Without Partners, and the Women's Electoral Lobby all pressured for changing benefits and eligibility rules. Through lobbying, protests, and media campaigns, these groups were able to influence the direction of welfare policy (Levi and Singleton, 1991:641).

7. Prime Minister Gough Whitlam, for example, appointed Elizabeth Reid as personal adviser on women's affairs following the election of the ALP in 1972. It was the first time that a women's policy portfolio was recognized as important.

8. The various renegotiated Accords were labeled by version; hence Mark 1 was the first Accord negotiated, while other versions followed (almost annually).

9. Childcare was the biggest item promised by the ALP in the 1984 election.

10. Within the government one source of pressure came from the "drys" or economic rationalists such as Senator Peter Walsh, the minister for finance, who argued that the state needed to crack down on benefit fraud or cheating.

11. Gail Reekie (1996) provides a very useful overview and analysis of the key conservative views on single parents in the contemporary Australian discourse. In particular she notes the diverse positions held by these various social scientists.

12. There is very little adequate research on Aboriginal families, welfare, and social policy. This is largely because, as Daley and Smith (1998) note, the categories that we use to discuss families in Australia do not apply to many Aboriginals. For example, conceptions of the family and responsibilities for children and their welfare do not fit the dominant patterns used in social policy research. It has also arisen because Aboriginal welfare has often been dealt with by a separate department and different levels of government, each with their own statistical protocols.

13. For example, John Hyde of the Australian Institute of Public Policy (Reekie 1996).

Chapter 9. Neoliberalism and *Tino Rangatiratanga*: Welfare State Restructuring in Aotearoa/New Zealand

Thanks to Maureen Baker, Catherine Kingfisher, Nan Seuffert, and Robert Webb for their comments.

1. Maori, the indigenous population of Aotearoa/New Zealand, comprise approximately 14 percent of the total population. People from neighboring Pacific Islands migrated to Aotearoa/New Zealand during the post-1945 period to fill labor shortages in the rapidly expanding manufacturing sector. People of Pacific Island descent now make up approximately 5.5 percent of the total population.

2. Established in 1975, the Waitangi Tribunal investigates Crown actions that are inconsistent with the spirit of the Treaty of Waitangi, which was signed by representatives of the British Crown and Maori in 1840.

3. Pakeha are descendants of European colonizing settlers.

4. This is not to underestimate the importance of the 1978 Tu Tanagata (Stand Tall) initiative as an initial model for a community-oriented and decentralized Department of Maori Affairs.

5. This was the report of a Ministerial Advisory Committee on a Maori Perspective for the Department of Social Welfare. The committee was established in response to long-standing complaints that the department was not sensitive to the needs of Maori.

6. Early childhood and primary school Maori immersion programs.

7. One study showed that 47 percent of women left the DPB to reenter a relationship and only 17 percent for paid work (Rochford 1993).

Chapter 10. Where to Next? Against and Beyond Neoliberalism

1. Other relevant articles of the Covenant include Article 3, which states that women and men must equally enjoy the rights set forth in the Covenant; Article 11, which states that all individuals have the right to social security, that women be provided with "special protection" prior and subsequent to childbirth, and that children be awarded special protection from exploitation; Article 12, which recognizes all persons' rights to physical and mental health; and Article 13, which recognizes all persons' rights to education (UN 1966).

Bibliography

Afshar, Haleh and Carolyne Dennis, eds. 1992. *Women and Adjustment Policies in the Third World.* New York: St. Martin's Press.

Aglietta, Michel. 1979. *A Theory of Capitalist Regulation.* London: New Left Books.

———. 1982. "World Capitalism in the Eighties." *New Left Review* 136:25–36.

Amin, Ash. 1997. "Placing Globalization." *Theory, Culture & Society* 14 (2):123–37.

Anderson, Elijah. 1996. "The Code of the Streets." *Hope Magazine*, March/April, 26–43.

———. 1999 *Code of the Street: Decency, Violence, and the Moral Life of the Inner City.* New York: W.W. Norton.

Andrews, Geoff. 1999. "New Left and New Labour: Modernisation or a New Modernity?" *Soundings* 13:14–24.

Appadurai, Arjun. 1996a. "Disjuncture and Difference in the Global Cultural Economy." In *Modernity at Large: Cultural Dimensions of Globalization.* Minneapolis: University of Minnesota Press.

———. 1996b. *Modernity at Large: Cultural Dimensions of Globalization.* Minneapolis: University of Minnesota Press.

———. 2000. "Grassroots Globalization and the Research Imagination." *Public Culture* 12 (1): 1–19.

Aschenbrenner, Joyce. 1975. *Lifelines: Black Families in Chicago.* New York: Holt, Rinehart and Winston.

Atkinson, Karen, Sarah Oerton, and Diane Burns. 1998. "Happy Families? Single Mothers, the Press, and the Politicians." *Capital and Class* 64: 1–11.

Auletta, Ken. 1982. "World Capitalism in the Eighties." *New Left Review* 136: 25–36.

———. 1983. *The Underclass.* New York: Vintage.

Australian Council of Trade Unions/Trade Development Council (ACTU/TDC). 1987. *Australia Reconstructed: ACTU/TDC Mission to Western Europe.* Canberra: Trade Development Council.

Australian Department of Industrial Relations. 1992. *Workplace Bargaining: A Best Practice Guide.* Canberra: Australian Government Publishing Service.

Australian Department for Social Security. 1986. *Social Security Review.* Canberra: Australian Government Publishing Service.

Baker, Dean, Gerald Epstein, and Robert Pollin. 1998. "Introduction." In *Globalization and Progressive Political Economy*, ed. Baker, Epstein, and Pollin. Cambridge: Cambridge University Press.

Bakker, Isabella. 1994a. "Introduction: Engendering Macro-Economic Policy Reform in the Era of Global Restructuring and Adjustment." In *The Strategic Silence: Gender and Economic Policy*, ed. Isabella Bakker. London: Zed Books/ North-South Institute.

———, ed. 1994b. *The Strategic Silence: Gender and Economic Policy*. London: Zed Books/North-South Institute.

———, ed. 1996. *Rethinking Restructuring: Gender and Change in Canada*. Toronto: University of Toronto Press.

Bane, Mary Jo and David Ellwood. 1994. *Welfare Realities: From Rhetoric to Reform*. Cambridge, Mass.: Harvard University Press.

Barlett, Donald L. and James B. Steele. 1994. *America: Who Really Pays the Taxes?* New York: Simon and Schuster.

Barlow, Maude and Bruce Campbell. 1995. *Straight Through the Heart: How the Liberals Abandoned the Just Society*. Toronto: HarperPerennial.

Barnes, Helen, Patricia Day, and Natalie Cronin. 1998. *Trial and Error: A Review of U.K. Child Support Policy*. London: Family Policy Studies Centre.

Barry, Andrew, Thomas Osborne, and Nikolas Rose, eds. 1996. *Foucault and Political Reason: Liberalism, Neo-Liberalism, and Rationalities of Government*. Chicago: University of Chicago Press.

Bates, Winton Russell. 1996. *The Links Between Economic Growth and Social Cohesion*. Wellington: New Zealand Business Roundtable.

Bateson, Gregory. 1972. "Minimal Requirements for a Theory of Schizophrenia." In *Steps to an Ecology of Mind*. New York: Balantine.

Bauman, Zygmunt. 1998. "On Glocalization: Or Globalization for Some, Localization for Some Others." *Thesis Eleven* 54: 37–49.

Beilhartz, Peter. 1994. *Transforming Labour: Labour Tradition and the Labour Decade in Australia*. Melbourne: Cambridge University Press.

Beilhartz, Peter, Mark Considine, and Rob Watts. 1992. *Arguing About the Welfare State*. Sydney: Allen and Unwin.

Bellah, Robert N., Richard Madsen, William M. Sullivan, Ann Swidler, and Steven M. Tipton. 1985. *Habits of the Heart: Individualism and Commitment in American Life*. Berkeley: University of California Press.

Beneria, Lourdes and Shelley Feldman, eds. 1992. *Unequal Burden: Economic Crises, Persistent Poverty, and Women's Work*. Boulder, Colo.: Westview Press.

Berkhoffer, Robert F., Jr. 1978. *The White Man's Indian: Images of the American Indian from Columbus to the Present*. New York: Vintage.

Blair, Tony. 1995. "The Rights We Enjoy Reflect the Duties We Owe." Spectator lecture, London, March 22.

———. 1997a. Speech given at Aylesbury Estate, Southwark, June 2.

———. 1997b. "The 21st Century Welfare State." Speech given at Rikjsmuseum, Amsterdam, January 24.

———. 1997c. "Seven Pillars of a Decent Society." Lecture, Southampton, April 16.

———. 1998. *The Third Way: New Politics for the New Century*. London: Fabian Society.

Bookman, Ann and Sandra Morgen, eds. 1988. *Women and the Politics of Empowerment*. Philadelphia: Temple University Press.

Boreham, Paul, Richard Hall, Bill Harley, and Gillian Whitehouse. 1996. "What Does Enterprise Bargaining Mean for Gender Equity? Some Empirical Evidence." *Labor and Industry* 7 (1): 51–68.

Boserup, Ester. 1970. *Woman's Role in Economic Development*. New York: St. Martin's Press.

Boston, Jonathan, Susan St. John, and Bob Stephens. 1996. "The Quest for Social Responsibility." *Social Policy Journal of New Zealand* 7: 2–16.
Boston, Jonathan and Paul Dalziel. 1992. *The Decent Society? Essays in response to National's Economic and Social Policies.* Auckland: Oxford University Press.
Boston, Jonathan, Paul Dalziel, and Susan St. John, eds. 1999. *Redesigning the New Zealand Welfare State.* Auckland: Oxford University Press.
Bourgois, Philippe. 1996. *In Search of Respect: Selling Crack in the Barrio.* Cambridge: Cambridge University Press.
Bradshaw, Jonathan, Steven Kennedy, Majella Kilkey, Sandra Hutton, Anne Corden, Tony Eardley, Hilary Holmes, and Joanna Neale. 1996. *The Employment of Lone Parents: A Comparison of Policy in 20 Countries.* London: Family Policy Studies Centre.
Brauner, Sarah and Pamela Loprest. 1999. *Where Are They Now? What States' Studies of People Who Left Welfare Tell Us.* New Federalism: Issues and Options for States A-32. Washington, D.C.: Urban Institute, May.
Bray, Mark and Peter Waring. 1998. "The Rhetoric and Reality of Bargaining Structures Under the Howard Government." *Labour and Industry* 9 (2): 61–79.
Brodie, Janine. 1994. "Shifting the Boundaries: Gender and the Politics of Restructuring." In *The Strategic Silence: Gender and Economic Policy,* ed. Isabella Bakker. London: Zed Books/North-South Institute.
———. 1995. *Politics on the Margins: Restructuring and the Canadian Women's Movement.* Halifax: Fernwood Publishing.
———. 1996a. "New State Forms, New Political Spaces." In *States Against Markets: The Limits to Globalisation,* ed. Robert Boyer and Daniel Drache. London: Routledge.
———. 1996b. "Restructuring and the New Citizenship." In *Rethinking Restructuring: Gender and Change in Canada,* ed. Isabella Bakker. Toronto: University of Toronto Press.
———. 1997. "Meso-Discourses, State Forms, and the Gendering of Liberal-Democratic Citizenship." *Citizenship Studies* 1 (2): 223–40.
———. 1999. "The Politics of Social Policy in the Twenty-First Century." In *Citizens or Consumers? Social Policy in a Market Society,* ed. Dave Broad and Wayne Anthony. Halifax: Fernwood Publishing.
Brodkin, Karen. 1998. *How Jews Became White Folks and What This Says About Race in America.* New Brunswick, N.J.: Rutgers University Press.
Brown, Wendy. 1995. *States of Injury: Power and Freedom in Late Modernity.* Princeton, N.J.: Princeton University Press.
Bryson, Lois. 1992. *Welfare and the State: Who Benefits?* London: Macmillan.
Buckley, Ken and Ted Wheelwright. 1988. *No Paradise for Workers: Capitalism and the Common People in Australia, 1788–1914.* Melbourne: Oxford University Press.
Burgess, John, William Mitchell, Duncan O'Brien, and Martin Watts. 1998. "Unemployment: Promises, Policies, and Progress." *Labour and Industry* 9 (2): 103–22.
Burghes, Louie and Ceridwen Roberts. 1995. "Scare in the Community: Britain in a Moral Panic: Lone Parents." *Community Care* (July): 6–12.
Burt, Sandra. 1994. "The Women's Movement: Working to Transform Public Life." In *Canadian Politics,* 2nd ed., ed. James Bickerton and Alain Gagnon. Peterborough, Ont.: Broadview.
Butler, Stuart and Anna Kondratas. 1987. *Out of the Poverty Trap: A Conservative Approach for Welfare Reform.* New York: Free Press.
Campbell, Iain and John Burgess. 1997. *National Patterns of Temporary Employment:*

The Distinctive Case of Casual Employment in Australia. National Key Centre for Industrial Relations Working Paper 53. Melbourne: Monash Univeristy

Campbell, Robert. 2000. "The Fourth Fiscal Era." In *How Ottawa Spends, 1999–2000: Shape Shifting: Canadian Governance Toward the 21st Century,* ed. Leslie A. Pal. Toronto: Oxford University Press.

Canada, Human Resources Development Canada (HRDC). 1994. *Improving Social Security in Canada: Paper on Working.* Hull, Quebec: HRDC.

———. 2000. *Poverty and Exclusion.* Hull, Quebec: HRDC.

Canada, Privy Council Office (PCO). 1999. *Policy Research Initiative: Sustaining Growth, Human Development, and Social Cohesion in a Global World.* Ottawa: PCO.

Cannan, Crescy. 1995. "From Dependence to Enterprise? Women and Western Welfare States." In *Women and Market Societies: Crisis and Opportunity,* ed. Barbara Einhorn and Eileen Janes Yeo. Aldershot: Edward Elgar.

Carney, Shaun. 1988. *Australia in Accord: Politics and Industrial Relations Under the Hawke Government.* Melbourne: Sun Books.

Carrier, James G., ed. 1997. *Meanings of the Market: The Free Market in Western Culture.* Oxford: Berg.

Carrithers, Michael, Steven Collins, and Steven Lukes, eds. 1985. *The Category of the Person: Anthropology, Philosophy, History.* Cambridge: Cambridge University Press.

Casper, Lynne M., Sara S. McLanahan, and Irwin Garfinkel. 1994. "The Gender-Poverty Gap: What We Can Learn from Other Countries." *American Sociological Review* 59: 594–605.

Castells, Manuel. 1996. *The Information Age.* Vol. 1, *The Network Society.* Oxford: Blackwell.

———. 1997. *The Information Age.* Vol. 2, *The Power of Identity.* Oxford: Blackwell.

Castles, Francis G. 1985. *The Working Class and Welfare: Reflection on the Political Development of the Welfare State in Australia and New Zealand, 1890–1980.* Sydney: Allen and Unwin.

Castles, Francis G., Rolf Gerritsen, and Jack Vowles, eds. 1996. *The Great Experiment: Labour Parties and Public Policy Transformation in Australia and New Zealand.* Auckland: Auckland University Press.

Castles, Francis G. and Ian Shirley. 1996. "Social Welfare Policy." In *The Great Experiment: Labour Parties and Public Policy Transformation in Australia and New Zealand,* ed. Francis G. Castles, Rolf Gerritsen, and Jack Vowles. Auckland: Auckland University Press.

Catley, Robert. 1978. "Socialism and Reform in Contemporary Australia." In *Essays in the Political Economy of Australian Capitalism,* ed. E. L. Wheelwright and Ken Buckley. Sydney: ANZ Books.

CBS News. 1999. "Project Strive." *Sixty Minutes,* October 17.

Cerny, Philip G. 1994. "The Dynamics of Financial Globalization: Technology, Market Structure, and Policy Response." *Policy Sciences* 27:319–42.

Chester, Robert. 1986. "The Myth of the Disappearing Nuclear Family." In *Family Portraits,* ed. Digby Anderson and Graham Dawson. London: Social Affairs Unit.

Cheyne, Christie, Mike O'Brien, and Michael Belgrave. 1997. *Social Policy in Aotearoa/New Zealand: A Critical Introduction.* Auckland: Oxford University Press.

Clark, Manning. 1976 Australian Broadcasting Commission Boyer Lecture. Sydney: Australian Broadcasting Commission.

Clarke, John and Janet Newman. 1998. "A Modern British People? New Labour and the Reconstruction of Welfare." Paper presented to the Discourse Analysis and Social Research Conference, Copenhagen, September.

Clarke, Karen, Gary Craig, and Caroline Glendinning. 1996. *Small Change: The Impact of the Child Support on Lone Mothers and Children.* London: Family Policy Studies Centre.

Cohen, Majorie. 1992. "The Canadian Women's Movement and its Efforts to Influence the Canadian Economy." In *Challenging Times: The Women's Movement in Canada and the United States,* ed. Constance Backhouse and David Flaherty. Montreal: McGill-Queen's University Press.

Collier, Jane F. and Sylvia J. Yanagisako. 1989. "Theory in Anthropology Since Feminist Practice." *Critique of Anthropology* 9 (2): 27–37.

Comaroff, Jean and John Comaroff. 1992. *Ethnography and the Historical Imagination.* Boulder, Colo.: Westview Press.

———. 2000. "Millennial Capitalism: First Thoughts on a Second Coming." *Public Culture* 12 (2): 291–343.

Commission on Social Justice (CSJ). 1994. *Social Justice: Strategies for National Renewal.* London: Vintage Press.

Connelly, M. Patricia. 1996. "Gender Matters: Global Restructuring and Adjustment." *Social Politics* 3 (1): 12–31.

Cook, Dee. 1997. "From Welfare to Work—and Back Again?" In *From Welfare to Work: Lessons from America,* ed. Alan Deacon. London: IEA Health and Welfare Unit.

Coulten, Claudia, Cara Pasqualone, Neil Bania, Toby Martin, Nina Lalich, Margaret Fernando, and Fang Li. 1999. *How Are They Managing? A Six Month Retrospective of Cuyahoga County Families Leaving Welfare.* Cleveland: Center for Urban Poverty and Social Change, Case Western University.

Council on Civil Society. 1998. *A Call to Civil Society: Why Democracy Needs Moral Truths.* New York: Institute for American Values.

Cowan, David. 1998. "Reforming the Homelessness Legislation." *Critical Social Policy* 18 (4): 435–64.

Cox, Robert W. 1987. *Production, Power, and World Order.* New York: Columbia University Press.

Cox, Robert. H. 1998. "The Consequences of Welfare Reform: How Conceptions of Social Rights Are Changing." *Journal of Social Policy* 27 (1): 1–16.

Cruikshank, Barbara. 1996. "Revolutions Within: Self-Government and Self-Esteem." In *Foucault and Political Reason: Liberalism, Neo-liberalism and Rationalities of Government,* ed. Andrew Barry, Thomas Osborne, and Nikolas Rose. Chicago: University of Chicago Press.

———. 2000. "Cultural Politics: Political Theory and the Foundations of the Democratic Order. In *Cultural Studies and Political Theory,* ed. Jodi Dean. Ithaca, N.Y: Cornell University Press.

Cushman, Philip. 1995. *Constructing the Self, Constructing America: A Cultural History of Psychotherapy.* Cambridge, Mass.: Perseus Press.

Daley, Anne and Diane Smith. 1998. "Indigenous Sole Parent Families: Welfare Dependency and Work Opportunities." *Australian Bulletin of Labour* 24 (1): 47–66.

Daniel, Paul and Elizabeth Burgess. n.d. *The Child Support Act: The Voice of Low Income Parents with Care.* London: Social Responsibility Department, Diocese of Southwark.

Davies, Bronwin. 1991. "The Concept of Agency: A Feminist Poststructuralist Analysis." *Social Analysis* 30: 42–53.

Davies, Jon. 1993. *The Family: Is It Just Another Lifestyle Choice?* London: IEA Health and Welfare Unit.

Day, Shelagh and Gwen Brodsky. 1998. *Women and the Equality Deficit: The Impact of Restructuring Canada's Social Programs.* Ottawa: Status of Women Canada.

Deacon, Bob. 1997. *Global Social Policy.* London: Sage.

Dean, Mitchell. 1992. "A Genealogy of the Government of Poverty." *Economy and Society* 21 (3): 215–51.

———. 1997. "Sociology After Society." In *Sociology After Postmodernism*, ed. David Owen. London: Sage.

de Goede, Marieke. 1996. "Ideology in the U.S. Welfare Debate: Neo-Liberal Representations of Poverty." *Discourse & Society* 7 (3): 317–57.

DeMartino, George. 1999. "Global Neoliberalism, Policy Autonomy, and International Competitive Dynamics." *Journal of Economic Issues* 33 (2): 343–49.

Dennis, Norman and George Erdos. 1992. *Families Without Fatherhood.* London: IEA Health and Welfare Unit.

DeParle, Jason. 1998. "Shrinking Welfare Rolls Leave Record High Share of Minorities." *New York Times*, July 27, 1998, A1, A12.

DeSipio, Louis and Rodolfo O. de la Garza. 1998. *Making Americans, Remaking America: Immigration and Immigrant Policy.* Boulder, Colo.: Westview Press.

Di Leonardo, Micaela. 1998. *Exotics at Home: Anthropologies, Others, American Modernity.* Chicago: University of Chicago Press.

Driver, Stephen and Luke Martell. 1998. *New Labour: Politics After Thatcherism.* Cambridge: Polity Press.

Drohan, Madelaine. 1998. "Grassroots Globalisation: How the Net Killed the MAI." *Women in Action* 2: 32–33.

Dumont, Louis. 1980. *Homo Hierarchicus: The Caste System and Its Implications.* Chicago: University of Chicago Press.

Duncan, Simon and Rosalind Edwards.1999. *Lone Mothers, Paid Work, and Gendered Moral Rationalities.* Basingstoke: Macmillan.

Durie, Edward. 1995. "Keynote Address." In *Kia Pumau Tonu: Proceedings of the Hui Whakapumau Maori Development Conference.* Palmerston North, N.Z.: Department of Maori Studies.

Durie, Mason. 1998. *Te Mana, Te Kawanatanga: The Politics of Maori Self-Determination.* Auckland: Oxford University Press.

Eames, Edwin and Judith Goode. 1973. *Urban Poverty in a Cross-Cultural Context.* New York: Free Press.

Easton, Brian. 1997. *The Commercialisation of New Zealand.* Auckland: Auckland University Press.

———. 1999. *The Whimpering of the State: Policy After MMP.* Auckland: Auckland University Press.

Edin, Kathryn and Laura Lein. 1997. *Making Ends Meet: How Single Mothers Survive Welfare and Low-Wage Work.* New York: Russell Sage Foundation.

Edwards, Rosalind and Simon Duncan. 1997. "Supporting the Family: Lone Mothers, Paid Work, and the Underclass Debate." *Critical Social Policy* 17 (4): 29–49.

Ehrenreich, Barbara. 1997. "Spinning the Poor into Gold." *Harper's* 295: 44–52.

Eisenstein, Zillah. 1996. "Stop Stomping on the Rest of Us: Retrieving Publicness from the Privatization of the Globe." *Indiana Journal of Global Legal Studies* 4 (1): 59–95.

Eisner, Jane. 2000. "Faith-Based Organizations: A Promise Still Untested." *Philadelphia Inquirer*, August 1, A17.

Elson, Diane. 1992. "From Survival Strategies to Transformation Strategies: Women's Needs and Structural Adjustment." In *Unequal Burden: Economic Crises, Persistent Poverty, and Women's Work*, ed. Lourdes Beneria and Shelly Feldman. Boulder, Colo.: Westview Press.

————. 1994. "Micro, Meso, Macro: Gender and Economic Analysis in the Context of Policy Reform." In *The Strategic Silence: Gender and Economic Policy*, ed. Isabella Bakker. London: Zed Books/North-South Institute.

————. 1995. "Male Bias in Macro-Economics: The Case of Structural Adjustment." In *Male Bias in the Development Process*, ed. Diane Elson. Manchester: Manchester University Press.

England, Paula. 1993. "The Separative Self: Androcentric Bias in Neoclassical Assumptions." In *Beyond Economic Man: Feminist Theory and Economics*, ed. Marianne A. Ferber and Julie A. Nelson. Chicago: University of Chicago Press.

England, Paula, Karen Christopher, Tim Smeeding, Katherin Ross, and Sara S. McLanahan. 1998. "The Role of the State, Family, and Market in the Gender Gap in Poverty in Modern Nations: Findings from the Luxembourg Income Study and Unresolved Methodological Issues." Paper prepared for the annual meeting of the American Sociological Association, San Francisco.

Enloe, Cynthia. 1989. *Bananas, Beaches, and Bases: Making Feminist Sense of International Politics*. Berkeley: University of California Press.

Esping-Andersen, Gøsta. 1990. *The Three Worlds of Welfare Capitalism*. Cambridge: Polity Press.

————. 1996. "After the Golden Age? Welfare State Dilemmas in a Global Economy." In *Welfare States in Transition: National Adaptations in Global Economies*, ed. Gøsta Esping-Andersen. London: Sage.

Fairbrother, P., S. Svensen, and J. Teicher. 1997. "The Ascendancy of Neo-Liberalism." *Capital and Class* 63: 1–11.

Fairclough, Norman. 1991. "What Might We Mean by 'Enterprise Discourse'?" In *Enterprise Culture*, ed. Russell Keat and Nicholas Abercrombie. London: Routledge.

————. 1992. *Discourse and Social Change*. Cambridge: Polity Press.

Finch, Helen, William O'Connor, Jane Millar, Jon Hales, Andrew Shaw, and Wendy Roth. 1999. The *New Deal for Lone Parents: Learning from the Prototype Areas*. Department of Social Security Research Report Summaries 92. London: DSS.

Finlayson, Alan. 1998. "Tony Blair and the Jargon of Modernisation." *Soundings* 10: 11–27.

Fitchen, Janet. 1991. *Endangered Spaces, Enduring Places: Change, Identity, and Survival in Rural America*. Boulder, Colo: Westview Press.

Fleras, Angie and Jean Leonard Elliott 1992. The *"Nations Within": Aboriginal-State Relations in Canada, the United States, and New Zealand*. Toronto: Oxford University Press.

Fogelson, Raymond D. 1982. "Person, Self, and Identity: Some Anthropological Retrospects, Circumspects, and Prospects." In *Psychosocial Theories of the Self*, ed. Benjamin Lee. New York: Plenum Press.

Ford, Reuben and Jane Millar, eds. 1998. *Private Lives and Public Responses: Lone Parenthood and Future Policy*. London: Policy Studies Institute.

Fortes, Meyer. 1987. *Religion, Morality, and the Person: Essays on Tallensi Religion*. Cambridge: Cambridge University Press.

Foucault, Michel. 1972. *The Archaeology of Knowledge and the Discourse on Language*. Trans. A. M. Sheridan Smith. New York: Pantheon.

———. 1977. *Discipline and Punish: The Birth of the Prison.* Trans. Alan Sheridan. New York: Vintage.

———. 1978. *The History of Sexuality.* Vol. 1, *An Introduction.* Trans. Robert Hurley. New York: Vintage.

———. 1979. "On Governmentality." *Ideology and Consciousness* 6: 5–21.

———. 1982. "The Subject and Power." In *Michel Foucault: Beyond Structuralism and Hermeneutics,* ed. Hubert L Dreyfus and Paul Rabinow. Chicago: University of Chicago Press.

Fox Harding, Lorraine. 1996. *Family, State and Social Policy.* Basingstoke: Macmillan.

Fraser, Nancy. 1989a. *Unruly Practices: Power, Discourse, and Gender in Contemporary Social Theory.* Minneapolis: University of Minnesota Press.

———. 1989b. "Women, Welfare, and the Politics of Need Interpretation." In *Unruly Practices: Power, Discourse, and Gender in Contemporary Social Theory.* Minneapolis: University of Minnesota Press.

———. 1993. "Clintonism, Welfare, and the Antisocial Wage: The Emergence of a Neo-liberal Political Imaginary." *Rethinking Marxism* 6 (1): 9–23.

———. 1997. "After the Family Wage: A Postindustrial Thought Experiment." In *Justice Interruptus: Critical Reflections on the "Postsocialist" Condition.* New York: Routledge.

Fraser, Nancy and Linda Gordon. 1992. "Contract Versus Charity: Why Is There No Social Citizenship in the United States?" *Socialist Review* 22: 45–67.

———. 1994. "A Genealogy of Dependency: Tracing a Key Word in the U.S. Welfare State." *Signs: Journal of Women in Culture and Society* 19 (2): 309–36.

Friedman, Jonathan. 1994. *Cultural Identity and Global Process.* London: Sage.

———. 1996. "Rethinking Poverty: Empowerment and Citizen Rights". *International Social Science Journal* 48 (2): 161–72.

Gallin, Rita S. 1998. "The Gendered Nature of Globalization." Paper presented at the annual meeting of the American Anthropological Association, December 2–6, Philadelphia.

Gans, Herbert. 1972. "The Positive Functions of Poverty." *American Journal of Sociology* 78 (2): 275–89.

Gardiner, Wira. 1996. *Return to Sender: What Really Happened at the Fiscal Envelope Hui.* Auckland: Reed.

Garnham, Alison and Emma Knights. 1994. *Putting the Treasury First: The Truth About Child Support.* London: Child Poverty Action Group.

Geertz, Clifford. 1975. "On the Nature of Anthropological Understanding." *American Scientist* 63: 47–53.

Gibson-Graham, J. K. 1996. *The End of Capitalism (As We Knew It): A Feminist Critique of Political Economy.* Oxford: Blackwell.

Giddens, Anthony. 1990. *The Consequences of Modernity.* Cambridge: Polity in association with Blackwell.

Gilder, George. 1981. *Wealth and Poverty.* New York: Bantam Books.

Gill, Stephen. 1995. "Globalisation, Market Civilisation, and Disciplinary Neo-liberalism." *Millennium: Journal of International Studies* 24 (3): 399–423.

Gills, Barry K. 2000. "Introduction: Globalization and the Politics of Resistance." In *Globalization and the Politics of Resistance,* ed. Barry K. Gills. New York: St. Martin's Press.

Ginsburg, Faye P. and Rayna Rapp. 1995. *Conceiving the New World Order: The Global Politics of Reproduction.* Berkeley: University of California Press.

Ginsburg, Norman. 1996. "Recent Changes in Social Housing." *Social Policy Re-*

view 8, ed. Margaret May, Edward Brunsdon, and Gary Craig. London: Social Policy Association.

Goldstein, Donna. 2001. "Microenterprise Training Programs, Common Sense, and the Discourses of Self-Esteem." In *New Poverty Studies: The Ethnography of Politics, Policy and Impoverished People in the U.S.*, ed. Judith Goode and Jeff Maskovsky. New York: New York University Press.

Goode, Jackie, Callender Claire, and Ruth Lister. 1998. *Purse or Wallet? Gender Inequalities and Income Distribution Within Families on Benefits*. London: Policy Studies Institute.

Goode, Judith. 1998. "The Contingent Construction of Local Identities: Koreans and Puerto Ricans in Philadelphia." *Identities* 5 (1): 33–64.

———. 2001. "Let's Get Our Act Together: How Racial Discourses Disrupt Neighborhood Activism." In *New Poverty Studies: The Ethnography of Politics, Policy, and Impoverished People in the United States*, ed. Judith Goode and Jeff Maskovsky. New York: New York University Press.

Goode, Judith and Jeff Maskovsky, eds. 2001. *New Poverty Studies: The Ethnography of Politics, Policy, and Impoverished People in the United States*. New York: New York University Press.

Goward, Pru. 1997. "Diversity, Opportunity and Choice." *Canberra Bulletin of Public Administration* 85: 56–58.

Graves, Frank. 2000. "Rethinking Government as if People Mattered." In *How Ottawa Spends, 1999–2000: Shape Shifting: Canadian Governance Toward the 21st Century*, ed. Leslie Pal. Toronto: Oxford University Press.

Green, David. 1993. Foreword to Norman Dennis, *Rising Crime and the Dismembered Family*. London: IEA Health and Welfare Unit.

———. 1995. Foreword to Patricia Morgan, *Farewell to the Family?* London: IEA Health and Welfare Unit.

———. 1996. *From Welfare State to Civil Society: Towards Welfare That Works in New Zealand*. Wellington: New Zealand Business Roundtable.

Grosz, Elizabeth. 1989. *Sexual Subversions: Three French Feminists*. Sydney: Allen and Unwin.

Guehenno, Jean Maria. 1993. *The End of the Nation State*. Minneapolis: University of Minnesota Press.

Hales, Jon, Carli Lessof, Wendy Roth, Mandy Gloyer, Andrew Shaw, Jane Millar, Matt Barnes, Peter Elias, Chris Hasluck, Abigail McKnight, and Anne Green. 2000a. *Evaluation of the New Deal for Lone Parents: Early Lessons from the Phase One Prototype*. Department of Social Security Research Report Summaries 108. London: DSS.

Hales, Jon, Carli Lessof, Wendy Roth, Mandy Gloyer, and Andrew Shaw. 2000b. *Evaluation of the New Deal for Lone Parents: Early Lessons from the Phase One Prototype—Findings of Surveys*. Department of Social Security Research Report Summaries 109. London: DSS.

Hall, Peter, ed. 1989. *The Political Power of Economic Ideas: Keynesianism Across Nations*. Princeton, N.J.: Princeton University Press.

Hall, Stuart. 1997. "The Local and the Global: Globalization and Ethnicity." In *Culture, Globalization, and the World-System: Contemporary Conditions for the Representation of Identity*, ed. Anthony King. Minneapolis: University of Minnesota Press.

Halperin, Rhoda. 1990. *The Livelihood of Kin*. Austin: University of Texas Press.

Hampson, Ian. 1996. "The Accord: A Post-Mortem." *Labour and Industry* 7 (2): 55–77.

Hannerz, Ulf. 1996. *Transnational Connections: Culture, People, Places.* London: Routledge.

Hantrais, Linda, and Marie-Therese Letablier. 1996. *Families and Family Policies in Europe.* London: Longman.

Harrington, Michael. 1962. *The Other America: Poverty in the United States.* Baltimore: Penguin.

Harris, Grace Gredys. 1989. "Concepts of Individual, Self, and Person in Description and Analysis." *American Anthropologist* 91 (3): 599–612.

Hart, Jeffrey A. and Aseem Prakash. 1997. "The Decline of 'Embedded Liberalism' and the Rearticulation of the Keynesian Welfare State." *New Political Economy* 2 (1): 65–78.

Harvey, David. 1989. *The Condition of Postmodernity.* Cambridge, Mass: Blackwell.

Hayek, Friedrich A. von. 1948. *Individualism and Economic Order.* Chicago: University of Chicago Press.

Hayward, Steven. 1998. "The Shocking Success of Welfare Reform." *Policy Review* 87: 6–10.

Higginbotham, Evelyn Brooks. 1996. "African-American Women's History and the Metalanguage of Race." In *Feminism and History,* ed. Joan Wallach Scott. Oxford: Oxford University Press.

Higgins, Jane. 1999. "From Welfare to Workfare." In *Redesigning the New Zealand Welfare State,* ed. Jonathan Boston, Paul Dalziel, and Susan St. John. Auckland: Oxford University Press.

Higgot, Richard. 1999. "Economics, Politics, and (International) Political Economy: The Need for a Balanced Diet in an Era of Globalisation." *New Political Economy* 4 (1): 23–36.

Hills, John. 1998a. *Income and Wealth: The Latest Evidence.* York: Joseph Rowntree Foundation.

———. 1998b. *Thatcherism, New Labour, and the Welfare State.* London: Centre for the Analysis of Social Exclusion.

Hindess, Barry. 1997. "A Society Governed by Contract?" In *The New Contractualism?* ed. Glyn Davis, Barbara Sullivan, and Anna Yeatman. Melbourne: Macmillan Education.

Hirst, Paul and Graham Thompson. 1996. *Globalization in Question.* Cambridge: Polity.

Ho, Elsie and Jacqueline Lidgard. 1996. "Give Us a Chance: The Employment Experiences of New Settlers from East Asia." In *Labour, Employment and Work in New Zealand: Proceedings of the Seventh Conference,* ed. Phil Morrison. Wellington: Victoria University.

Hobsbawm, Eric. 1994. *The Age of Extremes: The Short Twentieth Century.* London: Abacus.

Hobson, Barbara. 1994. "Solo Mothers, Social Policy Regimes, and the Logics of Gender." In *Gendering Welfare States,* ed. Diane Sainsbury. London: Sage.

Hollan, Douglas. 1992. "Cross-Cultural Differences in the Self." *Journal of Anthropological Research* 48 (4): 283–300.

Hum, Derek. 1993. "Exchange-Speak, Social Welfare Claims, and Economic Policy Discourse." In *New Approaches to Welfare Theory,* ed. Glenn Drover and Patrick Kerans. Hampshire: Edward Elgar.

Hunt, Paul. 1996. *Reclaiming Social Rights: International and Comparative Perspectives.* Aldershot: Dartmouth Publishing.

Hyatt, Susan Brin. 1995. "Poverty and Difference: Ethnographic Representation of 'Race' and the Crisis of the 'Social.'" In *Gender and Race Through Educa-*

tion and Political Activism: The Legacy of Sylvia Helen Forman, ed. Dena Schenk. Washington, D.C.: American Anthropological Association and Association for Feminist Anthropology.

———. 1997. "Policy in a Post-Welfare Landscape: Tenant Management Policies, Self-Governance, and the Democratization of Knowledge in Great Britain." In *The Anthropology of Policy,* ed. Sue Wright and Chris Shore. London: Routledge.

———. 2001. "From Citizen to Volunteer: Governance and the Erasure of Poverty." In *New Poverty Studies: The Ethnography of Politics, Policy, and Impoverished People in the United States,* ed. Judith Goode and Jeff Maskovsky. New York: New York University Press.

Ignatiev, Noel. 1996. *How the Irish Became White.* New York: Routledge.

International Bank for Reconstruction and Development (IBRD). 1992. *World Bank Report 1992.* Washington, D.C.: IBRD.

Jaggar, Alison M. 1983. *Feminist Politics and Human Nature.* Tatowa, N.J.: Rowman and Allanheld.

Jameson, Fredric. 1991. *Postmodernism, or the Cultural Logic of Late Capitalism.* Durham, N.C.: Duke University Press.

Jencks, Christopher and Joseph Swingle. 2000. "Without a Net: Whom the New Welfare Law Helps and Hurts." *American Prospect* 11 (4): 37–41.

Jenson, Jane. 1999. "Changing Citizenship Regimes: Concepts and Application." Keynote address to Symposium on Citizenship, Representation, and Neoliberalism. University of Auckland, July 24 1999.

———. 2000. "Reading the SUFA Through Policies for Children." *Policy Options,* (May).

Jesson, Bruce. 1985. *Behind the Mirror Glass: The Growth of Wealth and Power in New Zealand in the Eighties.* Auckland: Penguin.

Jones, John Paul III and Janet E. Kodras. 1990. "Restructured Regions and Families: The Feminization of Poverty in the U.S." *Annals of the Association of American Geographers* 80 (2): 163–83.

Kabeer, Naila. 1994. *Reversed Realities: Gender Hierarchies in Development Thought.* London: Verso.

Kahn, Joel S. 1997. "Demons, Commodities, and the History of Anthropology." In *Meanings of the Market: The Free Market in Western Culture,* ed. James G. Carrier. Oxford: Berg.

Katz, Michael. 1986. *In the Shadow of the Poorhouse: A Social History of Welfare in America.* New York: Basic Books.

———. 1989. *The Undeserving Poor: From the War on Poverty to the War on Welfare.* New York: Pantheon.

———, ed. 1993. *The Underclass Debate.* Princeton, N.J.: Princeton University Press.

Kearney, Michael. 1995. "The Local and the Global: The Anthropology of Globalization and Transnationalism." *Annual Review of Anthropology* 24:547–65.

Kelly, Paul. 1992. *The End of Certainty: The Story of the 1980s.* Melbourne: Allen and Unwin.

Kelsey, Jane. 1991. "Treaty Justice in the 1980s." In *Nga Take: Ethnic Relations and Racism in Aotearoa/New Zealand,* ed. Paul Spoonley, David Pearson, and Cluny MacPherson. Palmerston North, N.Z.: Dunmore Press.

———. 1993. *Rolling Back the State: Privatisation of Power in Aotearoa/New Zealand.* Wellington: Bridget Williams Books.

———. 1995. *The New Zealand Experiment: A World Model for Structural Adjustment?* Auckland: Auckland University Press/Bridget Williams Books.

———. 1999. *Reclaiming the Future: New Zealand and the Global Economy.* Wellington: Bridget Williams Books.

Kempson, Elaine. 1996. *Life on a Low Income.* York: Joseph Rowntree Foundation/York Publishing Services.

Kerr, Joanna. 1996. "Transnational Resistance: Strategies to Alleviate the Impacts of Restructuring on Women." In *Rethinking Restructuring: Gender and Change in Canada,* ed. Isabella Bakker. Toronto: University of Toronto Press.

Kiernan, Kathleen, Hilary Land, and Jane Lewis. 1998. *Lone Motherhood in Twentieth-Century Britain: From Footnote to Front Page.* Oxford: Oxford University Press.

Kimenyi, Mwangi S. and John Mukum Mbaku. 1995. "Female Headship, Feminization of Poverty and Welfare." *Southern Economic Journal* 62 (1): 44–52.

Kingfisher, Catherine. 1996. *Women in the American Welfare Trap.* Philadelphia: University of Pennsylvania Press.

———. 1999. "Rhetoric of (Female) Savagery: Welfare Reform in the United States and Aotearoa/New Zealand." *National Women's Studies Journal* 11 (1): 1–20.

———. 2001. "Producing Disunity: The Constraints and Incitements of Welfare Work." In *New Poverty Studies: The Ethnography of Politics, Policy and Impoverishment in the United States,* ed. Judith Goode and Jeff Maskovsky. New York: New York University Press.

Kingfisher, Catherine and Michael Goldsmith. 2001. "Reforming Women in the United States and Aotearoa/New Zealand: A Comparative Ethnography of Welfare Reform in Global Context." *American Anthropologist* 103 (3):714–732.

Kristeva, Julia. 1984. *Powers of Horror.* Trans. Leon S. Roudiez. New York: Columbia University Press.

La Fontaine, Jane S. 1985. "Person and Individual: Some Anthropological Reflections." In *The Category of the Person: Anthropology, Philosophy, History,* ed. Michael Carrithers, Steven Collins, and Steven Lukes. Cambridge: Cambridge University Press.

Lambert, Suzanne. 1994. "Sole Parent Income Support: Cause or Cure of Sole Parent Poverty?" *Australian Journal of Social Issues* 29 (10): 75–97.

Lannamann, John W. 1991. "Interpersonal Communication Research as Ideological Practice." *Communication Theory* 1 (3): 179–203.

Larner, Wendy. 1993. "Changing Contexts: Globalization, Migration, and Feminism." In *Feminism and the Politics of Difference,* ed. Sneja Gunew and Anna Yeatman. Sydney: Allen and Unwin.

———. 1996. "The 'New Boys': Restructuring in New Zealand, 1984–94." *Social Politics* 3 (1): 32–56.

———. 1997. "The Legacy of the Social: Market Governance and the Consumer." *Economy and Society* 26 (3): 373–99.

———. 1998. "Hitching a Ride on a Tiger's Back: Globalisation and Spatial Imaginaries in New Zealand." *Environment and Planning D: Society and Space* 16: 599–614.

———. 1999. "Sociologies of Neo-Liberalism: Theorising the New Zealand Experiment." *Sites* 36:5–21.

———. 2000. "Post-Welfare State Governance: Towards a Code of Social and Family Responsibility." *Social Politics* 7 (2): 244–65.

Lash, Scott and John Urry. 1987. *The End of Organized Capitalism.* Madison: University of Wisconsin Press.

Law, Ian. 1996. *Racism, Ethnicity, and Social Policy.* London: Prentice Hall/Harvester Wheatsheaf.

Leacock, Eleanor, ed. 1971. *The Culture of Poverty: A Critique.* New York: Simon and Schuster.

LeBlanc, Daniel. 1999. "UI Reform Hit Women Hardest." *Globe and Mail,* November 23.

Lee, Julie and Glenda Strachan. 1998. "Who's Minding the Baby Now? Child Care Under the Howard Government." *Labour and Industry* 9 (2): 81–101.

Levi, Margaret and Sara Singleton. 1991. "Women in 'The Working Man's Paradise': Sole Parents, the Women's Movement, and the Social Policy Bargain in Australia." *Social Research* 58 (3): 627–54.

Lévi-Strauss, Claude. 1969. *The Elementary Structures of Kinship.* Boston: Beacon Press.

Lewis, Jane. ed. 1997. *Lone Mothers in European Welfare Regimes.* London: J. Kingsley Publishers.

———. 1998. "The Problem of Lone Mothers in Twentieth Century Britain." *Journal of Social Welfare and Family Law* 20 (3): 251–83.

Lewis, Oscar. 1996. "The Culture of Poverty." In *Urban Life: Readings in Urban Anthropology,* ed. George Gmelch and Walter Zenner. Prospect Heights, Ill.: Waveland Press.

Lidgard, Jacqueline, Richard Bedford, and Joanne Goodwin. 1998. *Transformations in New Zealand's International Migration System: 1981–1996.* Population Studies Centre Discussion Paper 25. Hamilton, N.Z.: University of Waikato.

Liebow, Elliot. 1967. *Tally's Corner.* Boston: Little Brown.

Lipietz, Alain. 1994. "Post-Fordism and Democracy." In *Post-Fordism: A Reader,* ed. Ash Amin, Oxford: Blackwell.

Lister, Ruth. 1994. "The Child Support Act: Shifting Family Financial Obligations in the United Kingdom." *Social Politics* 1 (2): 211–22.

———. 1996. "In Search of the 'Underclass.'" In *Charles Murray and the Underclass: The Developing Debate,* ed. Ruth. Lister. London: Institute of Economic Affairs in association with the *Sunday Times.*

———. 1997a. *Citizenship: Feminist Perspectives.* London: Macmillan.

———. 1997b. "From Equality to Social Inclusion: New Labour and the Welfare State." *Critical Social Policy* 18 (2): 215–25.

———. 1998. "Vocabularies of Citizenship and Gender: The UK." *Critical Social Policy* 18 (3): 309–31.

———. 2002. "Towards a New Welfare Settlement?" In *British Politics Today,* ed. Colin Hay. Cambridge: Polity Press.

Lomawaima, K. Tsianina. 1993. "Domesticity in the Federal Indian Schools: The Power of Authority over Mind and Body." *American Ethnologist* 20 (2): 227–40.

Love, Ngatata. 1995. "The Hui Taumata and the Decade of Maori Development in Perspective." In *Kia Pumau Tonu: Proceedings of the Hui Whakapumau Maori Development Conference.* Palmerston North, N.Z.: Department of Maori Studies, Massey University.

Lukes, Steven. 1973. *Individualism.* Oxford: Blackwell.

Lutz, Catherine. 1988. *Unnatural Emotions: Everyday Sentiments on a Micronesian Atoll and Their Challenge to Western Theory.* Chicago: University of Chicago Press.

Lynch, Cecelia. 1998. "Social Movements and the Problem of Globalization." *Alternatives* 23: 149–73.

Lyon-Callo, Vincent. 2001. "Homelessness, Employment, and Structural Violence: Exploring Constraints on Collective Mobilization Against Systemic Inequality." In *New Poverty Studies: The Ethnography of Politics, Policy, and Impoverished People in the United States*, ed. Judith Goode and Jeff Maskovsky. New York: New York University Press.

Maaka, Roger. 1994. "The New Tribe: Conflicts and Continuities in the Social Organisation of Urban Maori." *Contemporary Pacific* 6 (2): 311–36.

Maaka, Roger and Angie Fleras. 1998. *Re-Constitutionalising Treaty Work: The Waitangi Tribunal.* Christchurch, N.Z.: University of Canterbury, mimeo.

Macdermott, Terri, Alison Garnham, and Sally Holterman. 1998. *Real Choices for Lone Parents and Their Children.* London: Child Poverty Action Group.

Macdonald, Martha. 1995. "Economic Restructuring and Gender in Canada: Feminist Policy Initiatives." *World Development* 23 (11): 2005–17.

MacFarlane, Alan. 1978. *The Origins of English Individualism.* Oxford: Blackwell.

MacLeod, Jay. 1995. *Ain't No Makin' It: Aspirations and Attainment in a Low-Income Neighborhood.* Boulder, Colo.: Westview Press.

Macpherson, C. B. 1962. *The Political Theory of Possessive Individualism: Hobbes to Locke.* Oxford and New York: Oxford University Press.

Maine, Sir Henry Sumner. [1861] 1998. *Ancient Law.* Holmes Beach, Fl.: Gaunt.

Malinowski, Bronislaw. [1922] 1961. *Argonauts of the Western Pacific: An Account of Native Enterprise and Adventure in the Archipelagoes of Melanesian New Guinea.* Prospect Heights, Ill.: Waveland Press.

Marcoux, Alain. 1997. *The Feminization of Poverty: Facts, Hypotheses, and the Art of Advocacy.* Rome: Food and Agriculture Organization (FAO) Population Programme Service.

Marcus, George E. 1995. "Ethnography in/of the World System: The Emergence of Multi-Sited Ethnography." *Annual Review of Anthropology* 24: 95–117.

Marks, Carol. 1991. "The Urban Underclass." *Annual Review of Sociology* 17: 445–66.

Marquand David. 1991. "Civic Republicans and Liberal Individualists: The Case of Britain." *Archive européenne de sociologie* 32: 329–44.

———. 1996. "Moralists and Hedonists." In *The Ideas that Shaped Post-War Britain*, ed. David Marquand and Anthony Seldon. London: Fontana.

Marsella, Anthony. 1985. "Culture, Self, and Mental Disorder." In *Culture and Self: Asian and American Perspectives*, ed. Anthony Marsella, George DeVos, and Francis Hsu. New York: Tavistock Publications.

Martin, Hans-Peter and Harald Schumann. 1996. *The Global Trap: Globalization and the Assault on Prosperity and Democracy.* Trans. Patrick Camiller. London and New York: Zed Books.

Maskovsky, Jeff and Catherine Kingfisher. 2001. "Introduction." *Urban Anthropology and Studies of Cultural Systems and World Economic Development*, Special Issue on Global Capitalism, Neoliberal Policy and Poverty 30 (2–3): 105–21.

Mauss, Marcel. [1938] 1985. "A Category of the Human Mind: The Notion of Person; the Notion of Self." Trans. W. D. Hall. In *The Category of the Person: Anthropology, Philosophy, History*, ed. Michael Carrithers, Steven Collins, and Steven Lukes. Cambridge: Cambridge University Press.

McArdell, Pania. 1992. "Whanaupani." In *Feminist Voices: Women's Studies Texts for Aotearoa/New Zealand*, ed. Rosmary Du Plessis, Phillida Bunkel, Kathie Irwin, and Alison Laurie. Auckland: Oxford University Press.

McClure, Margaret. 1998. *A Civilised Community: A History of Social Security in New Zealand, 1989–1998.* Auckland: Auckland University Press.

McDowell, Linda. 1991. "Life Without Father and Ford: The New Gender Order of Post-Fordism." *Transactions of the Institute of British Geography* 16: 400–19.

McIntosh, Mary. 1996. "Social Anxieties About Lone Motherhood and Ideologies of the Family: Two Sides of the Same Coin." In *Good Enough Mothering? Feminist Perspectives on Lone Mothering*, ed. Elizabeth Bortolaia Silva. London: Routledge.

Mead, Lawrence M. 1986. *Beyond Entitlement: The Social Obligations of Citizenship.* New York: Free Press.

———. 1992. *The New Politics of Poverty: The Non-Working Poor in America.* New York: Basic Books.

Mies, Maria. 1986. *Patriarchy and Accumulation on a World Scale: Women in the International Division of Labour.* London: Zed Books.

Mies, Maria, Veronica Bennholdt Thomsen, and Claudia von Werlhof. 1988. *Women: The Last Colony.* London: Zed Books.

Millar, Jane. 1996a. "Family Obligations and Social Policy: The Case of Child Support." *Policy Studies* 17 (3): 181–93.

———. 1996b. "Poor Mothers and Absent Fathers: Support for Lone Parents in Comparative Perspective." In *The Politics of the Family*, ed. Helen Jones and Jane Millar. Aldershot: Avebury.

———. 1998. "Social Policy and Family Policy." In *The Student's Companion to Social Policy*, ed. Pete Alcock, Angus Erskine, and Margaret May. Oxford: Blackwell.

———. 2000. "Welfare to Work for Lone Mothers in the U.K." Paper presented at What Future for Social Security? conference, University of Stirling, June 15–17.

Millar, Jane and Peter Whiteford. 1993. "Child Support in Lone-Parent Families: Policies in Australia and the United Kingdom." *Policy and Politics* 21 (1): 59–72.

Miller, S. M., Leonard Reissman, and Arthur Seagull. 1968. "Poverty and Self-Indulgence: A Critique of the Non-Deferred Gratification Pattern." In *Poverty in America*, ed. Louis A. Ferman, Joyce L. Kornbluh, and Alan Haber. Ann Arbor: University of Michigan Press.

Mink, Gwendolyn. 1995. *The Wages of Motherhood.* Ithaca, N.Y.: Cornell University Press.

Mishra, Ramesh. 1984. *The Welfare State in Crisis.* Brighton: Wheatsheaf.

———. 1999. *Globalization and the Welfare State.* Cheltenham: Edward Elgar.

Miyoshi, Masao. 1993. "A Borderless World? From Colonialism to Transnationalism and the Decline of the Nation-State." *Critical Inquiry* 19 (4): 726–51.

Morgen, Sandra and Jill Weigt. 2001. "Poor Women, 'Fair Work,' and Welfare-to-Work That Works." In *New Poverty Studies: The Ethnography of Politics, Policy and Impoverished People in the United States*, ed. Judith Goode and Jeff Maskovsky. New York: New York University Press.

Morris, Brian. 1991. *Western Conceptions of the Individual.* Washington, D.C.: Berg.

———. 1994. *Anthropology of the Self: The Individual in Cultural Perspective.* London: Pluto Press.

Moynihan, Daniel Patrick. 1965. *The Negro Family: The Case for National Action.* Washington D.C.: U.S. Government Printing Office for the Department of Policy, Planning, and Research of the Department of Labor.

Mullings, Leith. 1995. "Households Headed by Women: The Politics of Race, Class, and Gender." In *Conceiving the New World Order: The Global Politics of Reproduction*, ed. Faye Ginsburg and Rayna Rapp. Berkeley: University of California Press.

Murphy, Larry. 1999. "Housing Policy." In *Redesigning the New Zealand Welfare State*, ed. Jonathon Boston, Paul Dalziel, and Susan St. John. Auckland: Oxford University Press.

Murray, Charles. 1984. *Losing Ground: American Social Policy, 1950–1980.* New York: Basic Books.

———. 1994 "Does Welfare Bring More Babies?" *American Enterprise* 5 (1): 54–59.

———. 1996a. "The Emerging British Underclass." In *Charles Murray and the Underclass: The Developing Debate,* ed. Ruth Lister. London: Institute of Economic Affairs in association with the *Sunday Times.*

———. 1996b. "Underclass: The Crisis Deepens." In *Charles Murray and the Underclass: The Developing Debate,* ed. Ruth Lister. London: Institute of Economic Affairs in association with the *Sunday Times.*

Muscovitch, Allan. 1996. "Canada Health and Social Transfer: What Was Lost?" *CRSP/RCPS* 37: 66–75.

Naples, Nancy A. 1991. "Contradictions in the Gender Subtext of the War on Poverty: The Community Work and Resistance of Women from Low Income Communities." *Social Problems* 38 (3): 316–32.

———. 1997. "The New Consensus on the Gendered Social Contract: The 1987–1988 U.S. Congressional Hearings on Welfare Reform." *Signs* 22 (4): 907–45.

———. 1998. *Grassroots Warriors: Activist Mothering, Community Work, and the War on Poverty.* New York: Routledge.

National Commission on Civil Renewal. 1998. *A Nation of Spectators: How Civic Disengagement Weakens America and What We Can Do About It.* College Park, Md.: National Commission on Civil Renewal.

Navarro, Vicente. 1998. "Neoliberalism, 'Globalization,' Unemployment, Inequalities, and the Welfare State." *International Journal of Health Services* 28 (4): 607–82.

Naymik, Mark. 1998. "Tough Sell." *City Paper* (Philadelphia), December 11, p. 17.

Nederveen Pieterse, Jan. 1995. "Globalization as Hybridization." In *Global Modernities,* ed. Mike Featherstone, Scott Lash, and Roland Robertson. London: Sage.

———. 1997. "Globalisation and Emancipation: From Local Empowerment to Global Reform." *New Political Economy* 2 (1): 79–92.

Newman, Katherine. 1999. *No Shame in My Game: The Working Poor in the Inner City.* New York: Knopf and Russell Sage.

New Zealand Government. 1988. *He Tirohanga Rangapu/Partnership Perspectives.* Wellington: Government Printer.

———. 1996. Executive Government Speech Archive. July 30 and August 13, 1996. <www.govt.nz>.

———. 1997. Treasury. New Zealand Government Asset sales as at 31 December 1995. Wellington: Government Printer. <www.treasury.govt.nz/assetsales>.

———. 1998. Income Support Services (NZISS). Unpublished Figures: Applications by benefit, gender, and ethnicity, 1995–98. Wellington: New Zealand Government.

O'Connor, Julia S. 1996. "From Women in the Welfare State to Gendering Welfare State Regimes: Trend Report." *Current Sociology* 44 (2): 1–124.

O'Connor Julia, Ann Orloff, and Sheila Shaver. 1999. *States, Markets, Families: Gender, Liberalism and Social Policy in Australia, Canada, Great Britain, and the United States.* Cambridge: Cambridge University Press.

Offe, Claus. 1996. *Modernity and The State: East and West.* Cambridge: Polity.

Ong, Aihwa. 1999. *Flexible Citizenship: The Cultural Logics of Transnationality.* Durham, N.C.: Duke University Press.

Orloff, Ann. 1993. "Gender and the Social Rights of Citizenship: The Comparative Analysis of Gender Relations and Welfare States." *American Sociological Review* 58 (3): 303–28.

————. 1996. "Gender in the Welfare State." *Annual Review of Sociology* 22: 51–78.

Ozawa, Martha and Stuart A. Kirk. 1997. "Welfare Reform." In *Social Policy Reform Research and Practice*, ed. Patricia L. Ewalt, Edith M. Freeman, Stuart A. Kirk, and Dennis L. Poole. Washington, D.C.: National Association of Social Workers Press.

Pal, Leslie A., ed. 2000. *How Ottawa Spends 1999–2000: Shape Shifting: Canadian Government Towards the 21st Century.* Toronto: Oxford University Press.

Pandian, Jacob. 1985. *Anthropology and the Western Tradition: Toward an Authentic Anthropology.* Prospect Heights, Ill.: Waveland Press.

Pardo, Mary S. 1998. *Mexican American Women Activists: Identity and Resistance in Two Los Angeles Communities.* Philadelphia: Temple University Press.

Pateman, Carol. 1988. *The Sexual Contract.* Stanford, Calif.: Stanford University Press.

————. 1989. "The Patriarchal Welfare State." In *The Disorder of Women: Democracy, Feminism, and Political Theory.* Cambridge: Polity.

Peace, Robin. 1998. *Surface Tension: Place/Poverty/Policy.* PhD thesis, University of Waikato.

Pearce, Diane. 1978. "The Feminization of Poverty: Women, Work, and Welfare." *Urban and Social Change Review* 11 (1): 28–36.

Peters, Michael. 1997. "Neo-Liberalism, Welfare Dependency, and the Moral Construction of Poverty in New Zealand." *New Zealand Sociology* 12 (1): 1–34.

Philips, Susan Urmston. [1983] 1993. *The Invisible Culture: Communication in Classroom and Community on the Warm Springs Indian Reservation.* Prospect Heights, Ill.: Waveland.

Phillips, Susan. 1996. *How Ottawa Spends 1995–1996.* Ottawa: Carleton University Press.

Piven, Frances Fox. 1998. "Welfare Reform and the Economic and Cultural Reconstruction of Low Wage Labor Markets." *City and Society Annual Review, 1997*: 21–36.

Piven, Frances Fox and Richard Cloward. 1979. *Poor People's Movements: Why They Succeed and How They Fail.* New York: Vintage Books.

Plant, Raymond. 1993. "Free Lunches Don't Nourish: Reflections on Entitlement and Citizenship." In *New Approaches to Welfare Theory*, ed. Glenn Drover and Patrick Kerans. Hampshire: Edward Elgar.

Pocock, Barbara. 1998. "All Change, Still Gendered: The Australian Labour Market in the 1990s." *Australian Journal of Industrial Relations* 40 (4): 581–604.

Polanyi, Livia. 1989. *Telling the American Story: A Structural and Cultural Analysis of Conversational Storytelling.* Cambridge, Mass: MIT Press.

Prime Minister (UK). 1998. *The Government's Annual Report, 97/98.* London: Stationery Office.

Prince, Michael. 2000. "From Health and Welfare to Stealth and Farewell: Federal Social Policy: 1980–2000. In *How Ottawa Spends 1999–2000: Shape Shifting: Canadian Government Towards the 21st Century*, ed. Leslie A. Pal. Toronto: Oxford University Press.

Probyn, Elsbeth. 1998. "McIdentities: Food and the Familial Citizen." *Theory, Culture, and Society* 15 (2): 155–73.

Pujol, Michele A. 1992. *Feminism and Anti-Feminism in Early Economic Thought.* Aldershot: Edward Elgar.

Pulkington, Jane and Gordon Ternowetsky. 1999. "Neo-Liberalism and Retrenchment." In *Citizens or Consumers? Social Policy in a Market Society*, ed. Dave Broad and Wayne Anthony. Halifax: Fernwood Publishing.

Pusey, Michael. 1991. *Economic Rationalism in Canberra: A Nation-Building State Changes Its Mind.* Melbourne: Cambridge University Press.

Ramsay, Maureen. 1997. *What's Wrong with Liberalism? A Radical Critique of Liberal Political Philosophy.* Leicester: Leicester University Press.

Rata, Elizabeth. 1997. "The Theory of Tribal Capitalism." Paper presented to SAANZ: Sociological Association of Aotearoa, Massey University, Albany, December.

Reekie, Gail. 1996. "Single Parents and Social Scientists: Towards a Discourse Analysis of a Contemporary 'Problem'." *Australian Journal of Social Issues* 31 (3): 327–39.

Rei, Tania. 1998. "Te Triti o Waitangi, Maori Women and the State." In *Feminist Thought in Aotearoa New Zealand: Differences and Connections*, ed. Rosemary Du Plessis and Lynne Alice. Auckland: Oxford University Press.

Roberts, Ceridwen. 1998. Foreword to Helen Barnes, Patricia Day and Natalie Cronin, *Trial and Error: A Review of U.K. Child Support Policy.* London: Family Policy Studies Centre.

Robertson, Roland. 1992. *Globalization: Social Theory and Global Culture.* London: Sage.

———. 1995. "Glocalization: Time-Space and Homogeneity-Heterogeneity." In *Global Modernities*, ed. Mike Featherstone, Scott Lash, and Roland Robertson. London: Sage.

Rochford, Mike. 1993. *A Profile of Sole Parents from the 1991 Census.* Research Report Series 15. Wellington: Social Policy Agency.

Roe, Jill. 1988. "The End Is Where We Start From: Women and Welfare Since 1901." In *Women, Social Welfare, and the State in Australia*, ed. Cora V. Baldock and Betinna Cass. Sydney: Allen and Unwin.

Roediger, David. 1990. *The Wages of Whiteness: Race and the Making of the American Working Class.* London: Verso.

Rogers, Barbara. 1980. *The Domestication of Women: Discrimination in Developing Societies.* London: Kogan Page.

Rosaldo, Renato. 1989. *Culture and Truth: The Remaking of Social Analysis.* Boston: Beacon Press.

Rose, Nancy. 1995. *Workfare or "Fair Work": Women, Welfare, and Government Work Programs.* New Brunswick, N.J.: Rutgers University Press.

Rose, Nikolas. 1989. "Governing the Enterprising Self." In *The Values of Enterprise Culture: The Moral Debate*, ed. Paul Heelas and Paul Morris. London: Routledge.

———. 1996a. "The Death of the Social? Refiguring the Territory of Government." *Economy and Society* 25 (3): 327–56.

———. 1996b. "Governing 'Advanced' Liberal Democracies." In *Foucault and Political Reason: Liberalism, Neo-Liberalism, and Rationalities of Government*, ed. Andrew Barry, Thomas Osborne, and Nikolas Rose. Chicago: University of Chicago Press.

Roseneil, Sasha and Kirk Mann. 1996. "Unpalatable Choices and Inadequate Families: Lone Mothers and the Underclass Debate." In *Good Enough Mothering? Feminist Perspectives on the Lone Motherhood*, ed. Elizabeth Bortolaia Silva. London and New York: Routledge.

Rouse, Roger. 1995. "Questions of Identity: Personhood and Collectivity in

Transnational Migration to the United States." *Critique of Anthropology* 15 (4): 351–80.

Rowe, Audrey. 1991. "The Feminization of Poverty: An Issue for the 90's." *Yale Journal of Law and Feminism* 4 (73): 73–79.

Rowlingson Karen, Stephen McKay, and Richard Berthoud. 1998. *The Growth of Lone Parenthood: Diversity and Dynamics.* PSI Report 850. London: Policy Studies Institute.

Russell, Andrew and Iain R. Edgar. 1998. "Research and Practice in the Anthropology of Welfare." In *The Anthropology of Welfare*, ed. Ian R. Edgar and Andrew Russell. London: Routledge.

Sahlins, Marshall. 1972. *Stone Age Economics.* New York: Aldine.

———. 1976. *Culture and Practical Reason.* Chicago: University of Chicago Press.

Sainsbury, Diane. 1996. *Gender, Equality, and Welfare States.* Cambridge: Cambridge University Press.

Sargent, Lydia, ed. 1981. *Women and Revolution: A Discussion of the Unhappy Marriage of Marxism and Feminism.* Boston: South End Press.

Sassen, Saskia. 1996a. *Losing Control? Sovereignty in an Age of Globalization.* New York: Columbia University Press.

———. 1996b. "Toward a Feminist Analytics of the Global Economy." *Indiana Journal of Global Legal Studies* 4 (1): 7–41.

———. 1998. *Globalization and Its Discontents: Essays on the New Mobility of People and Money.* New York: New Press.

———. 2000. "Spatialities and Temporalities of the Global: Elements for a Theorization." *Public Culture* 12 (1): 215–32.

Saunders, Peter. 1994. *Welfare and Inequality: National and International Perspectives on the Australian Welfare State.* Melbourne: Cambridge University Press.

Schram, Sanford F. 2000. "Race, Riots, and Reform: Welfare Reform Politics from the 1960s to the 1990s." Paper presented at the Conference on Work, Welfare, and Politics. University of Oregon, Eugene, February 28–29.

Scott, C. M., Tammy E. Horne, and Wilfredo Enid Thurston. 2000. *The Differential Impact of Health Care Privatization on Women in Alberta.* Regina, Saskatchewan: Prairie Women's Health Centre for Excellence.

Scott, Kathleen. 1996. "The Dilemma of Liberal Citizenship: Women and Social Assistance Reform in the 1990s." *Studies in Political Economy* 50: 7–36.

Seabrook, Jeremy. 1997. "Convergence, Welfare, and Development." *Race and Class* 39 (1): 75–83.

Sharff, J. 1987. "The Underground Economy of a Poor Neighborhood." In *Cities in the United States*, ed. Leith Mullings. New York: Columbia University Press.

Sharp, Andrew. 1990. *Justice and the Maori: Maori Claims in New Zealand Political Argument in the 1980s.* Auckland: Oxford University Press.

Sharp, Andrew, ed. 1994. *Leap into the Dark: The Changing Role of the State Since 1984.* Auckland: Auckland University Press.

Shaver, Sheila. 1995. "Women, Employment, and Social Security." In *Women in a Restructuring Australia: Work and Welfare*, ed. Anne Edwards and Susan Magarey. Sydney: Allen and Unwin.

Shaw, Jenny. 1995. "Women, Time, and Markets: The Role of Feminization and Contradiction in the New Forms of Exploitation." In *Women and Market Societies: Crisis and Opportunity*, ed. Barbara Einhorn and Eileen Janes Yeo. Aldershot: Edward Elgar.

Shields, John and B. Michael Evans. 1998. *Shrinking the State: Globalization and Public Administration Reform.* Halifax: Fernwood Publishing.

Shirley, Ian and Maureen Baker. 1998. The Effects of Lone Parenthood on Child-hood Outcomes. Paper prepared for the Social Policy Agency, Wellington.

Shore, Bradd. 1982. *Sala'ilua: A Samoan Mystery*. New York: Columbia University Press.

Shweder, Richard A. and Edmund J. Bourne. 1984. "Does the Concept of the Person Vary Cross-Culturally?" In *Culture Theory*, ed. Richard A. Shweder and Robert A. LeVine, Cambridge: Cambridge University Press.

Sibley, David. 1995. *Geographies of Exclusion: Society and Difference in the West*. London: Routledge.

Silva, Elizabeth Bortolaia, ed. 1996. *Good Enough Mothering? Feminist Perspectives on Lone Motherhood*. London and New York: Routledge.

Sjolander, Claire Turenne. 1996. "The Rhetoric of Globalization: What's in a Wor(l)d?" *International Journal* 51 (4): 603–16.

Smart, Carol. 1995. *Law, Crime and Sexuality*. London: Sage.

Smith, Ruth L. 1990. "Order and Disorder: The Naturalization of Poverty." *Cultural Critique* 14: 209–29.

Smith, S. B. 1999. "Arguing Against Cuts in Lone Parent Benefits: Reclaiming the Desert Ground in the UK." *Critical Social Policy* 19 (3): 313–34.

Social Security Committee. 1993. *The Operation of the Child Support Act*. London: Stationery Office.

Song, Miri. 1996. "Changing Conceptualizations of Lone Parenthood in Britain: Lone Parents or Single Mums?" *European Journal of Women's Studies* 3 (4): 377–97.

Song, Miri and Rosalind Edwards. 1997. "Comment: Raising Questions about Perspectives on Black Lone Motherhood." *Journal of Social Policy* 26 (2): 233–44.

Sparr, Pamela. 1995. "From Nairobi to Beijing: Globalization, Women, and Poverty in the U.S." *Development* 1: 14–19.

Spiro, Melford E. 1993. "Is the Western Conception of the Self 'Peculiar' Within the Context of the World Cultures?" *Ethos* 21 (2): 107–53.

Stack, Carol. 1974. *All Our Kin*. New York: Harper and Row.

———. 1996. *Call to Home: African Americans Reclaim the Rural South*. New York: Basic Books.

Standing, Kay. 1999. "Lone Mothers and 'Parental' Involvement: A Contradiction in Policy?" *Journal of Social Policy* 28 (3): 479–95.

Starrels, Marjorie E., Sally Bould, and Leon J. Nicholas. 1994. "The Feminization of Poverty in the United States: Gender, Race, Ethnicity, and Family Factors." *Journal of Family Issues* 15 (4): 590–607.

State Services Commission. 1998. "Report to Respondents: Six Monthly Staffing Survey, Public Service Departments and Selected Crown Entities, as at 30 June 1998."

Stavrianos, Leften Starros. 1981. *Global Rift: The Third World Comes of Age*. New York: William Morrow.

Stefancic, Jean and Richard Delgado. 1996. *No Mercy: How Conservative Think Tanks and Foundations Changed America's Social Agenda*. Philadelphia: Temple University Press.

Stephens, Robert. 1999. "Poverty, Family Finances, and Social Security." In *Redesigning the New Zealand Welfare State*, ed. Jonathan Boston, Paul Dalziel, and Susan St. John. Auckland: Oxford University Press.

Strassmann, Diana. 1993. "Not a Free Market: The Rhetoric of Disciplinary Authority in Economics." In *Beyond Economic Man*, ed. Marianne A. Ferber and Julie A. Nelson. Chicago and London: University of Chicago Press.

Straw, Jack. 1998. Foreword to Home Office, *Supporting Families: A Consultation Document*. London: Stationery Office.

Susser, Ida. 1982. *Norman Street*. New York: Columbia University Press.

———. 1997. "The Flexible Woman: Regendering Labor in the Informational Society." *Critique of Anthropology* 17 (4): 389–402.

———. 1999. "Creating Family Forms: The Exclusion of Men and Teenage Boys from Families in the New York City Shelter System, 1987–1991." In *Theorizing the City*, ed. Setha Low. New Brunswick, N.J.: Rutgers University Press.

Susser, Ida and John Kreniske. 1987. "The Welfare Trap: A Public Policy for Degradation." In *Cities of the United States*, ed. Leith Mullings. New York: Columbia University Press.

Swan, Peter and Mikhail Bernstam. 1986. *The State as Marriage Partner of Last Resort: A Labour Market Approach to Illegitimacy in the United States, 1960–80*. Working Paper 29. Kensington, N.S.W.: Australian Graduate School of Management.

———. 1988. "The Political Economy of the Symbiosis Between Labour Market Regulation and the Social Welfare System." *Australian Journal of Management* 13 (2): 177–201.

Swimmer, Gene. 1996. *How Ottawa Spends, 1996–1997: Under the Knife*. Ottawa: Carleton University Press.

Takaki, Ronald T. 1979. *Iron Cages: Race and Culture in Nineteenth-Century America*. New York: Alfred A. Knopf.

Tahi, Brenda. 1995. "Biculturalism: The Model of Te Ohu Whakatupu." In *Justice and Identity: Antipodean Practices*, ed. Margaret Wilson and Anna Yeatman. Auckland: Bridget Williams Books.

Tapper, Alan. 1990. *The Family in the Welfare State*. Sydney: Allen and Unwin.

Teeple, Gary. 1995. *Globalization and the Decline of Social Reform*. Toronto: Garamond Press.

Te Puni Kokiri. 1996. Brief for the incoming minister of Maori Affairs. Wellington: New Zealand Government.

———. 1998. *Progress Towards Closing Social and Economic Gaps Between Maori and Non-Maori: A Report to the Minister of Maori Affairs*. Wellington: New Zealand Government.

Thatcher, Margaret. 1990. *The First NCH George Thomas Society Annual Lecture*. London: National Children's Homes.

Thomas-Emeagwali, Gloria T., ed. 1995. *Women Pay the Price: Structural Adjustment in Africa and the Caribbean*. Trenton, N.J: Africa World Press.

Thompson, E. P. 1971. "The Moral Economy of the English Crowd in the Eighteenth Century." *Past and Present* 50: 76–136.

Tinker, Irene. 1976. "The Adverse Impact of Development on Women." In *Women and World Development*, ed. Irene Tinker, Michele Bo Bramsen, and Mayra Buvinic. Washington, D.C.: Overseas Development Council.

———. 1982. *Gender Equity in Development: A Policy Perspective*. Washington, D.C.: Equity Policy Center.

Todorov, Tzvetan. 1984. *The Conquest of America: The Question of the Other*. Trans. Richard Howard. New York: Harper and Row.

Tomlinson, John. 1999. *Globalization and Culture*. Chicago: University of Chicago Press.

Tooze, Roger and Craig N. Murphy. 1996. "The Epistemology of Poverty and the Poverty of Epistemology in IPE: Mystery, Blindness, and Invisibility." *Millennium: Journal of International Studies* 25 (3): 681–707.

Topouzis, Daphne. 1990. "The Feminization of Poverty." *Africa Report* 35: 60–63.

Turok, Ivan and Nicola Edge. 1999. *The Jobs Gap in Britain's Cities: Employment Loss and Labour Market Consequences.* Bristol: Policy Press.

Turok, Ivan and David Webster. 1998. "The New Deal: Jeopardised by the Geography of Unemployment?" *Local Economy* 13: 309–28.

United Kingdom Department of Environment. 1995. *Our Future Homes.* White Paper. London: Stationery Office.

United Kingdom Department of Social Security. 1998. *New Ambitions for Our Country: A New Contract for Welfare.* London: Stationery Office.

———. 1999. *Households Below Average Income 1994/5 to 1997/8.* Leeds: Corporate Document Services.

United Kingdom Equal Opportunities Commission. 1996. *Pay, Briefings on Women and Men in Britain.* Manchester: Equal Opportunities Commission.

———. 1997. "Income and Personal Finance." In *Briefings on Women and Men in Britain.* Manchester: Equal Opportunities Commission.

———. 1999a. *Women and Men in Britain: Pay and Income.* Manchester: Equal Opportunities Commission.

———. 1999b. *Women and Men.* Manchester: Equal Opportunities Commission.

United Kingdom Home Office. 1998. *Supporting Families.* London: Stationery Office.

United Kingdom Office of National Statistics/EOC. 1998. *Social Focus on Women and Men.* London: Stationery Office.

United Nations Development Program (UNDP). 1995. *Human Development Report.* New York: Oxford University Press.

———. 1997. *Reinventing Government.* New York: United Nations.

———. 2000. *Human Development Report: 2000.* New York: Oxford University Press.

United Nations. 1966. International Covenant on Economic, Social and Cultural Rights. <www.unhchr.ch/html/menu3/b/a_cescr.htm>.

United States Congress. 1995. House Proceedings of the Record of March 24, 1995. Washington, D.C.: U.S. Government Printing Office.

———. 1996. House Proceedings of the Record of July 30, 1996. Washington, D.C.: U.S. Government Printing Office.

United States Department of Health and Human Services, Administration for Children and Families. 1999. "State-by-State Welfare Caseloads Since 1993." <www.acf.dhhs.gov/news/stats/caseload.htm>.

Valentine, Betty Lou. 1978. *Hustling and Other Hard Work.* New York: Free Press.

Valentine, Charles. 1968. *Culture and Poverty: A Critique and Counterproposals.* Chicago: University of Chicago Press.

van Drenth, Annemieke, Trudie Khijn, and Jane Lewis. 1999. "Sources of Income for Lone Mother Families: Policy Changes in Britain and the Netherlands and the Experiences of Divorced Women." *Journal of Social Policy* 28 (4): 619–41.

Waitangi Tribunal. 1998. *Te Whanau o Waipareira Report.* Wellington: Government Publications.

Walker, Ranginui. 1990. *Ka Whawhai Tonu Matou: Struggle Without End.* Auckland: Penguin.

Waring, Marilyn. 1989. *If Women Counted: A New Feminist Economics*. London: Macmillan.

———. 1990. *Counting for Nothing: What Men Value and What Women Are Worth*. Wellington, New Zealand: Bridget Williams Books.

Waters, Malcolm. 1995. *Globalization*. London: Routledge.

Watts, Jerry and Nan Marie Astone. 1997. "The Personal Responsibility and Work Opportunity Reconciliation Act of 1996." *Contemporary Sociology* 26 (4): 409–15.

Webb, Robert. 1998. "The Sealords Deal and Treaty Rights: What Has Been Achieved?" In *Fisheries and Commodifying Iwi*, ed. Leonie Pihama and Cheryl Waerea-I-te-rangi Smith. Economic, Politics, and Colonisation 3. Tamaki Makaurau: International Research Institute for Maori and Indigenous Education/Moko Productions.

Weber, Max. [1930] 1958. *The Protestant Ethic and the Spirit of Capitalism*. New York: Charles Scribner's Sons.

Weinroth, Michelle. 1997. "Deficitism and Neo-Conservatism in Ontario." In *Open for Business, Closed to People: Mike Harris's Ontario*, ed. Diana S. Ralph, André Régimbald, and Nérée St-Amand. Halifax: Fernwood Publishing.

White, Melanie. 1999. "Neo-Liberalism and the Rise of Consumer as Citizen." In *Citizens or Consumers: Social Policy in a Market Society*, ed. Dave Broad and Wayne Anthony. Halifax: Fernwood Publishing.

Williams, Brett. 1992. "Poverty Among African Americans in the United States." *Human Organization* 51 (2): 164–74.

Williams, Susan H. 1996. "Globalization, Privatization, and a Feminist Public." *Indiana Journal of Global Legal Studies* 4 (1): 97–105.

Wilson, William J. 1980. *The Declining Significance of Race: Blacks and Changing American Institutions*. Chicago: University of Chicago Press.

———. 1987. *The Truly Disadvantaged: The Inner City, the Underclass, and Public Policy*. Chicago: University of Chicago Press.

Wiseman, John. 1998. "Here to Stay? The 1997–1998 Australian Waterfront Dispute and Its Implications." *Labour and Industry* 9 (1): 1–15.

Yeatman, Anna. 1990. *Bureaucrats, Femocrats, Technocrats: Essays in the Contemporary Australian State*. Sydney: Allen and Unwin.

———. 1993. "Women's Citizenship Claims, Labour Market Policy, and Globalisation." *Australian Journal of Political Science* 27: 449–61.

———. 1994. *Postmodern Revisionings of the Political*. New York: Routledge.

———. 1996. "Interpreting Contemporary Contractualism." *Australian Journal of Social Issues* 31 (1): 39–54.

———. 1997. "Contract, Status and Personhood." In *The New Contractualism?* ed. Glyn Davis, Barbara Sullivan, and Anna Yeatman. Melbourne: Macmillan Education.

———. 2000. "Mutual Obligation: What Kind of Contract Is This?" In *Reforming the Australian Welfare State*, ed. Peter Saunders. Melbourne: Australian Institute of Family Studies.

Young, Iris Marion. 1986. "The Myth of the Disappearing Nuclear Family." In *Family Portraits*, ed. Digby Anderson and Graham Dawson. London: Social Affairs Unit.

———. 1990a. "Pregnant Embodiment: Subjectivity and Alienation." In *Throwing like a Girl and Other Essays in Feminist Philosophy and Social Theory*. Bloomington: Indiana University Press.

————. 1990b. *Throwing like a Girl and Other Essays in Feminist Philosophy and Social Theory.* Bloomington: Indiana University Press.

————. 1997. "Mothers, Citizenship, and Independence: A Critique of Pure Family Values." In *Intersecting Voices: Dilemmas of Gender, Political Philosophy, and Policy.* Princeton, N.J.: Princeton University Press.

Contributors

Janine Brodie is Chair of the Department of Political Science, University of Alberta and former Robarts Chair in Canadian Studies and Director of the Centre for Feminist Research at York University, Toronto. She is the author of several books on Canadian political economy and gender and politics, and is currently focusing her research on globalization and neoliberal governance.

Judith Goode is Professor of Anthropology and Urban Studies at Temple University. For several decades she has been engaged in research and teaching about the ethnography of race, ethnicity, and class in Philadelphia and the United States. She is the recipient of the 2000 SANA Prize for Distinguished Achievement in the Critical Anthropology of North America and the coeditor of *The New Poverty Studies: The Ethnography of Power, Politics, and Impoverished People in the United States*.

Catherine Kingfisher is Associate Professor of Anthropology at the University of Lethbridge. Her research focuses on gender, poverty, neoliberalism, and globalization, and her previous publications include *Women in the American Welfare Trap* (University of Pennsylvania Press), and articles in *Discourse & Society* and *American Anthropologist*. She is currently conducting research on neoliberalism and welfare reform in small-town Canada.

Wendy Larner is Senior Lecturer in the Sociology Department, University of Auckland, Aotearoa/New Zealand. She has published widely in the areas of globalization, governance, and gender, including articles in *Economy and Society, Environment and Planning A, Social Politics*, and *Society and Space*. Current projects include research on local partnerships (funded by the New Zealand Foundation for Research, Science, and Technology) and research on the spaces and practices of globalization (funded by a Royal Society of New Zealand Marsden Grant).

Ruth Lister is Professor of Social Policy at Loughborough University. She is a former director of the Child Poverty Action Group and has published extensively on issues of poverty, welfare, gender, and citizenship. Her latest book is *Citizenship: Feminist Perspectives*.

Susan Robertson is Reader in Sociology of Education at the University of Bristol. She has held academic posts in Australia, Canada, and, until recently, New Zealand. Her research has focused on theorizing changing state formations, governance, labor, discourse and identity, and the changing role of social institutions in that. She has recently published *A Class Act: Changing Teachers' Work, Globalization and the State.* Her current work on globalization focuses on regional (NAFTA, APEC, EU) and global institutions (WTO) and their relationships to national states.

Index

Acknowledgments

This book is the outcome of a collective endeavor, and I feel privileged to have been able to work with my collaborators: Janine Brodie, Judith Goode, Wendy Larner, Ruth Lister, and Susan Robertson. I also owe a debt of gratitude to those who listened to my ideas and/or read portions of the manuscript: Doreen Indra, Jeff Maskovsky, Michael Goldsmith, Wendy Larner, Rita Gallin, Sandra Bamford, Sandra Morgen, Norman Buchignani, Wallace Clement, Pat Armstrong, and Daiva Stasilius, and to those who provided less tangible but no less important emotional support and sustenance: Heidi Macdonald, Carol Williams, Charlene Janes, Virginia McGowan, and Arlene Daisley. Students in my graduate seminar on globalization, welfare state restructuring, and women's poverty at Carleton University and in my senior seminar on globalization at the University of Lethbridge participated in fertile discussions at key junctures in the development of this project. Allison Dobek, research assistant extraordinaire, contributed both intellectual feedback and word processing skills. Financial support was provided by a University of Lethbridge Research Excellence Grant and a Canadian Department of Foreign Affairs and International Trade Faculty Research Award, and editorial support at the University of Pennsylvania Press was provided by Peter Agree, Audra Wolfe and Alison Anderson. Last but not least, I would like to thank my beautiful son, Levi, who always reminds me about what's important in life.